CROSSING THE THRESHOLD OF DIVINE REVELATION

Crossing the Threshold of Divine Revelation

William J. Abraham

WILLIAM B. EERDMANS PUBLISHING COMPANY
GRAND RAPIDS, MICHIGAN / CAMBRIDGE, U.K.

Wm. B. Eerdmans Publishing Co.
255 Jefferson Ave. S.E., Grand Rapids, Michigan 49503 /
P.O. Box 163, Cambridge CB3 9PU U.K.

Printed in the United States of America

11 10 09 08 07 06   7 6 5 4 3 2 1

Library of Congress Cataloging-in-Publication Data

Abraham, William J. (William James), 1947-
Crossing the threshold of divine revelation / William J. Abraham.
p.   cm.
ISBN-10: 0-8028-2958-9 / ISBN-13: 978-0-8028-2958-0 (pbk.: alk. paper)
1. Christianity — Philosophy.   2. Philosophical theology.
3. Revelation.   I. Title.

BR100.A27 2006
230.01 — dc22

2006032808

www.eerdmans.com

To Patrick Roche

Contents

—⟨⟨⟨⟩⟩⟩—

Acknowledgments

—⌘—

At the outset I want to thank the Lilly Endowment for a generous grant that enabled me to spend a sabbatical to write a first draft in the academic year 2002-3. I also want to thank my colleagues in the canonical theism project whose own independent research, encouragement, and insights have enriched my thinking. In particular, I want to thank Frederick Aquino, Pavel Gavrilyuk, Chuck Gutenson, Douglas Koskela, Mark Powell, Natalie Van Kirk, Jason Vickers, and David Watson. Equally, I am extremely thankful for the ongoing response to some of the ideas developed here in the Polycarp Fellowship. Thus I thank Vaughn Baker, Terisa Clark, Keefe Cropper, Timothy Davenport-Herbst, Tom Davis, John Feagins, Michael Gehring, Andrew Kinsey, Elizabeth Moreau, Scott Sager, and John Wilson. I also thank Chad Wilkes for spotting a serious problem of presentation. I am very grateful for the feedback received from my students at Perkins School of Theology over the years, and most especially to the students in my seminar on the epistemology of theology in the spring semester of 2004. They convinced me (if ever I needed it) that theological students are deeply interested in epistemology, and that they relish the chance to read and think in this arena. I also pay tribute to my faculty colleagues at Perkins School of Theology for conversation in and around the topics covered here, especially to James Kirby, William Babcock, and Bruce Marshall. Outside Perkins I am grateful to Jerry Walls, Frank Gourley, Patrick Roche, Andrew Walker, Bill Marsh, and Basil Mitchell for their critical comments. Parts of chapter 5 have appeared in "The Offense of Divine Revelation" in the *Harvard Theological Review* 95, no. 3 (2002): 251-64, and as "Revelation Revisited," in *Revelation*, edited by Paul Avis (Grand Rapids: Eerdmans, 1999). I am grateful for permission to use this material here. Last but not least, I want to thank Mary Ann Marshall for indispensable help in the final stages of the work that went into this volume. Needless to say, the mistakes and weaknesses are all mine, but there would be many more but for the assistance of these wonderful people. Finally, I am grateful to my family, who gladly leave me to my intellectual pursuits without complaint.

Preface

—∞∞∞—

This work needs a word or two of explanation as it sallies forth into the world. More particularly, it is important for the reader to get a feel for the landscape, or better, the manifold landscapes, that this work occupies.

First, this essay takes its place in the cracks and tensions between philosophy and theology. The dangers that go with this placement are obvious. It will come across as too theological for philosophers and too philosophical for theologians. Equally, it may come across as too technical for the student and the general reader and not technical enough for the professional scholar. Yet I dare to believe that all concerned will find the central thesis developed worthy of their attention.

One of my aims is to familiarize Christian theologians with some of the fruits of recent developments within epistemology. This is not intended in a condescending spirit; happily, many theologians show a healthy and persistent interest in the justification of theological claims. So I hope to encourage them to take a look at what has emerged in recent work in epistemology, yet to do so with a sense of real freedom, realizing that they have a real stake in the conversation. Theologians do not need to see themselves as taking crumbs from the philosopher's table but as genuine agents in the conversation. So I hope to draw theologians into a conversation they have resisted. The central topic of the book, divine revelation, clearly belongs first and foremost within theology, so I hope theologians will see that they have a stake in the argument as a whole.

I also hope to garner the interest of philosophers. This constitutes a second aim. I seek in this volume to deploy the rich network of insights that have emerged in recent analytical philosophy in thinking about the rationality of the Christian faith. It will be clear from the outset that, though I think the work of recent philosophers has been exceptionally fertile and original in its treatment of theism, much still needs to be done in this arena. In particular I hope philosophers will revisit the whole topic of divine revelation and mine it for epistemic insight. If there is anything I want to lift up at the beginning, it is that revelation is a fascinating epistemic concept; it deserves attention in its own right; and it makes a deep difference in how we think about the rationality of Christian belief and related topics. So I hope to rouse the philosophers to further reflection. I trust that those in the Reformed tradition who have complained that I have been more inclined to cursing the darkness than lighting a candle will note that I have heeded their admonition.[1]

I also hope to make available to students and nonspecialist readers a way of thinking about the content and rationality of the Christian faith that they will find both illuminating and persuasive. The issues I take up are neither esoteric nor secondary; they are intrinsically interesting and relevant to the whole of our existence. Hence I have sought to write in a way that is accessible to students and to the general reader. I am convinced that the central thesis worked out in this volume is one that will make sense of some of their bafflement in thinking about issues of faith.

Second, this work is part of a bigger project that really began back in the mid-1980s and that has continued tacitly and now explicitly in this volume. The centerpiece of this larger project is the articulation and defense of a vision of Christianity that I have identified as canonical theism. By canonical theism I mean here very simply the vision of theism adopted publicly, intentionally, and explicitly by the church as it was initially driven to articulate, celebrate, and live out its fundamental convictions on the other side of conversion and the gospel. I refer to this theism as "canonical theism" because it is indeed canonical; it was the theism, the beliefs about God, listed and officially adopted by the church prior to the schism between East and West.

To my astonishment, I first hit upon something akin to canonical

---

1. The challenge is delightfully expressed by Alvin Plantinga in his *Warranted Christian Belief* (New York: Oxford University Press, 2000), 200 n. 1.

theism when trying to work through what happened in the evangelization of the Roman Empire.[2] It was there that I came across the critical place of catechesis in Christian conversion, the pivotal and agreed place of the early creeds for understanding the faith, and the diversity of judgment in epistemology represented by the great theologians of the faith. More particularly, I became convinced that becoming a Christian — or better, Christian initiation — was not first and foremost gaining a theory of knowledge but was coming to love the God identified in the rich canonical heritage of the church. In bringing people to faith the church articulated a very particular vision of God, creation, and redemption that had to be seen as a whole and received as a whole. It was that vision that over time I came to name and identify as canonical theism.

The wider project really took off in the research that resulted in a radical rereading of the nature of canon across the centuries. In particular, I became convinced that there was a very important shift from canon to criterion in Christian theology that had destroyed the richness of the Christian vision from within in the West.[3] Friend and foe have objected that I need to come clean on my own epistemological commitments, if they are to give up the conventional way of thinking about canon in the West. In this book I hope I have met this request, even though I am well aware of the challenge involved. Once we get hold of the distinction between canon and criterion, between the faith of the church and any epistemology developed to defend it intellectually, it is relatively easy to make the radical shift in orientation that I think is critical for the future of the church and of theology. Here I propose one way forward on the epistemological front. Thus I trust I have met a pressing challenge that arises when folk first hear of canonical theism as a serious option for the future but are puzzled about how to fill the intellectual vacuum they feel once they stop reducing canon to scripture and cease thinking of canon as a criterion.

Yet in meeting this challenge, I remain convinced that it is a deep mistake to canonize any epistemological theory in the life of the church. Thus this book needs to be read alongside my more recent work on the renewal of the church. I have argued at length elsewhere how tempting and

---

2. At the time I was working on the issues that were developed in *The Logic of Evangelism* (Grand Rapids: Eerdmans, 1988).

3. The fruit of this work can be found in my *Canon and Criterion in Christian Theology: From the Fathers to Feminism* (Oxford: Clarendon, 1998).

unsatisfactory it is to look to epistemology (often disguised as a theory of scripture or a new method in theology) for renewal or salvation.[4] I am convinced that canonical theism can help to spur fresh thinking on renewal, on ecumenism, on evangelism, on theological education, and on mission. One way it does so is by keeping epistemology in its place.

Yet crucial work remains to be done on several fronts. We need not just a fresh vision of canon and of the epistemology of theology; we also need to rethink how best to proceed in systematic theology, so that we can abandon habits of thinking and criteria of success that have been in place for centuries. Until this work is done, the goal of presenting canonical theism will remain as an interesting promissory note. Happily, we are making progress on this front, but the task itself will require extensive collaborative research across the generations.[5]

4. See *The Logic of Renewal* (Grand Rapids: Eerdmans, 2003).
5. For an initial effort to make clear what is at stake, see William J. Abraham, Natalie B. Van Kirk, and Jason E. Vickers, eds., *Canonical Theism*, forthcoming from Eerdmans.

Chapter One

Reorientation

—◦◦◦—

The Current Scene

Popular culture is currently swamped with divine revelations. Traditional visions of divine revelation in Judaism, Christianity, and Islam continue to flourish; the more recent claims to divine revelation represented by Mormonism and various New Age gurus have no shortage of devotees.[1] To be sure, such flourishing is an astonishing phenomenon, given the dire predictions of the end of religion that have been commonplace in the twentieth century. Happily sociologists are now coming to terms with reality in this arena. Moreover, while we are still trying to sort through the impact of militant forms of Islam that clearly make appeal to divine revelation, it is obvious that we can no longer pretend that divine revelation can be shunted aside as marginal or irrelevant. Claims to divine revelation are here to stay. We need all the help we can muster if we are to come to terms with them intellectually.

Yet in theology we have been given next to no help in sorting through claims to divine revelation. The very idea of adjudicating competing claims to divine revelation is alien to the sensibility of contemporary

---

1. See, for example, Neale Donald Walsch, *The New Revelations* (New York: Atria Books, 2002). My favorite example outside the West is described in Jonathan Spence, *God's Chinese Son: The Taiping Heavenly Kingdom of Hong Xiuquan* (London: Flamingo, 1997).

1

theology. In my experience students tend to approach the topic with skepticism. Even if they believe in divine revelation, they do not expect to be able to explain why. They simply hold to it as a matter of faith; that is, they believe in divine revelation without evidence. And they have little or no idea how they might defend their commitment to a specific divine revelation as rational or plausible. Nor do they think that, in appealing to divine revelation, revelation might constitute good evidence for their claims. This is a radical change from the day when faith was construed as believing on the basis of divine revelation, and precisely because of this, on the basis of exceptionally good evidence. In some student circles it is morally objectionable to ask critical questions about the proper location of divine revelation in that such questioning is seen as attacking the cherished beliefs of friends or as a form of intellectual oppression. The whole topic has been set aside or become thoroughly privatized and swept into the corner of personal piety.

Within professional theology, divine revelation is assumed, rejected, or ignored. We can detect three major schools of thought. First, while a host of conservative theologians believe that they do indeed possess divine revelation and rely on it in their fundamental deliberations, they offer little help in justifying their claim to possess divine revelation. Given the endemic tendency to collapse divine revelation into scripture, their primary work consists in working through problems thrown up by contemporary forms of historical criticism, spelling out various models of divine revelation, and defending the material theology they see lodged within divine revelation.[2]

Second, other theologians find the whole idea of justifying claims to divine revelation otiose or wrongheaded. Here the great hero is Karl Barth,

2. One of the best pieces of recent work on divine revelation is to be found in *Dei Verbum* from Vatican II. Currently evangelicals in North America, who have been deeply committed to divine revelation, appear to be more interested in preserving a doctrine of inerrancy and in keeping at bay the impact of open theism than they are in tackling issues related to the epistemology of divine revelation. David K. Clark pursues the topic of revelation in an oblique way in *To Know and Love God* (Wheaton, Ill.: Crossway, 2003), folding the topic under his vision of scripture. One of the most interesting treatments of the topic of divine revelation that is intentionally theological but philosophically rigorous can be found in Keith Ward, *Religion and Revelation* (Oxford: Clarendon, 1994). David Brown's singular and extraordinary work is also exceptionally interesting. See his *Tradition and Imagination, Revelation and Change* (Oxford: Clarendon, 1999). Avery Dulles's *Models of Revelation* (New York: Image Books, 1985), with all of its irenic shortcomings, remains a classic in the field.

whose massive work on divine revelation has outlawed the very idea of providing any kind of rational defense for the identification of divine revelation. While Barth's work at certain levels remains unsurpassed, his central epistemological claims about divine revelation have been a disaster, leaving its adherents stripped of help in confronting competing claims.[3] The best that can be done is to stick to sophisticated expositions of the internal grammar or content of the Christian faith and leave the rest to God.[4] Echoes of this view show up in those who rest in the power of the biblical text to open up a new world or who appeal to the internal histories and perspectives of their faith communities to carry the day.[5] Efforts to hitch Barth's vision to analogies with natural science display a desperate attempt to salvage something from the ruins.[6]

Third, mainstream theologians have turned to deal with other worries. The primary concern has been moral and has been located in finding ways to address issues of exclusion, oppression, poverty, and discrimination. In this arena, outside a rather tepid commitment to forms of Marxist

---

3. I have discussed Barth's views at some length in *An Introduction to Philosophy of Religion* (Englewood Cliffs, N.J.: Prentice-Hall, 1985), chap. 7, and *Canon and Criterion in Christian Theology* (Oxford: Clarendon, 1998), chap. 14.

4. This has been a marked feature of the Yale school developed by Hans Frei, Paul Holmer, David Kelsey, and George Lindbeck. For a fine essay in this tradition see Ronald F. Thiemann, *Revelation and Theology: The Gospel as Narrated Promise* (Notre Dame: University of Notre Dame Press, 1985). Written prior to the emergence of the New Yale School, H. Richard Niebuhr's *The Meaning of Revelation* (New York: Macmillan, 1941) remains a landmark study.

5. See especially Paul Ricoeur, "Toward a Hermeneutic of the Idea of Revelation," in his *Essays in Biblical Interpretation* (Philadelphia: Fortress, 1980), 73-118. For a very helpful discussion of Ricoeur's fundamental moves in the epistemology of theology, see Mark I. Wallace, "Ricoeur, Rorty, and the Question of Revelation," in *Meaning in Texts and Actions: Questioning Paul Ricoeur*, ed. David E. Klemm and William Schweiker (Charlottesville: University of Virginia Press, 1993), 235-53. Rowan Williams, somewhat like Ricoeur, is drawn to a vision of revelation that focuses less on the unveiling of God and more on the generating of new perspectives. See his "Trinity and Revelation," *Modern Theology* 2 (1986): 197-211.

6. This project shows up aggressively in the work of Thomas F. Torrance and Alister McGrath. See Thomas F. Torrance, *Transformation and Convergence in the Frame of Knowledge: Explorations in the Interrelations of Scientific and Theological Enterprise* (Grand Rapids: Eerdmans, 1984), and Alister E. McGrath, *A Scientific Theology*, vol. 1, *Nature* (Grand Rapids: Eerdmans, 2001). I have provided a critical assessment in "Revelation and Natural Theology," in *Alister E. McGrath and Evangelical Theology*, ed. Suun Wook Chung (Carlisle: Paternoster, 2003), 264-79. My reservations about Barth do not mean I think students and admirers of his work will not be able to come through with a new defense of his position; at the moment, however, we have, at best, strong assertions and promissory notes.

and neo-Marxist philosophy, skepticism, suspicion, or diffidence reigns. In some circles enlightenment consists in accepting the privileged position of the poor and the oppressed in giving access to the truth about God.[7] It is rare to find an extended articulation of this thesis as a serious epistemological option. For the most part we are given reiterated assertions accompanied by sharp questions about the motivations for our critical questions.[8] It is as if epistemology is a taxi that the theologian can rudely dismiss once the driver has been paid for the relevant services.

The wider horizon in contemporary theology fits naturally with the dilapidated state of discussion of divine revelation within contemporary philosophy. It is simply assumed for the most part that divine revelation is not an option.[9] Here both mainstream analytical philosophy and the more complex strains of postmodernity stand together. The few exceptions that exist prove the rule.[10] Happily, these exceptions are wedged in

7. This theme has been persistently pursued with elegance by Joerg Rieger in his *Remember the Poor* (Harrisburg, Pa.: Trinity, 1998) and *God and the Excluded* (Minneapolis: Fortress, 1998). In the feminist tradition see Monika Hellwig, *Whose Experience Counts in Theological Reflection?* (Milwaukee: Marquette University Press, 1982).

8. For a splendid counterexample to this generalization see Clodovis Boff, *Theology and Praxis* (Maryknoll, N.Y.: Orbis, 1978). As a Thomist, Boff makes it very clear that work in fundamental theology cannot appeal to the poor as a privileged site of truth.

9. Consider the following comments of John Searle and Richard Rorty. Speaking of the scientific and naturalist worldview, Searle claims: "This world view is not an option. It is not simply up for grabs along with a lot of competing world views. Our problem is not that somehow we have failed to come up with a convincing proof of the existence of God or that the hypothesis of afterlife remains in serious doubt, it is rather that in our deepest reflections we cannot take such options seriously. When we encounter people who claim to believe such things, we may envy them the comfort and security they claim to derive from these beliefs, but at bottom we remain unconvinced that either they have heard the news or they are in the grip of faith" (*The Rediscovery of the Mind* [Cambridge: MIT Press, 1992], 90-91). Rorty shows his hand in his vision of culture. "For in its ideal form, the culture of liberalism would be one which is enlightened, secular, through and through. It would be one in which no trace of divinity remained, either in the form of a divinized world or a divinized self. Such a culture would have no room for the notion that there are nonhuman forces to which human beings should be responsible. It would drop or drastically reinterpret, not only the idea of holiness but those of 'devotion to truth' and of 'fulfillment of the deepest needs of the spirit'" (*Contingency, Irony, and Solidarity* [Cambridge: Cambridge University Press, 1989], 45).

10. Two outstanding discussions can be found in George Mavrodes, *Revelation in Religious Belief* (Philadelphia: Temple University Press, 1988), and Richard Swinburne, *Revelation: From Metaphor to Analogy* (Oxford: Clarendon, 1992).

an extraordinary flourishing of new work in epistemology and the philosophy of religion. While such work continues to be ignored within much of contemporary theology, it is hard to believe that it will not bear significant fruit over time. Clearly, patience is the order of the day at this stage, not least because current challenges to long-standing assumptions require time if they are to be sifted. Moreover, even if recovery of a robust commitment to divine revelation is a real option, progress is likely to be slow and scattered.

In this book I shall argue that divine revelation exists and that our possession of such revelation constitutes knowledge. Not surprisingly, it will soon become apparent that this claim cannot stand in stark isolation from a wider network of epistemological claims. Hence I shall locate this claim in a wider vision of the epistemology of theology. So while I have opened this chapter with a brief word on the current fortunes of divine revelation, we cannot reach our goal without striking further afield. Thus it will take some time before I can begin to make good on this assertion about the status of divine revelation.

Given that I think we can have knowledge in this arena, it will come as no surprise that I also think belief in divine revelation can also be both rational and justified. This too is a bold thesis that can easily be dismissed out of hand. I take comfort from the fact that in the long history of philosophy and theology a positive epistemic estimate of divine revelation has been taken as commonplace.[11] Thus I view the current orthodoxy within theology and philosophy as an aberration. Aberrations in this instance arise because of serious problems in the prevailing modes of thought. Hence our first task will be to clear the decks by raising queries against current ways of thinking about the epistemic status of theological claims. This will detain us in the middle section of this opening chapter. In pursuing our quarry at this point I shall limit my observations to strategies for articulating the rationality or justification of religious belief. We shall come to the question of knowledge soon enough. For the purposes of ex-

---

11. This is obviously the case throughout the Middle Ages, but it extends at least up until the work of John Locke. It is a sign of the times that contemporary philosophers have enormous difficulty coming to terms with the commitment to divine revelation both in theory and fact in the life of Socrates. For a splendid treatment of this topic see Mark L. McPherran, "Socratic Reason and Socratic Revelation," *Journal of the History of Philosophy* 29 (1991): 345-73. This essay, while exegetical and historical in orientation, bears close pondering by those interested in the epistemology of divine revelation.

position I shall need to modify this policy, but initially we need not be excessively fussy about terminology.

The Standard Strategy

I begin with a simple observation. Virtually all attempts to secure the rationality of theism develop a shared strategy that we can neatly name as the standard strategy. It can be formulated as follows. Develop a general account of rationality or justification and then apply it to theism to see how far belief in God is rational or justified. The obvious rationale for this strategy is that without something like this our approach to belief in God will appear insecure and question begging. We need a vision of rationality or justification that will stand independently of the beliefs it secures; otherwise the whole exercise looks like special pleading. At the least we need a foothold outside of theology, whether wholly or by analogy, to gain what we need in the epistemology of theology.

We can see this strategy exemplified in the most important visions of the epistemology of theology that have surfaced in twentieth-century philosophy. Initially it is good to see them in their simplest forms, leaving aside our worries about misrepresentation. Consider the following catalogue of options.

1. Rationality or justification is secured by proof or disproof of the relevant propositions. Thus classical natural theologians have developed deductive proofs of the existence of God and thereby hoped to establish the rationality of belief in God. In this vision, in the absence of proof and disproof, there is nothing but subjective opinion or emotional and prudential commitment. This schema has dominated discussions of the rationality of religious belief from Aquinas until the middle of the twentieth century.[12]

2. Rationality or justification consists in ultimate language games or framework beliefs. Discourse about God is a language game or a

---

12. The great exception to this until recently is to be found in the work of Joseph Butler and John Henry Newman. Neither has received the attention he deserves. For a notable exception see William J. Wainwright, *Reason and the Heart: A Prolegomenon to a Critique of Passional Reason* (Ithaca, N.Y.: Cornell University Press, 1995).

framework belief that requires no justification. Language games constitute the boundaries of rationality and knowledge. Given that many people play the religious language game, the rationality and justification of theism are as secure as anything could be. There is nothing above or below religious discourse that can call it into question; theological discourse stands on its own feet. Broadly speaking, this is a position that has flown under the flag of Wittgensteinian fideism.[13]

3. Rationality or justification is established by basing a belief on universal human experience. Theistic belief is based on the universal human experience of trust, therefore it is rational. While this constitutes a minority report, Schubert Ogden has made it with exemplary clarity.[14]

4. Rationality or justification can be attained by the provision of cumulative case arguments. Theism can be well supported by cumulative case arguments, therefore belief in God is rational and justified. Basil Mitchell and Richard Swinburne have both made this case with telling originality.[15]

5. Rationality or justification can be secured by perceptual experience accompanied by testimony. Theism can be shown to be grounded in religious experience accompanied by testimony. John Hick has argued in this manner with verve and rigor.[16]

6. Warrant is secured by properly basic belief. Christian theism is constituted by a network of properly basic beliefs, therefore Christian

---

13. One of its most notable exponents is D. Z. Phillips. See, for example, his *Faith after Foundationalism* (London: Routledge, 1988).

14. See Schubert Ogden, "The Reality of God," in his *The Reality of God and Other Essays* (New York: Harper and Row, 1963), 1-70.

15. See Basil Mitchell, *The Justification of Religious Belief* (Basingstoke: Macmillan, 1973), and Richard Swinburne, *The Existence of God* (Oxford: Clarendon, 1979; rev. ed. 1991). For a fine discussion of the differences between Mitchell and Swinburne see Robert Prevost, *Probability and Theistic Explanation* (Oxford: Clarendon, 1990). Often the strategy identified here involves a network of arguments to the best explanation. For a fine collection of essays that develop this version of the cumulative case argument position, see Paul Copan and Paul K. Moser, eds., *The Rationality of Theism* (London: Routledge, 2003).

16. See John Hick, *Faith and Knowledge* (Ithaca, N.Y.: Cornell University Press, 1966), *The Interpretation of Religion* (New Haven: Yale University Press, 1989). It might be thought that William P. Alston in his widely acclaimed *Perceiving God* (Ithaca: Cornell University Press, 1991) belongs in this category. It is clear, however, that his work belongs in the previous, fourth option.

theism is warranted. Reformed epistemology, led by the indefatigable and splendid work of Alvin Plantinga, operates from this angle.[17]

This bald summary of the main options in the contemporary epistemology of theology cannot begin to do justice to the care with which they have been developed and articulated. Nor can it do justice to the progress that has been made in the literature as a whole. I shall gladly have recourse in the work that follows to a variety of insights, conceptual discoveries, and particular arguments that have emerged of late in the literature. Yet there is merit in standing back and noting the simple strategy that is at work in virtually every case, for the great diversity and fecundity of proposals can easily mask the large measure of agreement in place. There is at work here a standard intellectual procedure that is rarely examined or questioned. The fundamental move is to work out a general theory of rationality, justification, knowledge, warrant, and the like, that we can then take on the road and use to work out the status of theism. Virtually all the crucial work goes into working out the details of the relevant general epistemology; once this is in place, it is relatively simple to see how the proposed epistemology does or does not apply to theism. The work as a whole represents nothing short of a golden era in the epistemology of religion. It is such a vast improvement on the dismissive and simpleminded veto on theology within philosophy that was prevalent in the middle of the twentieth century, that it may seem churlish to find fault. Yet it is time to identify and come to terms with a network of problems within it that naturally arise.

Problems in the Current Strategy

Note at the outset that there is no agreement on the general epistemology or theory of justification to be deployed. Given that virtually everything in philosophy is contested, this does not take us very far. However, at the very least, lack of agreement opens the door for tackling the relevant questions from a radically different angle. If the major protagonists cannot agree on the general epistemology to be deployed, we can take leave of the

17. See Alvin Plantinga, *Warranted Christian Belief* (New York: Oxford University Press, 2000).

standard option with a good conscience and begin again from a different angle.

Furthermore, we do not know a priori what sort of criteria or general theory should be invoked in dealing with the epistemology of theology. This is in fact the case in dealing with contested disciplines and issues outside of theology. Again and again general criteria have been proposed, but invariably they rule out claims to truth that should rightly detain us. Thus history has been faulted because it does not fit the paradigm supplied by natural science; or belief in the external world has been found wanting because it does not meet with the requirements of empiricism; or beliefs about other minds have been found shaky because they cannot be established deductively. Theology itself has become marginalized precisely because it has failed this or that test of credibility or good reasoning. Yet the content and status of the theory deployed often turn out to be every bit as speculative and complicated as theology itself has ever been. Thus we need to cultivate more modesty and to take more time to sort through the kind of claim that is on offer in theology.

We should also note that within theology itself the impact of more general theories is all too apparent. Thus crucial theological claims are systematically ignored or set aside because they would not fit the schema in hand. Protagonists of this or that theory remain satisfied if they can secure this or that favored element within theism; they leave the rest on one side, or interpret the adopted theological claim in a bald and insensitive manner, or simply remap the internal claims of theology as "myth," "symbol," or "metaphor" to fit the required schema. Taking the latter option to a higher level, it is not uncommon for central theological claims to be reworked and radically reinterpreted to make them fit. This leaves theology at the mercy of the theories in hand. More broadly, it leaves theology at the mercy of the prevailing options in contemporary philosophy. Within this horizon there is next to no way to find ample space for the kind of robust theism that is found in the lifeblood of the Christian tradition or that may be needed to fit the complexity and raggedness of human existence. The epistemological theory is primary; theology itself is secondary and treated as subservient; theology's central claims are seen as guilty until proven innocent.

A further consideration in the neighborhood of canonical theism is this: rarely, if at all, do these proposals secure the deep content of Christian belief. Generally theists are satisfied to provide a justification for a minimalist version of theism that does not come close to the complexity and rich convictions that are central to the living core of the Christian faith. They leave vast tracts of crucial theological assertions unattended, as if they are to fend for themselves or to be relegated to the margins of belief. Sometimes the favored schema creates intellectual conditions in which it would be impossible to take seriously, much less believe, whole networks of theological assertions. Even taking the offending materials seriously is seen as a mark of superstition or credulity.

In addition, it is far from clear how the standard strategy can do full justice to the way in which a host of Christian believers actually believe. There are characteristic features of Christian belief, namely, its firmness, persistence, and sureness, that do not get attention or fit into the proposal as a whole. One of the most neglected but interesting challenges facing the epistemologist of theology is the kind of certainty believers often exhibit in their commitments and assent. On any serious reading of the tradition, we need an account that will begin to do justice both to the faith of the ordinary believer and to the faith of the saints and martyrs. Presently the latter tend to be seen as irrational fanatics; there is next to no natural place for them in the standard schema.

Lastly, the standard strategy rarely if ever attends to the welter of epistemic suggestions and insight that lies buried in the Christian tradition. There are in fact extremely interesting epistemological insights and ideas to be found there. They represent a serious engagement with the rationality of beliefs inside faith that need to be explored and pondered in their own right, whether or not they fit our standard strategy. We shall come to several of them in due course. For the moment I want to register that it is not enough to set them aside; they deserve to be articulated and evaluated on merit rather than dismissed as question begging.

In the light of these considerations, we should set aside the standard strategy and work from a radically different angle. The standard strategy has served us well in ensuring that theology not be given any special privileges, but we need to take a different path.[18] We can move in the right di-

18. I am deeply sympathetic to the standard strategy in that it was the only real option in a cultural situation where one first had to establish one's credentials in philosophy more generally before one could tackle the challenges of philosophy of religion. In part, this stems from a sense that epistemology is constituted by a tradition of rationality and critical inquiry that came into existence by setting itself in opposition to myth, religion, and tradition. Thus the dice have long been loaded in a secularist direction. In part, this strategy

rection by adopting a very different epistemological principle. Our vision of rationality, justification, knowledge, warrant, and the like should be appropriate to the subject matter in hand. Let's call this the principle of appropriate epistemic fit. Thus, rather than beginning with a general strategy that we apply to the subject before us, we should look to the actual subject matter that claims our allegiance and, starting afresh, see where that takes us. Certainly this is a relatively secure, alternative epistemic principle. We do not dismiss history because it does not fit the requirements of geometry. Inductive arguments about the world should not be cast aside because they do not satisfy the conditions essential to deductive arguments. Faith is not to be thrown out because it fails to satisfy the normative conditions related to sight.

Of course, the standard strategy has its own characteristic way of resolving the identity of the issue in hand. With few exceptions, the issue at hand is reduced to two simple alternatives, theism or atheism. We then look around for a good epistemology to find out which of these yields the best epistemic results. Having found a satisfactory epistemology, we apply it to the debate between theists and atheists and check the results. We can understand how the quest for simplicity and the desire to manage the data drive us in this direction. However, the results have left us at a stalemate. Moreover, the options are mere paper options; they do not constitute the

---

stemmed from having to address philosophers committed in their own way to a vision of "pure reason" abstracted from culture and tradition. For a fine exposure of the situatedness in the heart of all modern European philosophy, see Merold Westphal, "Whose Philosophy? Which Religion? Reflections on Reason as Faith," in James E. Faulconer, *Transcendence in Philosophy and Religion* (Bloomington and Indianapolis: Indiana University Press, 2003), 13-34. Westphal cogently argues that traditions of pure reason have their own basic beliefs about the human condition that are set in wider historical and often metaphysical narratives and are embedded in their particular practices or *Welt-Praxis*. Westphal's suggestions go a long way to explaining why much contemporary philosophy has until recently been so prejudiced against problems in philosophy of religion and why those committed to working in philosophy of religion had to hide their interest and talents and bide their time before turning to the field. In these circumstances the standard strategy was a good one. Moreover, the gains for epistemology in following the standard strategy have been enormous, as can be seen in the general epistemological work of William P. Alston, Alvin Plantinga, Robert Audi, Nicholas Wolterstorff, Richard Swinburne, Paul Moser, George Mavrodes, Eleonore Stump, Philip L. Quinn, Keith Yandell, and many others. Philosophy of religion, if only indirectly, has its own way of generating fresh thought within philosophy more generally. I see the work of the last forty years as truly extraordinary in its impact and fecundity. It will remain as landmark work for a long time.

kinds of robust versions of theism and atheism that we find in history or real life. In reality there are very different versions of theism and atheism on offer.

Failure to acknowledge the complexity of rival theistic and atheistic worldviews, while it may have made the argument look more rigorous and elegant, has given the whole debate an air of unreality. This is especially so on the atheist side of the discussion. Generally atheists have been content to sit back, let the theists make a case, and then simply refute it as elegantly as possible. Presumably the atheism embraced is then the negation of the theism refuted; the atheist becomes identified simply as the one who does not believe in the god identified by his opponent. This strategy depends, of course, on the virtually impossible task of establishing a negative proposition. As Alvin Plantinga has argued to telling effect, it may well need a version of evidentialism to keep it afloat.[19] That is, the atheist's position involves a highly questionable assumption that insists that rationality and kindred goals can be secured only if one has propositional evidence in hand. The really important point to make here, however, is that this makes life far too easy for the atheist, for serious versions of atheism are much richer and far more interesting and important than this strategy permits. One is rarely a mere atheist. One is a Marxist atheist, an existentialist atheist, a humanist atheist, a Buddhist atheist, a Nietzschean atheist, a Nazi atheist, a Chekovian atheist, a materialist atheist, and the like. Thus genuine, living forms of atheism never gain the exposition much less the critical evaluation they deserve. Atheists rarely if ever properly defend positive, world-orienting forms of atheism.

One way to bring out the wealth of the options on offer is to note that atheists have their own network of beliefs about creation, their own vision of the human situation, their own view of and prescription for righting the ills of the world, their own characteristic way of living, and their own vision of the future. The same applies to theism. One is a Christian theist, a Jewish theist, a Unitarian theist, a process theist, and the like. Each has its own vision of creation, human nature, salvation, the future, and the like. So we now see that the standard strategy has yet one more problem to contend with beyond the ones enumerated above. Much of the debate is a kind of sophisticated

19. See his seminal essay "Reason and Belief in God," in *Faith and Rationality*, ed. Alvin Plantinga and Nicholas Wolsterstorff (Notre Dame: University of Notre Dame Press, 1983), 16-93.

shadowboxing that leaves most people outside a network of professionals bored and dissatisfied. It is as if the real subject is never seriously joined. The protagonists fail to connect to the life of either belief or unbelief.[20]

An Alternative Strategy

If there are serious difficulties in the standard strategy, it is time to look for an alternative. What I propose is quite simple. Let us reverse the way we proceed. Rather than securing a method and then seeing what results it gives us, let us identify a particular brand of theism and then ask what would be the appropriate way to adjudicate its intellectual status. In this scenario we begin with a robust vision of theism; we then stand back and ask what would be the appropriate way to think about working out whether it is rational or irrational, justified or unjustified, knowledge or illusion. This is in fact how much of our thinking develops. We find ourselves already believing a network of theistic propositions, and when challenged we are forced to think through which kinds of considerations should come into play in thinking through queries about its epistemic status. Alternatively, we find ourselves presented with a robust Christian vision of the world and then pursue how best to get a handle on its rationality and justification. Note that what is at issue here is not the material reasons or considerations that may come into play but which kinds of reasons and considerations should come into play.

Once we pose the problem in this fashion, the next question is which theistic vision to put on the table. The obvious way to meet this issue head-on is to specify more carefully the particular expression of theism that is being evaluated from an epistemic point of view. In this work I shall take as our target the vision of theism embodied in the canonical heritage of the church. By this I mean the theism that was officially adopted by the church over time and deliberately embodied in its scriptures, its creed, its sacraments and liturgy, its iconography, its saints, and in the writings of its canonical teachers. As I have suggested elsewhere, we might designate this

20. One can readily understand why in the recent cultural climate theists have been satisfied to get the central proposition that God exists out on the table again for discussion. Getting this far is an enormous achievement, and I in no way want to belittle the great progress that has been made.

theism as canonical theism.[21] It represents the theism officially developed in the church prior to the great schism and which continues to shine through in the canonical materials, practices, and persons that were designated as its best carriers and exemplars. While it is impossible to avoid the shadow of artificiality here, this strategy of highlighting this particular expression of theism avoids the tempting simplicities of mere theism and mere atheism.

In adopting this option we can immediately register some preliminary benefits. To begin, we avoid any form of theism that has been cut back to fit some favored epistemological vision. We allow the theism on offer to stand independently of its defense. Furthermore, we are dealing with a version of theism that remains alive and well across the generations. Its canonical status was wrung from the struggles of history. In part or in whole it has sustained countless simple believers and many saints and martyrs across space and time. Moreover, given the richness of its contents, we have plenty on offer by way of epistemic insight and suggestion. While it is first and foremost constituted by a vision of creation and redemption, it has buried within it a vision of revelation that can be freshly articulated in the present. In addition, once we begin to see its contours, we can note that there are ways to think of its epistemic status that are outside the boundaries of the standard strategy. Finally, we gain ground in securing the principle of appropriate fit in our work in epistemology. By starting with a robust vision of theism, we can begin to explore the kinds of considerations and arguments that are relevant to adjudicating its epistemic status. In pursuing our quarry in this manner, we do not of course rule out the development of other epistemological strategies that would help in making progress on the epistemology of theology; nor do we for a moment disparage work on other versions of theism. Our claim is more modest in that we are content to open up a rival option to the standard strategy that currently prevails in the field.

Canonical Theism

It remains in this chapter to explore further what is at stake in working with that form of theism that I have designated as canonical theism. It is the version of theism embodied in the rich canonical heritage of the church. Thus

---

21. See the collection of essays bearing this title forthcoming from Eerdmans.

canonical theism is dispersed in the scriptures, the Nicene Creed, the iconography, and the liturgy; it is enacted in the lives of the saints; it is summarized and worked through in the work of the canonical teachers of the church prior to the great schism; it is implicitly received in baptism; and it is handed over in ordination to the diaconate, priesthood, and episcopate from generation to generation. The intellectual core of canonical theism is a rich vision of God, creation, and redemption. At heart it involves the claim that the one and only God, the creator of the universe, has redeemed the world from sin and death through the life, death, and resurrection of Jesus Christ through the working of the Holy Spirit. In and around these themes there slumbers a vast network of other themes and proposals that will emerge as we proceed. This refusal to begin with a simple, short vision of theism will be something of a handicap for those that want to work with a tidy form of theism, but as I have already indicated, for too long tidiness has been privileged at the expense of complexity and depth. It will become relatively clear as we proceed what is and what is not included in canonical theism. Even then, I have no desire to cut away the ragged edges.

It will suffice for now to keep the following points in mind as we proceed. The interpretation of canonical theism, together with the teachings and practices that relate to it, is not a static affair. The handing over of the canonical heritage is accompanied by intense discussion, by legitimate internal disagreement, by extensive commentary, and the like.[22] Inevitably it will reflect the personalities, perspectives, and locations of its adherents.

Thus it is a mistake to confuse canonical theism with orthodoxy, or with classical or traditional theism, and then assume that we are dealing with some sort of inert dogma that cannot connect with the real world or with our contemporary situation. There are a time and place to make use of the ideas of orthodoxy or traditional forms of theism as shorthand for ca-

---

22. John Henry Newman, with characteristic felicity, exaggerates only a little when he writes: "Nor is it an inferior faculty to discriminate, rescue, and adjust the truth, which a fierce controversy threatens to tear in pieces, at a time when the ecclesiastical atmosphere is thick with the dust of the conflict, when all parties are more or less in the wrong, and the public mind has become so bewildered so as not to be able to say what it does or does not hold, or even what it held before the strife of ideas began. *In such circumstances, to speak the word evoking order and peace, and to restore the multitude of men to themselves and to each other, by a reassertion of what is old with a luminousness of explanation which is new, is a gift inferior only to that of revelation itself*" (*Rise and Progress of Universities and Benedictine Essays* [Notre Dame: Gracewing, 2001], 476, emphasis added).

nonical theism, but we should not be misled at this point. Our interest is the faith of the church, and this faith should not be confused with handy summaries, polemical shortcuts, or categories drawn from the history of ideas.

Further, while there has been a long-standing and disastrous tendency to rework parts of the canonical heritage of the church so that they operate as items in epistemology, the canonical heritage is not and never has been an epistemology. I have argued the case for this elsewhere and will not belabor the point afresh here.[23] Suffice it to insist that the canonical heritage is constituted by a network of materials, practices, and persons brought into being by God within the church and intended to heal our wounded and rebellious selves. Thus from the outset we have a rich set of theological claims; we have first-order discourse about God, creation, the human situation, redemption, and the like; we do not have an epistemology.

This last point needs to be emphasized. If it had so desired, the church could well have canonized a particular theory of knowledge. We know that from at least the thirteenth century on the temptation to do this has been well nigh irresistible. Modern Western theology has been marked to the point of obsession by the persistent reduction of the canonical heritage of the church to its canon of scripture, by the conceiving of this canon as a criterion of truth secured initially by a theory of divine revelation, and then by looking hither and yon for an alternative when this vision breaks down. But I am convinced that the church as a whole, prior to the great schism, did not take this route. It never developed an agreed theory of reflective rationality, much less canonize such a theory. We can see this plainly when we recall that the church, while resolute, for example, in adopting a specific trinitarian vision of God and a particular Christology, never adopted a particular doctrine of the atonement or a specific vision of divine inspiration, even though we can find lots of material on these topics in the history of theology. Likewise, while the teachers and evangelists of the church deployed a wealth of argument, insight, and even large-scale epistemological theories, the church did not canonize this material.[24] This is a subtle but crucial point that bears repeating from another angle.

23. *Canon and Criterion in Christian Theology.*
24. I exaggerate here in saying that teachers deployed large-scale epistemological theories. Even in the case of figures like, say, Origen, Augustine, the Cappadocians, and Boethius, who were intellectuals of the first rank, the epistemological work is often incomplete and operates more as an assumption than a required commitment. Their first commitment was to the faith of the church.

The church claims to hand down the truth about God. Thus it claims to provide pivotal information about creation, the human situation, the healing activity of God in history, his promises for the future, and the like. The core of the faith from a cognitive angle is simply the truth about our origins, our alienation from God, and our redemption through the work of the triune God. Moreover, in teaching this faith the teachers and members of the church may give all sorts of reasons to support the claim that it possesses such pivotal information or that what it teaches is true. However, what the canonical theist asserts is that the church offers no formal theory as to how it knows that it possesses the truth about God, the human situation, the activity and purposes of God, and the like. More importantly, canonical theists insist that the failure to canonize an epistemology was a wise omission both for the good of the church and for the good of epistemology.

Consider some neighboring examples. Compare a historian giving information about the past without mentioning or even possessing a theory of historical knowledge. Indeed, the historian's account of the epistemology of history, were she to have one, might turn out to be thoroughly inadequate. Yet the historian could still provide genuine information. Or compare an observer of the Holocaust insisting on the heinous nature of the deeds done, even though she does not have to hand any theory of moral discourse and its justification. Clearly, the observer could be right about the immorality of the Holocaust without signaling which epistemology of morality, if any, was embraced. Or compare someone recognizing and reveling in the beauty of Mozart's music without having given any thought to the nature of beauty or to how to demarcate good music from vulgar music. She could still provide significant information about the beauty of Mozart's music to, say, her children without having any of this kind of material to hand.

To put the matter grandly, we can and do make good judgments about the world, about the quality of deeds wrought in history, and about the beauty of this or that object, without having a theory of truth, goodness, or beauty. Further, we can give all sorts of persuasive and telling reasons for our judgments and our beliefs without having a theory of why these constitute good reasons for them.[25] In regard to the case in hand, the

---

25. Even then, when we are given a theory, it is not clear if we have made much progress intellectually. Thus, suppose we are told that we should accept that two plus two equals

church teaches that its core beliefs are true, that eternal life in Christ is worth securing, that the lives of its saints are conspicuously good, without at the same time insisting that any particular theory of truth or goodness is correct. Moreover, in teaching the faith, the church can provide all sorts of reasons and evidence for its beliefs and practices without having to hand a theory as to what constitutes good or relevant evidence.

Canon and Epistemology

This distinction between success in providing good arguments and having to hand a theory of good arguments may appear elementary, but we are mistaken if we do not see the depth and import of this simple observation. It is easy to be misled here. At one level it might seem obvious that we should canonize the theories that have proved useful in supporting the church's first-order commitments. John Locke, for example, was convinced that a rule of faith, his term for an agreed criterion of truth in theology, was essential for the identity of a religious community. "For since all things that belong to that religion are contained in that rule, it follows necessarily that those who agree in one rule are of one and the same religion, and vice-versa. Thus, Turks and Christians are of different religions because these take the holy scripture to be the rule of their religion and those the Alcoran."[26] Religious communities were, in his view, picked out and identified by the rule of faith they embraced, so that the difference between Christianity and Islam was captured by their different rules of faith. Moreover, a religious community might seem underdeveloped or incomplete if it did not have an official criterion of truth. Surely if truth really

---

four because this is a self-evident proposition, or that it is true that there is now a desk in front of me because it is evident to the senses; it is not all that clear how far this gets us. Would we stop believing these propositions if we were to find a flaw in these second-order claims? Does the second-order claim do anything beyond describing something we already implicitly accepted before we thought about the issue? There is indeed virtue in sorting through the assumptions that may be operating and organizing them as best we can, but we need to be wary of making too much of what we have done. Sometimes in epistemology it is tempting to think that all we achieve is preventing a certain kind of intellectual rot from getting a grip on our thinking; perhaps in epistemology we have an odd kind of intellectual therapy on our hands.

26. John Locke, "A Letter Concerning Toleration," in *Works* (London: John Pemberton, 1727), II, 250.

matters, the argument goes, each community will officially identify and deploy its agreed epistemology, especially when doing so will resolve current and future disputes by securing the truth on contested issues. Thus a good epistemology seems like a useful instrument to have to hand.

The historical evidence counts seriously against this kind of argument. The church lived for centuries without any such agreement. Christian intellectuals have invented and deployed a host of competing epistemic positions. They have been able to be fully committed, say, to the Nicene vision of God and yet hold to a host of competing epistemological proposals. Drawing on the current technical language, we can safely say that Christian intellectuals have been foundationalists and coherentists, contextualists and foundherentists, evidentialists and anti-evidentialists, internalists and externalists, particularists and methodists, realists and idealists, rationalists and empiricists. It is odd in the extreme to make these kinds of commitments constitutive or essential to the content or identity of the Christian faith. It may not even be possible to articulate the canonical heritage of the church without displaying one's epistemological commitments, but this in no way makes the particular epistemology on display canonical. It simply shows that a particular expression of the Christian faith is better expounded in, with, and through epistemic commitments; it does nothing to show that canonical content and epistemic strategy are identical.

Moreover, once we make epistemological commitments canonical, then the likelihood of schism within the church is immediately multiplied. If the church's identity and unity now depend on adopting the favored epistemology, then we can expect division not just on the gospel or the creed, but on issues of epistemology as well. Certainly insisting on the infallibility of the pope, a move that was later enriched to shore up the failing fortunes of the doctrine of *sola scriptura*, was one crucial element in the split between East and West. It remains a massive stumbling block to Christian unity today. Equally, the attempts within the Roman Catholic tradition to canonize the epistemology of Aquinas in the 1870s have recently fallen on hard times given the competing visions of Thomism that have emerged over the last century or so.[27] Canonizing Aquinas as the theologian of theologians has

27. It is well known that the initial doctoral work of Karl Rahner and Pope Benedict XVI barely made it through the university system of examinations because they challenged the prevailing interpretations of Aquinas. For the difficulties in appeal to Thomas

simply increased divisions rather than reduced them. In addition, the deep splits within modern Protestantism often hinge on competing epistemological theories. Thus the big split between conservatives and liberals revolves around the relative merits of religious experience as the foundation of Christian belief. Current disputes about the status of postmodernism are also disputes about the content of epistemic theory. They may begin with debates about meaning, but they quickly evolve into debates about the nature of truth and justification.[28]

In addition, it is illusory to think that the adoption of a rule of faith secures agreement on the kinds of issues that hold a religious community together. The Reformers agreed to a rule of faith in scripture and fell apart because they could not agree on its content. More recently, attempts by Anglicans to rally around the triad of scripture, tradition, and reason, or by United Methodists to agree to the quadrilateral of scripture, tradition, reason, and experience, have proven barren in securing unity. Epistemologies of theology, given their radical diversity, do not at all secure agreement on what really matters in the life of faith. On the contrary, they have been disastrous when pressed into service in this arena; they foster division rather than unity.

Furthermore, there is something categorically odd going on when Christian communities or denominations claim to possess some sort of expertise in epistemology. The Christian faith is first and foremost a message of healing from spiritual sickness, despair, and evil. Its leaders do not come equipped with any special expertise in epistemology. It is odd to think of Jesus conducting seminars on epistemology for his disciples. Epistemology, insofar as it exists at all, is a serious and complex subdiscipline within philosophy.[29] It requires its own expertise and training,

---

Aquinas see Gerald A. McCool, S.J., *From Unity to Pluralism: The Internal Evolution of Thomism* (New York: Fordham University Press, 1989). Similar attempts to make John Wesley an epistemological mentor within Methodism have also failed, though the effort to keep this alive still lingers on in some circles. See my "The End of Wesleyan Theology," *Wesleyan Theological Journal* 40 (Spring 2005): 7-25.

28. I leave aside here the possibility that semantics, epistemology, and truth may be integrally related, a claim that has many adherents in contemporary philosophy.

29. Within theology, it does not really take on a full life of its own until the later Middle Ages. Even so, I have been chastened but not convinced by conversations with my colleague Bruce Marshall on how little interest there is, for example, in divine revelation in the work of Thomas Aquinas.

yet surely not the kind of expertise or training vouchsafed in baptism or ordination. The church's expertise, thankfully, lies elsewhere. Focusing on epistemology as integral to its identity or to the content of its canonical heritage strikes me as fatally damaging. The church is first and foremost in the business of holiness. It is failure within this horizon, that is, lasting failure in spiritual formation, that is the root cause of its current troubles. The church has lost faith in its own canonical heritage, much of it engendered by insisting on the propriety of this or that epistemological vision.[30] Worse still, the church in the West has transformed its canonical heritage into a network of epistemic theory and thereby damaged the use of its own most fundamental means of grace.

It might be objected at this point that we are missing out on the fullness of faith. What if God has given the church a full-dress epistemology? We are to suppose here that we have available a divinely authorized epistemology, supplied by a prophet who has received it by divine revelation. We can think of either a generic epistemology designed to take care of all manner of issues and disputes, or a more regional epistemology designed, say, to apply only to theology. In either case we would not need the labor of philosophers; or if we did, their role would be one of mere confirmation. We might think of the purported epistemology to be analogous to what fundamentalists claim to possess in the realm of science, namely, a divinely authorized account, say, of the origin of species delivered by divine inspiration and now available in a sacred text. Thus we might think of an epistemology of theology given to us in a divine revelation. We only have to mention the possibility to reject it. The appeal to divine revelation is itself one more epistemological proposal, so the plan to secure a particular epistemology by an appeal to divine revelation is to extend the epistemology on offer; it does not secure its status. Spiritually speaking, the whole operation is absurd on its face. Only someone obsessed about epistemology would venture such a suggestion; only someone already in the grip of the primacy of epistemology and cut off from the treasures of the church would invent and then crave such an esoteric option.[31]

---

30. I explore this topic in *The Logic of Renewal* (Grand Rapids: Eerdmans; London: SPCK, 2003).

31. It has to be bluntly stated at this point that many theists continue to be obsessed with not just epistemology but with a certain kind of epistemology. The very possibility of knowledge is predicated on having to hand some theory of knowledge that shows that we possess knowledge. We cannot claim to be justified or claim to possess knowledge, it is said,

Eschewing the desire for a divinely authorized epistemology does not preclude Christian theologians from taking a stand against this or that epistemological theory, as Augustine and Luther in their own ways did against skepticism. For excellent reasons Christian evangelists and teachers may reject all sorts of epistemological proposals like positivism, relativism, nihilism, and the like, and argue with skill and flair against them. They may also deploy all sorts of epistemological proposals in their work. However, this is a far cry from the church adopting any particular epistemological theory. Such negative, polemical, or constructive work belongs to the ongoing exposition and articulation of the gospel in the world as it is; the church can well do so without overreacting and overcommitting itself to some grand theory of knowledge. When the church goes that far, it risks its own best treasures and undermines the delicate economy of its welfare.

We need to tread carefully here. Insisting on the noncanonical status of epistemological proposals as they relate to theology does not mean that we should be indifferent about epistemological issues. Indeed, doing good epistemology, even right on the borders of the canonical heritage of the church, as shall detain us in this work, helps to keep matters in perspective. Such work helps to highlight precisely the difference between the canonical heritage of the church and epistemology. The alert observer can readily perceive the difference once we move into the field of epistemology and set to work. In addition, epistemologists have their own modest work to do for the sake of the church's ministry in the world. In its own time and place epistemology will even be spiritually and pastorally beneficial. Epistemologists can clarify a network of important questions, resolve much confusion, help believers and unbelievers get clear on what is at stake in disputes between them, and clear many a roadblock on the road to holiness. Moreover, it is right and proper that we pursue questions about the rationality and justification of theology for its own sake.[32]

---

without having appropriate criteria of justification or of knowledge in place and without showing how we meet them. For such readers the whole thrust of this text will appear bizarre and even perverse. They will want to know up front what criteria or theory we are deploying. If this is not available, they will insist that the pertinent criteria are masked from view or hidden away below the surface. This whole essay rejects this prior epistemological assumption, insisting that we can know all sorts of things without knowing how we know them. In making this move I am not rejecting epistemology; I am simply calling into question one popular way of thinking of epistemology.

32. It is surely also the case that epistemological issues crop up very naturally both in

Our concern in what follows is more modest. I want to relocate the appeal to divine revelation within a wider vision of the epistemology of theology. To that end I have given a brief survey of the current state of play within significant tracks of recent theology and philosophy of religion. Beyond that I have suggested that there is a standard strategy in dealing with the justification of theism that starts from the wrong end of the terrain. While this strategy has borne enormous fruit, it does not begin to do justice to the robust forms of theism that operate in people's lives. Canonical theism is one such form of Christian theism that can serve as a useful instrument in reworking the terms of the discussion. This is constituted by a rich network of world-orienting beliefs that has had a lasting impact across the centuries and that is enshrined in a deep vision of creation and redemption. With this in hand we are now ready to move to the next stage by exploring which kinds of considerations are relevant to exploring its epistemic status. Before we can get there, however, we must look more generally at the topic of epistemology.

---

everyday thinking and in all sorts of disciplined inquiry; thus it is futile to wish epistemology out of existence or to kill it off by writing obituary notices.

Chapter Two

Epistemic Platitudes and Theology

———❧———

Resisting Skepticism

While contemporary theologians are generally uninterested or impatient with current work in epistemology, those who do venture forth in this arena are very tempted to develop a full-blown epistemology. By epistemology I mean here a systematic account of rationality, justification, and knowledge.[1] If God is to be related to everything, and if theology is the study of God and of everything else as it relates to God, it would seem odd not to have a theology that did not at least speak to the general issues in epistemology. How could something as ubiquitous, as substantial, as vital as rationality, justification, and knowledge not be a matter for theological reflection? How could a theologian concerned with God and with everything insofar as it relates to God not desire, for example, to think of knowledge insofar as it relates to God, the creator and sustainer of all things? Moreover, given that epistemology tends to be a seamless whole in which a network of proposals is developed, it is difficult to stop short of a full-scale theory. One of the fascinations of medieval theology is the extent to which this kind of persistent quest was pursued with flair and rigor.[2]

1. This is somewhat broader than standard definitions that restrict epistemology to the study of justification and knowledge.

2. Gordon Leff, *Medieval Thought, Augustine to Ockham* (London: Penguin Books, 1958), remains an older but superb review of the terrain.

24

In the modern period this quest for comprehension in epistemology is visible in the very terms in which the debate is pursued. On the one hand we gravitate toward big umbrella concepts that will have maximum spread. Thus we note the search for an account of the relation between faith and reason, or faith and experience, or faith and rationality, or faith and science, and the like.[3] Equally we note the inclination to reach for broad concepts, like scripture, tradition, reason, and experience, and we witness the desire to find a satisfactory account of their nature and inter-relation. We become worried about bulky entities like objectivity, subjec-tivity, rationality, skepticism, meaning, power, and language.

On the other hand the temptation to short-circuit the discussion is acute. Thus there is a besetting temptation to take care of things by settling, say, for or against foundationalism, or by latching on to an original but mar-ginal figure, like Michael Polanyi.[4] Certainly this kind of move can provide breathing space for the theologian, but it cannot be a final resting place.

Another way forward is hermeneutics. After all, the interpretation of sacred texts is central to theology, so it is natural to look to hermeneu-tics for relief. Originally hermeneutics was confined to the task of under-standing texts, which, on the surface at least, would appear to be a rela-tively straightforward exercise. Virtually all scholarship, and most especially scholarship in the humanities, is taken up with interpreting and understanding texts, so the practice of interpretation lies close to hand. As readers and students of texts, we have immediate access to the practice we are seeking to understand. So with moderate effort, it will be argued, we can quickly assemble the kind of data that are pertinent to understanding texts. We can make progress, say, by turning to such categories as authorial intention, grammar, literary genre, historical and social con-texts, and the like. Things become genuinely murky, on this analysis, only when we move from what the text meant in the past to what the text means, for then we face all the complications of relating the meaning of ancient texts to contemporary values and commitments. At that point we are immediately immersed in epistemology because our contemporary

3. The medieval theologians preferred to deploy generic umbrella terms like "being," "act," "potency," "necessity," "contingency," and the like.

4. It would be a major study in itself to track down the extraordinary influence of his *Personal Knowledge* (London: Routledge and Kegan Paul, 1958) in late twentieth-century theol-ogy. Equally interesting would be a tracking of the use made of Thomas S. Kuhn's *The Struc-ture of Scientific Revolutions* (Chicago: University of Chicago Press, 1970).

values and commitments are constituted in part by our current norms regarding truth, credibility, justification, warrant, and the like. So working out what the given text means today cannot be done without committing ourselves to a network of epistemic standards that we are devoted to in the present. Thus hermeneutics is as good a place as any to lodge our epistemological endeavors.

This basic two-step process (first work on what the text meant and then on what it means) has been seriously challenged of late in that the first step is seen as fraught with epistemic overtones and queries that cannot be postponed to the second step of fresh interpretation and application. For one thing, to distinguish between literal and figurative discourse we will need to rely on background information about the world. Thus we will take the sentence "It is raining cats and dogs" to be metaphorical because of our background beliefs about how the world operates. Furthermore, the evidence for an interpretation of a text, it will be said, underdetermines the understanding of any text. Different readers provide very different interpretations of the same text, so that the very existence of a stable text is in question. Thus interpretation is saturated with inescapable instability. Expressed graphically, any interpretation is in some sense a misinterpretation. Any interpretation of necessity must omit elements of the text; thus it can be challenged and replaced with a competing interpretation with intellectual impunity. There are no secure proofs or decisive foundations like, say, the author's intention, to call a halt to this inexorable process. The upshot is that theology as an exercise in interpretation is unstable, thoroughly dependent on the reader, intimately related to the relevant community of interpretation, necessarily incomplete, and permanently revisable. It is construction more than it is discovery.

The result is skepticism. While it would be exaggerated to claim that one interpretation is as good as another, there is no finally secure ground on which to stand. And secure grounds, it is assumed, are essential to knowledge. Stated bluntly, the evidence radically underdetermines every move; hence we are left with opinion rather than knowledge, with subjective alternatives rather than objective conclusions, with doubt rather than assertion, with uncertainty rather than certainty. If we are troubled by this bleak outcome, then we can take comfort in the fact that we are all in the same boat. To switch metaphors, we are all at the bottom of the epistemic food chain and cannot climb higher, so let's be content with the crumbs we have; nobody in this world has any red meat. The skeptic is right in the end, and there is no escape; we do not know, we can only opine; at best we know that we do not know.[5]

This is an amazing turn of events. Note what has happened. First, we have reduced theology to the study of texts and thus evaded the responsibility of speaking openly and self-critically about God. Second, we have been given an illusory word of assurance. In a world of interpretation without facts, we are suddenly offered the fact that we are all in the same boat. However, there can be no facts in this world of interpretation; so we cannot help ourselves to facts without obvious self-contradiction. Nor can we even claim that we know that we do not know, for that claim too is a contradiction. We are now making a claim to know while at the same time claiming that knowledge is not possible. Thirdly, and most importantly, we have been given our epistemology of theology on the cheap. With a few swift moves we have landed ourselves in skepticism. The deep reason for this is obvious. We have set up for ourselves impossibly high and unrealistic standards for the correct or best interpretation of texts and then become disillusioned when we cannot meet them. At that point we settle for the lowest of the low and seek to drag everyone else down with us. This becomes in reality a counsel of despair, a rejection of the light of the moon when the light of the sun has been taken from us. If we allow the reduction of theology to hermeneutics, we do of course have an epistemology of theology. It can be expressed in one simple sentence: there is no knowledge in theology and related disciplines.

---

5. Michael Williams is right to suggest that skeptical ideas often underpin "such widely accepted doctrines as 'social constructivism,' according to which what people believe is wholly a function of social, institutional, and political reasons, so that 'reason' is the only mask for power; relativism which says that things are only 'true for' a particular person or 'culture'; and 'standpoint epistemologies,' according to which social differentiation by gender, race, class, or tribe gives rise to distinct 'ways of knowing,' there being no possibility of justification according to common standards" (*Problems of Knowledge: A Critical Introduction to Epistemology* [Oxford: Oxford University Press, 2001], 10). He rightly goes on to note: "While skepticism fades in the light of day, it continues to exert a subterranean influence beyond the narrow confines of purely theoretical inquiry. One index of our culture's being pervaded by skeptical doubt is a tendency to stridency and suspiciousness. We continue to judge and to argue, while suspecting that such practices are really a sham. The less confident we feel, the more insistent we become. Or see opponents, not as fellow inquirers, but as driven by disreputable motives, which it is our duty to expose. Argument gives way to unmasking (though if skepticism is correct, why suppose that there is anything to explanations like this?)" (10).

Once the search for an epistemology has reached this impasse, we need to stop and start again. Theologians should resist the temptation to develop a general epistemology. Theology is better served if it is content to be more modest and contract out some of the services on which it depends.[6] Like historians and natural scientists, theologians should not worry overmuch if they do not have a full-blown epistemology. Historians do not get intellectually distraught if they fail to have to hand an account of why they should rely on perception, memory, inference, cumulative case arguments, hunches, intuitions, or even testimony. Equally, natural scientists do not complain if they cannot explain in any great detail the nature of scientific inference, explanatory power, simplicity, confirmation, falsification, and the like. Historians and scientists do not feel under an obligation to resolve, say, disputes between foundationalists and antifoundationalists. They are none the worse off if they refuse to grant that there is some first philosophy or first epistemology that they must internalize and satisfy before they can get on with their work. Historians and natural scientists are permitted to assume a whole network of epistemic principles.

To be sure, it would be improper for epistemologists to ignore the reflection of historians and scientists on their own crafts. Historians and scientists have provided extremely insightful material on the nature of their deliberations.[7] Courses on method have a place in the relevant curricula of history and science. Yet, we are rightly careful about the status and value of this work. The nature of historical or scientific thinking is not discovered by mere introspection on historical investigation and scientific inquiry. Moreover, what constitutes relevant evidence in history is not itself a purely historical investigation. Nor is what constitutes a good explanation in science subject, say, to experimental investigation. There are matters that belong in epistemology that are rightly the province of the philosopher. Historians are generally content to get on with their work and dig up what happened in the past; outside the temptation to reach for some version of relativism, they tend to stick to resolving worries about the past.[8] The

6. We really need a subdiscipline within theology, namely, the epistemology of theology, to sort out the issues and keep a sense of proportion about what is at stake for theology.

7. For history, R. G. Collingwood's *The Idea of History* (Oxford: Clarendon, 1946) remains a classic.

8. See, for example, Hayden White, *The Content of the Form: Narrative Discourse and Historical Representation* (Baltimore: Johns Hopkins University Press, 1987).

temptation for scientists to go beyond their specialist inquiries and reach for the big picture and provide a scientific explanation of everything may be greater, but it is no less mistaken. At the very least, it is clear that a fully naturalized epistemology is first and foremost a philosophical proposal.[9] The merits or demerits of such a theory are not something that can be decided the way we resolve scientific queries. There are no scientific experiments to settle the claims at issue. Nor can they be determined by pursuing theological queries.

Theologians should help themselves to the same liberties as the historian and the natural scientist. They should be content to take for granted a whole network of epistemic platitudes that can be assumed or defended relatively easily. I have already deployed an epistemic platitude that is as old as Aristotle.[10] With Aristotle I have insisted that we should accept the principle of appropriate epistemic fit. We should let the subject matter in hand shape what kinds of considerations should be brought to bear on the rationality of the issue under review. For example, we do not look to the paradigm of geometry or natural science to be the standard for disputes in history or economics. I take this as a platitude not just because it is obvious on its face, but also because it is a conclusion that naturally arises from a review of several centuries of epistemological reflection. Perhaps calling such a principle a platitude masks the hard work that goes into securing such a principle, but the great advantage of this way of speaking is that we do not need at present to prove it or establish it rigorously to get on with our work. Platitudes surely need not be self-evident; it is enough that they be relatively secure.

As with the historian and scientist, we should certainly pay heed to the second-order reflections of theologians on the nature of their deliberations. As we proceed we can even make room for the supernaturalizing of epistemology.[11] I shall argue in due course that theology has its own insights to add to epistemology. This applies not just to the way special reve-

9. See W. V. Quine, "Epistemology Naturalized," in his *Ontological Relativity and Other Essays* (New York: Columbia University Press, 1969), 68-90.

10. Aristotle makes the point in this manner: "It is a mark of an educated man to look for precision in each class of things so far as the nature of the subject admits; it is evidently equally foolish to accept probable reasoning from a mathematician and to demand from a rhetorician scientific proofs" (*Nicomachean Ethics* 1094.24-25).

11. Plantinga's work in Reformed epistemology hints at this possibility from time to time, but it remains underdeveloped.

lation rightly plays a role in disputes about God, but also to the way theology will rule out certain options and underwrite others in robust and surprising ways. We do not, however, begin there; we allow these matters to arise naturally as we proceed. For now we are content to explore a network of epistemic platitudes that the theologian is at liberty to embrace. In this arena theologians should not be held to standards that do not apply to everyone else. This is not a request for special treatment; it is at heart an appeal to epistemic equity. So we should embrace the platitude of appropriate epistemic fit without apology.

Particularism and Methodism

Another platitude that has already been deployed and that should be formally articulated at this point is this. Particularism is to be preferred to methodism. As its name suggests, methodism in epistemology is the claim that we can never know anything to be true unless we already possess the right method for demarcating truth from falsehood. Particularism reverses this order and insists that it is far better to begin with particular claims to knowledge and then work up from there to proposals about method or theories of knowledge.[12]

In the history of epistemology, methodism naturally arose in the cultural crisis of post-Reformation Europe. It arose, that is, in and around competing theological claims. Whole nations took to killing each other over competing theological commitments. Both René Descartes and John Locke sought to get beyond the warring options by looking for a more general, even universal, method that would resolve disputes.[13] Descartes opted for intuition or reason; Locke opted for sense experience. The hope was that by securing agreement on a criterion of truth they could then go

12. The best discussion remains that of Roderick Chisholm. See his "The Problem of the Criterion," in *The Foundations of Knowing* (Minneapolis: University of Minnesota Press, 1982), 61-75.

13. Happily historians of epistemology are now taking with much greater seriousness the social and political contexts of past work in epistemology. See, for example, in the case of Descartes, Stephen Toulmin, *Cosmopolis* (Chicago: University of Chicago Press, 1990). I am not here rejecting accounts that bring out the relation between, say, the Cartesian tradition and the emergence of science; I am drawing attention to features of the tradition that clearly relate to theological considerations.

back and resolve the first-order issues that troubled them and their friends. In hindsight we can now see that this solution represents in part a secularization of the earlier theological commitment to have one single foundation for all theological truth represented by an exclusive appeal to scripture. As in the appeal to scripture, when an exclusive appeal to reason or experience gets a grip on the mind, it is exceedingly difficult to dislodge this kind of monothematic theory. One suspects that the pleasing simplicity manifested is the chief attraction. Moreover, the hope of finding, once and for all, one way of settling disputes dies hard.

The difficulties in methodism did not take long to surface, however. We are immediately confronted with the obvious stalemate between rationalists and empiricists. While we are attracted to the certainty secured in intuition, we are equally drawn to the deliverances of sense experience, not least because the latter looks like ordinary common sense.[14] So, if we let both proposals stand, we now have two methods, not one, and it is not entirely clear how they should be prioritized. Even then, suppose we want to know why we should accept either option in the search for foundations. If we appeal to either reason or experience, we beg the question at issue, or end up arguing in a circle. And how can we establish reason by appealing to reason, or experience by appealing to experience? How is either reason or experience to establish the priority of one over the other? We are simply going round in circles.

We then face a further query. What if these methods exclude what most people would take to be intellectually permissible beliefs? Depending on how we interpret reason and experience, it is not clear that these methods will permit us to believe in the past, in other minds, in material objects, in causation, or in simple moral truisms, like it is wrong to roast babies alive at three o'clock in the morning for fun. It is notorious that neither rationalism nor empiricism has been able to secure the existence of the external world.[15]

14. This was how Locke's work struck me when I first read it as a student. Locke lures us into his position by making it look natural and obvious as an account of our cognitive practices.

15. We read the great classic of A. J. Ayer, *The Problem of Knowledge* (Harmondsworth: Penguin Books, 1957), and lay it aside wondering what we would do if we were convinced that Ayer's argument seeking to establish the existence of the external world did not carry the day. We could, and should, still admire the elegance and originality of the argument, but it is highly unlikely that we would give up belief in the existence of the external world were we to conclude that Ayer had failed to make his case.

We become even more unsure of ourselves when we reach for complex theoretical beliefs, say, about the natural world, about the mental states of our neighbors, about the unconscious, or even about the higher reaches of mathematics. By the time we have fine-tuned our original position in epistemology to meet our expanded list of examples, the method turns out to be so speculative and shaky that it is no more secure than the examples we use to test its adequacy. Thus we find ourselves drawn by degrees to reject methodism and to embrace particularism. So in epistemology we begin again by turning to the particular propositions we think are rational, justified, warranted, and the like, and then move from these to systems of classification or to proposals about method.

This radical shift in perspective does not come without its own problems. Thus, epistemology instantly becomes person-relative. We are thrown back on how things appear to us; we are not able to reach out to some transcendent realm of "pure reason" that is not subject to the vicissitudes of human existence. Initially, we have to take much on trust. Our position is also person-relative in the narrower sense that we now begin with the particular beliefs we take to be rational, justified, warranted, and the like, and these may differ quite radically in content. Different people begin with different intuitions on the relevant set of particular beliefs.

An additional problem is that we may let in too many beliefs at the outset. What if someone wants to include astrological claims? We rightly become worried at where to draw the line, at where the relevant boundaries lie. The temptation to backtrack and find the right criterion or method can become very strong at this point. Worse still, we may be drawn to a version of radical particularism that eschews any attempt to classify our beliefs or to work out pertinent theories to explain our commitment to the particular beliefs from which we started. After all, the argument will go, there is little point in going on to that second level of inquiry if our theories are to be tested against the particular beliefs we use to test them. All we would be doing is making explicit what is already implicit; we would not find out anything radically new; so let's sit pat on the particulars we already possess. This simply looks like the end of epistemology altogether, for it omits the normative side of our inquiry; it sticks to how things already are and ignores how they ought to be.

Furthermore, however we proceed, we would not be overturning skepticism, and skepticism has long been considered the silent elephant in the room in epistemology. Rather than securing this or that belief against skeptical attack, we would be positing a whole network of beliefs as worthy of belief from the outset. Thus, even if we avoided the peril of radical particularism, it looks as if we are not serious about epistemology as commonly understood.

There is a convincing rejoinder to these latter worries. The skeptic is a useful agent in epistemology, but he makes a bad household inspector. There is more to epistemology than satisfying the skeptic. We can surely register significant progress if we can clarify certain crucial concepts in the field as we find them in ordinary usage and if we can render our common practices and convictions intelligible. In this arena we should not shy away from borderline cases or working with a variety of initial intuitions and judgments.[16] The default position is not that we know nothing until we can show that we can know something, but that we know far more than we are able to show that we know. This is the great merit of particularism. The skeptic and the methodist prefer to start as epistemic misers. They have been disappointed so often, or they have set for themselves such high standards of success in epistemology, that they come to think they know next to nothing until they find some surefire method of knowing. Skeptics and methodists suffer from a failure of nerve that is masked as courageous self-criticism.[17]

16. Richard Swinburne captures the situation nicely as follows. "Philosophers have given many different accounts of warrant that — on the assumption that knowledge is a clear concept — they have represented as alternative accounts, at most one of which can be the true account of warrant. But I suggest that knowledge and so warrant are not clear concepts. The situation rather is that, as with the case of justification, the philosopher is faced with a vast number of actual and possible cases where we all say that someone knows something, and a vast number of actual and possible cases where we all say that someone believes (strongly) some true proposition, although he does not know it. The philosopher seeks a general formula for warrant that will yield the answer that we all give in these agreed cases for whether or not someone knows something. There are, however, many different formulae that will yield the answers we all give for these cases, but disagree in their verdicts about the answers to other possible cases about which we differ in our intuitive judgements" (*Epistemic Justification* [Oxford: Clarendon, 2001], 192).

17. It should be noted that there is another side to skepticism that is rarely if ever noted. Moderate skeptics advise us to return to the conventions of our culture and society and to stop worrying about a knowledge that cannot be attained. In this they are in fact trying to find a place for considerations that do not figure in utopian conceptions of justification, warrant, and the like. However, they too readily accept the opponents' terms of reference and hence have no way to secure their own commitments at this stage of the discussion. Thus skepticism bears witness not just to despair in the search for knowledge

The particularist is not an epistemic miser. Nor is she credulous, naive, or gullible; she is properly confident and generous. For the particularist the central problem in epistemology is radically different from that posed by the skeptic or methodist. She finds herself puzzled not by how little she knows but by how much she knows. She knows that she is the daughter of her mother, that Ireland is an island, that two plus two equals four, that innocent people ought not to be punished, that terrorism is a great evil, that there are atoms, that human beings die, that there are flowers in the garden, that there are thoughts and sensation, that other minds exist, that the love of money is the root of much evil, that she has two feet, that there are fish in the ocean, that there can be much pain in love, that it is better to be happy than miserable, and the like. The list is interminable. What puzzles the particularist is a quite different issue from what bothers the methodist and the skeptic, namely, how do we know that we know this welter of material. The particularist is sure she has good money; she does not know exactly how it was minted but is eager to explore the options. The skeptic and the methodist have seen so much bad money that they want to build a new mint from scratch, which will print nothing but fully certified, universally accepted currency. With suitable adjustments we can express a similar conclusion for rationality and justification.

Particularism is not some covert appeal to common sense; it is a serious epistemological position.[18] Common sense is what it is. It is a useful summary of the kind of consensus that shows up in most cultures or that appears as a continuous commitment within a single culture. Common sense does nothing to resolve epistemological worries. It is constituted, more or less, by the wisdom of the ages or of a particular culture. The particularist is happy that such shorthand summaries of what we think we know abound. However, the particularist is very clear that any appeal to common sense is not in itself an argument. To appeal to common sense is simply to repeat what appears to be obvious. Common sense is as strong or as weak as appearances are.

---

but also to a desire to accommodate what is all too readily dismissed by philosophers with hard-line attitudes and impossible standards of success.

18. One wonders if the work of Thomas Reid, a perceptive particularist, was lost for well over a century in epistemology because it was reduced in vulgar version to common sense and sold in the market of ideas in that form. Happily we can leave this to the historians. For a fine treatment of Reid, see Nicholas Wolterstorff, *Thomas Reid and the Story of Epistemology* (Cambridge: Cambridge University Press, 2001).

As we saw above, the deep argument in favor of particularism is that theories in epistemology can be overthrown, and indeed should be overthrown, by appeal to particular propositions. Put differently, when confronted with some method that rules out some particular proposition as false, we may challenge the method precisely because it calls the particular proposition into question. The method deployed may be no more secure than the initial proposition ventured; indeed, the method may be far less secure than the proposition it challenges. If some moral theorist presents a general epistemology that calls into question the claim that it is wrong to roast babies alive at three o'clock in the morning for fun, I would not hesitate to reject the moral theory on offer. If some brilliant philosopher argues on the basis of some theory that I am wrong to believe that I have two feet, then something has gone radically wrong with the theory developed. I have more confidence in the particular claim that I have two feet than I have in any theory that would call it into question. We argue similarly on down the line from a host of particular beliefs.

This vision dovetails snugly with the principle of appropriate epistemic fit. Once we give up the search for a single, monothematic, all-encompassing theory of knowledge, we pay as much attention to the subject in hand as we do to the epistemic reflection that relates to it. Particularism thus provides additional reason for taking our time and exploring what kinds of considerations apply when we are exploring the justification of canonical theism. What is at stake here is a change in perspective. We cease to be gripped by the standard strategy identified in the last chapter. We do not worry if we do not have to hand a single method of resolving disputed issues. I am not claiming that all those committed to the standard strategy are methodists; this would be claiming too much. Yet there is a natural affinity between the two; certainly it is unclear how methodists in epistemology could avoid being committed to the standard strategy.

A Network of Epistemic Platitudes

Now that we have broken the spell of the standard strategy and of methodism, the way is clear to embrace a number of other epistemic platitudes. I propose that the wise theologian, again like the historian and the scientist, will cheerfully commit to the following principles.

1. We can and should accept the general reliability of our senses, to-gether with the belief-forming mechanisms and practices that ac-company them. Thus we can rely on introspection, intuition, and perception, unless we have good reason to believe otherwise. There is no noncircular justification for our reliance on these ex-traordinary capacities, mechanisms, and practices. These are basic to the life of the mind in the sense that any attempt to justify them will itself presuppose their reliability. They involve different mo-dalities of operation, so that we cannot secure the reliability of one by appeal to that of another; nor can we fault one because it does not fit the pattern we associate with another. Introspection is dif-ferent from perception; yet we rely on one as much as we do on the other.

2. We can and should accept that propositions gain in epistemic status insofar as they can be supported by deductive inference, by induc-tive or abductive argument, by cumulative case arguments, by tacit judgments, and by arguments to the best explanation. These too are basic to the life of the mind. We either accept them as legitimate and trustworthy or we do not. In this case also, we cannot reduce one modality of argument either to secure or overturn the modality of another. Deduction is not induction, and it is futile to fault the latter because it does not meet the standard of the former. Equally, it is fu-tile to play off reason against reliance on the senses.[19]

3. We should also rely on memory. There is no noncircular justifica-tion for relying on our memories. Any appeal we make to some-thing outside of memory in order to defend reliance on memory, say, to perception or inference, will itself depend on memory. Memory is a pervasive, bedrock feature of our intellectual existence; its loss is

---

19. Thomas Reid's memorable expression of this bears repeating. "The skeptic asks me, Why do you believe in the existence of the external object which you perceive? This be-lief, sir, is none of my manufacture; it came from the mint of Nature; it bears her image and superscription; and, if it is not right, the fault is not mine: I even took it upon trust, and without suspicion. Reason, says the skeptic, is the only judge of truth, and you ought to throw off every opinion and every belief that is not grounded on reason. Why, sir, should I believe the faculty of reason more than that of perception? — they come from the same shop, and were made by the same artist; and if he puts one piece of false ware into my hands, what should hinder him from putting another?" (*An Inquiry into the Human Mind* [Chi-cago: University of Chicago Press, 1970], 207).

devastating from a cognitive point of view; its existence is a standing marvel.[20]

4. We can and should accept testimony. We rightly accept what others tell us without having first established that they are worthy of trust. David Hume's efforts to overturn this principle have proven inadequate.[21] Without testimony we would never be able to learn a language, we would have to give up everything we have learned from others whom we have not checked out for ourselves, and hence we would be radically impoverished intellectually.[22]

5. Our linguistic formulations have extremely complex originating causes, yet this fact does not preclude access to the truth about reality. Thus I cannot claim to have seen a car in my driveway unless I have already acquired and learned how to apply the concepts of car, driveway, and spatial relation. If I lived in a culture from which these concepts were absent, I would not be able to say that my green Honda was in the driveway. It is one thing to acquire and apply these concepts; it is another to use them to make assertions about the way things are on particular occasions in specific contexts. Concept acquisition is a presupposition of particular assertions; it is not a barrier to making assertions.

6. Some of our beliefs are rightly or properly basic. We are permitted to hold them without having to hand either in fact or in principle inferential evidence for them. Such beliefs may be supported and confirmed by other beliefs, and they may cohere with other beliefs, but we rightly believe them naturally or immediately on inspection. They can be defeated and undermined; they are neither infallible nor incorrigible; but they can also stand full square on their own without propositional evidence.

---

20. The place of memory even in our sense of touch is well brought out in Hans Jonas, *The Phenomenon of Life: Towards a Philosophical Biology* (New York: Harper and Row, 1966), 140. More generally Jonas rightly comments: "In the form of immediate short-term retention, memory rightly enters into the very constitution of sensibility, and is thus coeval with it" (140).

21. Most famously perhaps in his discussion of miracles. See David Hume, *Enquiries concerning Human Understanding and concerning the Principles of Morals* (Oxford: Clarendon, 1975), 127-28.

22. The best study available is C. A. J. Coady, *Testimony: A Philosophical Study* (Oxford: Clarendon, 1992).

7. To get access to relevant information or argument it may be essential to make use of specialized epistemic practices. Thus in natural science we assign a special role to experiment; in history we may have to learn how to read old coins; in literary studies much depends on the practice of exegesis. These practices may come naturally to us, or they may not. They may involve the cultivation of virtue and the elimination of vice, or they may not. They may require assistance and dependence on others, or they may not.[23]

8. Our epistemic obligations are person-relative. They depend on how much information we have, on how strong we think the pertinent arguments are, on our general background knowledge, on how much time we have to think things over, on how far we have defeaters for the propositions under consideration, on how much intellectual capacity we possess, on which other obligations we must meet, and the like.

9. Our beliefs are not generally under our control. Doubt is not a vice; it is something that naturally happens to us; on occasion it is an invaluable asset and operates as a warning light that something is amiss intellectually. However, we can indirectly control our beliefs by attending to evidence or avoiding objections, by suppressing or cultivating doubt, or by engaging in pertinent epistemic practices. There is generally an appropriate relation between the level of assent we give to a proposition and both the kind and amount of evidence we possess.

10. The stronger the evidence, the greater the level of assent permitted; the weaker the evidence the lesser the level of assent permitted. Exceptions, of course, may prove the rule here, but we properly begin with this apt generalization.

11. Judgment is a vital part of our epistemic capacity or equipment. We may well know what is the case without being able to identify all the relevant considerations that have had a role in the formation of our belief or without being able to provide a determinate analysis of the identity and weight of the relevant evidence.

This laundry list of platitudes should not be taken as in any way comprehensive. The list is deliberately laid out in an ad hoc manner, and

23. The place of social practices in epistemology is explored with great skill in Alvin Goldman, *Knowledge in a Social World* (Oxford: Clarendon, 1999).

no attempt has been made to weave its various elements into full-scale epistemology. Observant readers will note that the list does not in fact include an analysis of three central concepts of epistemology, namely, rationality, justification, and knowledge. While I shall continue to knock on the door of these concepts and even open the door and enter from time to time, I shall leave any formal analysis until later. We have enough on the table to detain us for now.

None of these epistemic platitudes rides on the acceptance of any theological premise. Think of what it would mean to start with the divine and then establish these platitudes. First, we would need to have secure in hand some vision of God. Second, we would then need to move from the available vision of God by way of argument or connecting theory to these platitudes. We would immediately run into insuperable difficulties on both fronts. Thus we would need a language in which to express the relevant vision, but we could not secure this if we could not rely on memory. We could not move to establish our conclusion by way of argument unless we already had some kind of reliable inference or epistemic vision to take us there. Hence we already presuppose one or several elements in the platitudes.

For this reason it is not just exaggerated but misleading to think that without some version of theism we are doomed to nihilism in epistemology. We will explore later why a theist might genuinely suffer a serious and even searing loss of epistemic confidence in conversion to unbelief. What we must challenge is the claim that theism is essential to secure our network of epistemic platitudes. The order is the reverse. We move from the epistemic platitudes to theism; then we can explore what difference, if any, theism makes to epistemology.[24]

Our epistemic platitudes do little more than codify what is implicit in healthy forms of believing and in good intellectual practices. They are received or accepted insofar as they make sense of crucial features of our ordinary concepts, insofar as they can be captured by pertinent example, insofar as they can be enriched over time, and insofar as we can defend

24. For this reason I do not find the current efforts by proponents of radical orthodoxy to meet various versions of postmodernity by a return to Neoplatonic and medieval metaphysics at all convincing. Much postmodernism strikes me as hopelessly indebted to a modernism that set the standards for success in epistemology ridiculously and impossibly high. Perhaps postmodernists are disillusioned and dissatisfied modernists. A retrieval of Neoplatonism does not really address the problem of inappropriate standards of success.

them against this or that objection. They are neither absolute nor relative. They do not admit of philosophical or any other kind of proof. Any or all of them can in principle be overturned by argument and evidence. They are the product of our fallible observation, reflection, and discussion. Every one of them can be contested; few if any of them can be avoided in our intellectual endeavors. They are as secure as anything can be in this domain of inquiry.

Theologians are in the same boat as everybody else at this point. Initially they are in no position either to prove or to overthrow the kinds of epistemic platitudes I have enumerated. The wise theologian will accept them as given. So too will the historian, the scientist, the local dentist, and the ordinary person in the street. Such worries as they engender can for now be left in the hands of the philosopher. The theologian should simply contract them out without a bad conscience and not look for any final, decisive, intellectual bill of health. There are no final bills of health in this arena, and it is a mistake to accept any on offer.[25]

What can and should detain theologians is the particular claims they offer to the world. Are there features of these claims that call for special attention? Here generalizations are risky. Theologies differ radically in what they claim. As we noted in the last chapter, one is never a mere theist except in the abstract or for the purposes of academic argument. The overall argument for fundamentalist theism will be radically different from that needed, say, for process theism. It is a mistake to think there is a generic method that we can simply lift and apply in either case. We need to allow the protagonists to articulate which kind of argument they think is needed and allow them intellectual space to make good on their respective proposals.

Of course, there may be all sorts of analogies and overlaps in these proposals. Fundamentalist theists and process theists may make similar kinds of arguments in both form and content. They may both, for instance, deploy a version of the ontological argument. Nothing can be precluded in advance. Moreover, there is no need to confine the debate to the relevant protagonists. Outsiders who have sympathetically explored the option on offer, or who may have at one time adhered to it, may well be

25. One suspects that it was the goal of both positivism and phenomenology to eliminate this feature of our epistemic situation by finding an irrefutable foundation in experience.

able to note features readily missed by insiders. Objections no doubt will be launched from all sides; mature and astute believers will learn from them as they proceed to make their case. So there is lots of room for enriching collaboration and pungent criticism.

The strategy up ahead is clear. We shall narrow our query and explore what the canonical theist should say at this point to move us forward in our deliberations about the epistemology of theology. In the next chapter I want to explore a network of basic observations on the logic of canonical theism that bring into sharp relief the particular insights that relate to the justification of canonical theism. I want to identify features of what is on offer so that we shall have an appropriate sense of the kinds of considerations that are relevant to its truth or falsehood. In short, we shall explore what emerges when we apply the principle of appropriate epistemic fit to canonical theism.

In moving to this level it is vital not to confuse canonical theism with either the arguments in its favor or the epistemic suggestions I am about to develop. Canonical theism, seen in its intellectual content, is at its core a network of assertions about God, creation, and redemption. It is not a set of arguments or an epistemology. Canonical theists will differ on what are the relevant reasons for its truth and on what is the best epistemology to embrace. There is nothing odd or unusual about this. Anselm and Aquinas both believed in the same God, but they differed on why they did so. Anselm clearly considered the ontological argument to be both sound and valid; Aquinas did not and preferred a network of inductive arguments when he discussed the justification of theism with unbelievers. In recent times, we can note that William P. Alston, Paul Moser, Alvin Plantinga, Eleonore Stump, Nicholas Wolterstorff, and Richard Swinburne all believe in God, but they do not at all agree on the epistemology they develop or assume when they defend the rationality of theism. Equally it will be possible for canonical theists to develop competing visions of the justification of canonical theism.

It is simply a mistake to think that the rationality of any and all forms of theism depends on the epistemology embraced by their adherents. The only forms of theism in this predicament are those that build epistemological proposals into the content of their theism. It is interesting to note how readily this can happen. Three great versions of Christianity in the West have done so with enthusiasm. Fundamentalism, liberal Protestantism, and Roman Catholicism make epistemic proposals constitutive of their identity. Fundamentalist theism is unthinkable without the doctrine of the inerrancy of scripture; liberal Protestant theism makes the appeal to religious experience a hallmark of its identity; Roman Catholicism requires commitment to papal infallibility. It may well be that the prevalence of these leading forms of Christianity in the West has made it easier for theists to assume that somehow it is impossible to be a theist without at the same time being devoted to a particular epistemology of theology. It is surely fascinating that Reformed Christians are eager to develop a Reformed epistemology and that United Methodists have come within a hairbreadth of embracing the so-called Wesleyan Quadrilateral. The assumption that somehow a network of canonized or constitutive epistemological commitments is essential to one's theism dies very hard.

Canonical theists rightly make no such assumption, for they are very clear that the church in its canonical commitments eschewed this kind of luxury. This does not mean that canonical theists are not interested in epistemology or take it lightly. The best defense of this interest at this point is its execution. For now it is enough to say that we have in this chapter laid out a network of epistemic platitudes. If the reader has made it this far and has not given up, then we are well on our way. If he or she does not yet find the exercise worthwhile, then we can still live in hope that future chapters will repay his or her attention and perseverance.

Chapter Three

Canonical Theism and Proper Epistemic Fit

———✺———

In Search of Epistemic Suggestions

We are now in a position to explore the kind of intellectual entity we have in hand when we are committed to canonical theism, as contrasted, say, with mere theism. En route we shall mark out the epistemic issues posed; that is, we shall note features of this version of theism that indicate which kinds of considerations are relevant to the assessment of its rationality or justification. We shall pursue this course both negatively and positively. Hence we shall identify inappropriate arguments and signal the way one might begin to make a case in its favor. In due course we shall note that divine revelation is a critical component of any adequate epistemology relevant to the truth or falsehood of canonical theism.

We begin with the observation that, like all forms of serious and living theism, canonical theism is constituted by a network of interrelated propositions that need to be taken as a whole. We noted this earlier by summarizing canonical theism as that rich vision of God, creation, and redemption developed over time in the scriptures, articulated in the Nicene Creed, celebrated in the liturgy of the church, enacted in the lives of the saints, handed over and received in the sacraments, depicted in iconography, articulated by canonical teachers, mulled over in the Fathers, and treasured, preserved, and guarded by the episcopate. The full exposition of this, together with its unity and diversity, is properly the task of systematic theology.[1] What is at issue, then, is a vision of God, of the human situation, of the healing of the world, and the like, set in the context of a rich ontology. In fact, canonical theism is first and foremost a rich ontology.

Another way to press this point is to note that while the appropriation of canonical theism can be seen as the gradual embrace of its varied components, the whole is more than the sum of its parts. As a whole, it constitutes a rich, world-orienting network of beliefs. There is no generic intellectual apparatus for the adjudication of the truth of worldviews. To be sure, we can appeal to broad criteria like explanatory power, simplicity, fit with the world, internal consistency, overall coherence, and the like.[2] But these are very general, they shade off into the aesthetic, and they are only of partial assistance in reaching our goal. In the end we are faced with a unique web of material beliefs that is incommensurable with other webs of material beliefs on offer from rival versions of theism and atheism. While there are overlapping contents and significant analogies across metaphysical visions, there are also radically different kinds of claims on offer that cannot be inserted into some sort of truth-detection machine. Indeed, there are not just radically different networks of claims on offer, there are also different kinds of arguments that are appropriate, and different modes of assent and believing. Hence we have to take the internal features of the relevant proposals with radical seriousness.[3]

It is also illuminating to attend to the epistemic suggestions that emerge within the theism on offer, that is, to attend to the considerations that often lead folk to believe. Within the canonical heritage of the church we find all sorts of epistemic insights relative to the truth or falsehood of the theism on offer. In reviewing the most obvious reflections on offer, we

1. For the canonical theist a critical but not exclusive task of systematic theology is the work of hermeneutical retrieval and renewal as represented in a vision of systematic theology as university-level catechesis.

2. For a very penetrating discussion of one way to pursue this option, see the neglected work of Basil Mitchell in *The Justification of Religious Belief* (London: Macmillan, 1973). For a fine discussion see Robert Prevost, *Theism and Probabilistic Explanation* (Oxford: Clarendon, 1990).

3. Consider the different kinds of claims about human nature that show up, say, in atheistic Buddhism over against Freudian atheism. Even within the family of atheism there are radically different proposals on the table, and there will be very different sorts of positive arguments relevant to their adjudication. Each case will have to be examined carefully on its merits.

are not asking for a free ride in epistemology. We are following the general practice of exploring phenomenologically and intuitively the relevant constraints and factors that need to be taken seriously by the adherents and opponents of canonical theism.

This is nothing new in epistemology. Thus in exploring perceptual claims we begin with those we actually have and see where that takes us. In exploring the nature of reasoning in science or history, we begin by paying attention to the kinds of moves that are made, the intellectual constraints that are in play, and the kind of arguments that are deployed. So in theology we can begin from within and then work our way outward and upward. We have particularized this strategy with respect to canonical theism.

In doing so we need to note that epistemic fit as conventionally understood will have to be expanded. Generally and quite properly the principle of appropriate epistemic fit has been taken to mean that we look for relevant differences in the way we adjudicate different kinds of claims. Hence we do not expect historical claims to be measured by the kinds of arguments that would apply to mathematics or the natural sciences. There are characteristic ways of making historical explanations with appropriate ways of resolving disputes where this is possible. With various forms of theism and atheism, as we have just noted, we may indeed apply general evaluations that explore consistency, coherence, simplicity, explanatory power, and the like. Yet in the end each network of beliefs must be taken in its radical particularity. The fit between the claims advanced and the positive intellectual case made may be singular and unique. We are thus entitled to work our way outward from within the theism on offer, take seriously the kind of epistemic suggestions advanced by the ordinary believer and in the canonical heritage of the church, and see where this takes us in the discussion.

Some General Epistemic Observations

We can record immediately that there can be no single proof of this vision, that is, some valid and sound deductive argument, or some sort of inductive proof. In the former, deductive case we would need a set of premises and a conclusion where the argument form is both valid and sound, that is, where the premises are true and we cannot commit to them and deny the conclusion without contradiction. In the latter, inductive case the premises would raise the plausibility or probability of the conclusion. A proof invariably has to be directed at weighing the worth of single propositions. Once we lay out a proof, its validity and soundness can be settled more or less objectively, that is, by critical inspection or by appropriate investigation of the premises, the conclusions, and their logical properties. This is not to say that settling these matters may be easy to follow, or that we may not have extended argument in and around them. What is clear is that the procedures we need to deploy are relatively uncontested. Given that canonical theism is a cluster of propositions that hang together in some sense as a whole, the idea of some kind of single proof for it makes no sense.[4]

We should also immediately note, however, that there is a place for disproof. Canonical theism is not a set of beliefs insulated from searching criticism. It can be disproved, for example, by showing that its central concepts are incoherent. Were we to show that the idea of an invisible or incorporeal agent was internally self-contradictory, or that the doctrine of the Trinity was not just a mystery but utterly incoherent, we would have a disproof of canonical theism. Equally, were we to show by historical investigation that Jesus of Nazareth never lived, or that he did not rise from the dead, canonical theism would be decisively refuted. Or were we to show that human beings are nothing more than complex physical and chemical organisms produced merely by chance events, the anthropology implicit within it would simply collapse. Indeed, given that canonical theism is a network of diverse claims, it can be readily attacked by focusing on this or that element and subjecting it to searching criticism.

4. We do not at this point rule out the possibility of a series of proofs, moving from mere theism up the line to canonical theism. I am skeptical that any such series of rigorous deductive or inductive proofs would be at all successful. As I shall attempt to show, we can indeed have arguments that would gradually take us from one position to another. This is commonplace in our thinking and in our modes of justification, but the material arguments to be deployed lie ahead of us. In a way this is clearly the project carried out with vigor, clarity, dexterity, and thoroughness by Richard Swinburne in a network of very important volumes. See *The Coherence of Theism* (Oxford: Clarendon, 1997), *The Existence of God* (Oxford: Clarendon, 1979), *Faith and Reason* (Oxford: Clarendon, 1981), *Revelation: From Metaphor to Analogy* (Oxford: Clarendon, 1992), *The Evolution of the Soul* (Oxford: Clarendon, 1986), *Responsibility and Atonement* (Oxford: Clarendon, 1989), *The Christian God* (Oxford: Clarendon, 1994), *Providence and the Problem of Evil* (Oxford: Clarendon, 1998), *The Resurrection of God Incarnate* (Oxford: Clarendon, 2003).

Along similar lines, it is possible to bring canonical theism under acute intellectual strain. Were we to establish that Jesus of Nazareth died accidentally when hit by a falling brick while preaching in the temple in Jerusalem, the deep convictions concerning the grace and love of God expressed in its vision of the death of Christ would become implausible. Equally, were we to show convincingly that the world is not just marked by gratuitous and horrendous suffering but that it is utterly pervaded from top to bottom by such suffering, then canonical theism would be severely challenged. Or were it established that the world's ills are due simply to a bad virus that could be cured by a routine vaccination, or that they could be put right by exclusive manipulation of the structures of society, there would be very good reason to abandon canonical theism and look for a better network of world-orienting beliefs and practices.

One positive way forward in assessing the status of canonical theism would be to claim that belief in the triune God can be held as rational, justified, warranted, and the like, in the absence of evidence.[5] Belief in the triune God would, on this analysis, be like belief in the external world, belief in the past, belief in other minds, or belief in the platitudes of arithmetic. The warrant for canonical theism would be secured by the proper functioning of the *sensus divinitatis* implanted within us at creation by God and repaired in redemption by the work of the Holy Spirit.[6] We are to imagine in this instance the sum and substance of canonical theism arising under various circumstances, triggered by this or that experience, but ultimately secured epistemically by the inner witness of the Holy Spirit God, the believing agent.[7]

Given that the canonical theist welcomes any and every attempt to provide an epistemic defense of canonical theism, there is no need in principle to rule out this option. However, its prospects look especially daunting for the following reasons.

---

5. I continue to leave the distinctions between these epistemic desiderata aside for the moment, even though, strictly speaking, there may be crucial differences between them that would permit other possibilities to emerge at this point in the rational defense of Christian theism.

6. The full-scale articulation of this position has been brilliantly developed by Alvin Plantinga in *Warranted Christian Belief* (New York: Oxford University Press, 2000).

7. Plantinga makes the case at this point for a kind of broad-version orthodox Christianity shared across the church as a whole. It is close enough at this point to canonical theism to make the thought experiment involved relatively easy.

We cannot discover the truth or falsehood of the doctrine of the Trinity by inspection, as we might for such propositions as two plus three equals five, or there is a pain right now in my left arm, or it is morally wrong for male soldiers to rape women in combat, or it appears to me now that God has forgiven me my sins. The doctrine of the Trinity was wrung from the history of the church's struggle with a variety of alternatives and was secured as much by the soteriology it addressed as by any kind of inferential argument, say, from this or that text of scripture. Its adoption and retention, its purchase on the mind of believers, was intimately related to the deep plausibility of an accompanying vision of the human condition, alienated from God and gripped by the love of God brought near in the good news about Jesus Christ.

Further, to appeal to the *sensus divinitatis*, to its repair in redemption, and to the inner testimony of the Holy Spirit as the agency of cognitive healing is to rely on various, selected components of the canonical heritage to support other components. There are in fact three distinct theological proposals on offer. (a) There is an appeal to the *sensus divinitatis*. We are offered a complex spiritual anthropology, that is, a vision of human beings as made in the image of God, who have built into them, as it were, a network of spiritual sensors that detect or discern the presence of God in creation. (b) There is an appeal to redemption. This claim posits that we have been alienated from God by sin, that God has intervened in Jesus of Nazareth to save the world, and that the Holy Spirit heals us from cognitive malfunction in the formation of our theological beliefs. We are already deeply enmeshed in the topics of soteriology, Christology, and pneumatology. (c) There is an appeal to the inner testimony or witness of the Holy Spirit. This claim proposes that this witness is the critical agent or process whereby our *sensus divinitatis* is repaired of its cognitive malfunction. Again we are deeply implicated in a particular vision of pneumatology. Clearly, all around we are deeply immersed in a network of theological commitments. Prima facie, it seems very odd to privilege these three theological claims as if they were somehow secure in and of themselves. Surely we need to know why, say, the claim about the inner witness of the Holy Spirit is more secure or privileged than, say, the doctrine of the Trinity.

To rework these theological claims into a network of proposals about God's design plan for proper cognitive functioning is a major stretch. While we can readily envisage such a design plan theologically, we can surely imagine other design plans as well. We can think of other ways in which God might have created us so that we fulfill our epistemic duties, gain access to the truth, properly proportion assent to evidence, and the like. In reality we have no access to God's intentions in this matter at all beyond our epistemic speculations. God has not sent along a set of explanations and instructions with the instrument at this point, say, by divine revelation. Thus it is not surprising that Christian philosophers from Augustine, to Bonaventure, to John Locke, and to Alvin Plantinga tend to plug their epistemic moves into whatever theological concepts, themes, or doctrines lie to hand. Augustine and Bonaventure developed an illuminationist vision,[8] Locke annexed a theory of divine workmanship,[9] and Plantinga deploys a vision of the image of God.[10] While each can lay claim more or less to some measure of plausibility theologically, none of them are fully convincing as an exposition of the relevant theological materials they embody.

Moreover, consider what is proposed in the option we are entertaining. We are being invited to bear in mind that we have a doxastic practice or a reliable belief-producing mechanism that stands alongside and logically independent of perception, intuition, reason, memory, and testimony as an appropriate source of rationality, justification, warrant, and the like. Thus the believer need not lean, for example, on the church's testimony to Jesus Christ, or on any divine guidance in the church, say, on the doctrine of the Trinity, to be warranted in believing Christian theism. Perhaps the believer was listening to a harangue on the poisonous nature of Christian doctrine by an ardent atheist who rejected traditional Christian theism. In the course of the harangue, on hearing the exposition of the doctrine of the Trinity, the Holy Spirit triggered in the believer the convic-

---

8. Consider Laura A. Smit's summary of Bonaventure's position. "God's design for human beings is that we will understand, will grasp the truth of things around us. In doing this, we reflect the image of Christ, who, as the Exemplar, contains or grasps the essential forms of all that exists. In perceiving the world, we are able to reflect and understand what we perceive in the same way that we are reflected and understood by Christ, and so in our knowing we are being like Christ" ("'In Your Light, We See Light': The Continuing Viability of a Christocentric Epistemology," in *Realism and Antirealism*, ed. William P. Alston [Ithaca, N.Y.: Cornell University Press, 2002], 167-82).

9. Locke sees our understanding as the most excellent part of God's workmanship in *An Essay concerning Human Understanding* (Oxford: Clarendon, 1975), 4.18.5.

10. This comes out very clearly in his attack on naturalism at the end of his *Warrant and Proper Function* (New York: Oxford University Press, 1993), 236.

tion that God is triune. In addition, the believer knows of no good defeaters for her beliefs thus formed, or has found good defeaters for the defeaters with which she is acquainted. If she actually believes the doctrine of the Trinity with strong assent, if the doctrine of the Trinity is true, then she has knowledge.

This is a bizarre scenario, epistemically speaking. For one thing it seems odd to rely on the inner testimony of the Holy Spirit and say nothing about reliance, implicitly or otherwise, on the testimony of the church or the biblical writers. Further, to rework a previous point, it is not likely that one will find appeal to the inner witness of the Holy Spirit as somehow more epistemically privileged than appeal to, say, the doctrine of the Trinity. There may be epistemic connections between the two, but by making the connection direct and unidirectional, that is, straight from the inner witness to the Trinity, the process strikes one as much too abrupt and short-circuited. Finally, the result is lame and disappointing. We began our journey hoping to gain epistemic purchase for the believer, but we end very close to where we started. If the believer is already convinced that traditional theism is true, then she has warrant and hence knowledge. Provided we can buy into the claim that warrant is what we need for knowledge, that truth secures warrant rather than vice versa, and that warrant is secured by relevant proper functioning, then we may indeed have made epistemic progress. Yet the eventual payoff seems slim despite the massive initial investments. Everything hinges on the measure of assent we already give to the theistic option.[11]

It would be too strong to claim here that I have refuted the claim that canonical theism might be secured by seeing the fundamentals of such theism as properly basic beliefs. I have said enough, I trust, to register why I am not persuaded by this option. We can put it aside for now, leaving room to come back around and harvest those insights within this position that might be better deployed in a very different epistemic scenario.

---

11. The closing paragraph to Plantinga's *Warranted Christian Belief* is surely anticlimactic in the extreme. "But *is* it true? This is the really important question. And here we pass beyond the competence of philosophy, whose main competence, in this area, is to clear away certain objection, impedances, and obstacles to Christian belief. Speaking for myself and of course not in the name of philosophy, I can say only that it does, indeed, seem to me to be true, and to be the maximally important truth" (498, emphasis added).

Closer Epistemological Inspection

Thus far I have argued that there are no proofs of canonical theism, that there can be disproof, that it can be subject to acute intellectual strain, and that it is not possible to secure it by appealing to properly basic beliefs. What else can we say that would help us get as clear a picture as possible of the relevant epistemic considerations that come into play in the assessment of canonical theism? I shall begin with some psychological comments with epistemological overtones and then shift to more explicit epistemological commentary. My aim is to lay bare the epistemic suggestions that naturally but not necessarily emerge in the exposition of, appropriation of, and engagement with the epistemic proposals that lie below the surface of canonical theism.

On the positive side one may come to believe in canonical theism virtually by fits and starts. This reflects the teaching process of the early church, where the faith was handed over in a delicate process of catechesis, for it took time to assimilate its central claims. The intellectual gains in believing are often piecemeal and haphazard. The church rightly works on a principle of reserve, for some elements can be appreciated only after other pieces are in place. From the viewpoint of the believer, the process is a journey marked by internal and external conversation. In the light of this, proof and disproof may appear as a refined parlor game that can readily distract and be seized upon to keep the more challenging components of the faith at bay. There may indeed be proofs, or decisive arguments, along the way. However, we need to include in our epistemic narrative softer components like cultivated insights, particular intuitions, specific experiences of God, the intellectual effects of conspicuous sanctity, and the like.

Newman captured the tone and mode of this intellectual possibility in a memorable passage.

> Reason, according to the simplest view of it, is the faculty of gaining knowledge without direct perception, or of ascertaining one thing by means of another. In this way it is able, from small beginnings, to create to itself a world of ideas, which do or do not correspond to the things themselves for which they stand, or are true or not, according as it is exercised soundly or otherwise. One fact may suffice for a whole theory; one principle may create and sustain a system; one

minute token is a clue to a large discovery. The mind ranges to and fro, and spreads out, and advances forward with a quickness which has become a proverb, and a subtlety and versatility which baffle investigation. It passes from point to point, gaining one by some indication; another on a probability; then availing itself of an association; then falling back on some received law; next seizing on testimony; then committing itself to some popular impression, or some inward instinct, or some obscure memory; and thus it makes progress not unlike a clamberer on a steep cliff, who, by quick eye, prompt hand, and firm foot, ascends how he knows not himself, by personal endowments and by practice, rather than by rule, leaving no track behind him, and unable to teach another. It is not too much to say that the stepping by which great geniuses scale the mountain of truth is as unsafe and precarious to men in general, as the scale of the skilful mountaineer up a literal crag. It is a way which alone they can take; and its justification lies in their success. And such mainly is the way in which all men, gifted or not gifted, commonly reason, — not by rule, but by an inward faculty.[12]

Newman's remarks dovetail with the observation that the intellectual substance of canonical theism comes arrayed in complexity, mystery, density, and paradox. Essential to its content is the claim that there is a radical distinction between the Creator and the creature, so there are limits to how far the human mind can understand the divine, and so coming to faith at some stage involves dissonance and suffering. The doctrines of the Trinity and the incarnation clearly stretch both the mind and the imagination to their limits, evoking a silent wonder that cannot be eradicated. Understanding the internal content of canonical theism is profoundly self-involving. To meet God is to meet one's creator, redeemer, and judge; thus one sees oneself not as autonomous but as radically dependent.

The invitation in the gospel to commitment naturally evokes either devotion or rebellion; indifference is itself rejection. Progress in commitment is intimately related to the operation of divine grace, for once one begins to grasp one's alienation or indifference to God, then one realizes

12. *Fifteen Sermons Preached before the University of Oxford between* A.D. *1826 and 1843* (Notre Dame: University of Notre Dame Press, 1997), 256-57.

that there can be no journey to God and to full human dignity without radical, divine assistance.

Within this journey, coming to grasp and embrace the truth may involve dramatic conversion.[13] Initially what was dark and obscure may suddenly become clear and compelling. Personal encounter with God within and without the sacraments of the church may completely reorder a network of tacit judgments that suddenly strike one as a whole with persuasive force. Where before conspicuous sanctity in the saints appeared to be humanly odd and unnatural, now this phenomenon reappears as deeply human and as morally inspiring. Thus if we limit the justification of canonical theism merely to what currently passes for synchronic and diachronic justification, we will miss that kind of diachronic justification that is available not after pertinent investigation but only after one has come to terms with certain experiences and encounters that are not under our control and that cannot be investigated at will.[14]

Furthermore, reliance on the testimony of the church and on the scriptures she has canonized is unavoidable. This stems from the historical claims about divine action in Christ at the core of the faith. Canonical theism insists on the efficacy of once-for-all events in the past recorded in scripture. Hence, it is not at all accidental that intellectual opponents of canonical theism focus on the unreliability of the Gospels and of the church that produced and canonized them. Once this arrow has been shot, the next attack naturally moves to undermining the capacity of the church to arrive at good judgments about the nature of God and his work in the world. Often the core of the intellectual opposition at this point focuses on the welter of supposedly better options developed in the ancient world; or more simply, the strategy concentrates on highlighting the vices, the morally damaged abilities, and the contextual handicaps of the

---

13. I pursue the topic of conversion in chapter 7.

14. Richard Swinburne introduces the distinction between synchronic and diachronic justification and makes extensive use of it in his most recent work. "Theories of justification that analyse what it is for a belief to constitute a justified response to the situation in which the believer finds herself at a given time, I shall call theories of synchronic justification. I contrast them with theories . . . that are theories of what it is for a synchronic justified belief to be based on adequate justification over time, which I call theories of diachronic justification" (*Epistemic Justification* [Oxford: Clarendon, 2001], 9). However, we need to think of the justification that may become possible simply in the course of the journey of faith itself, independently of intentional investigation.

canonical theologians of the church. Over against this, canonical theists operate eventually with a principle of charity toward the witness of the church. There is an inescapable social dimension to what they believe. Testimony is unavoidable and, in its own way, welcomed. Potential defeaters of the church's testimony will be taken seriously, depending on time and circumstances, just as the case for the church's positive abilities and specific judgments will be investigated seriously. Debate is unavoidable with respect to testimony; challenges and rebuttals will ideally be weighed without fuss or defensiveness.

We might summarize the gains of these initial reflections on the content of canonical theism and its embrace in the following manner. First, canonical theism is not readily subject to proof by either deductive or inductive argument. Second, canonical theism can be disproved. Third, canonical theism can be subjected to severe intellectual strain either by cogent single arguments or by an accumulation of negative appraisals.[15] Fourth, canonical theism cannot be secured by appeal to properly basic beliefs. Fifth, making epistemic progress is not an all-or-nothing affair. It requires that we look at the issues both synchronically and diachronically. Sixth, testimony is inescapable.

Further Epistemological Commentary

In the last section of this chapter we can add a further network of explicit epistemic comments.

We begin by noting that the content of canonical theism will naturally and initially appear absurd in the eyes of the world. The content of God's stooping into human existence is frankly astonishing. As Celsus displayed in the second century, it is not difficult to transform this claim into something pathetic and ridiculous.[16] The whole idea of the Creator of the world showing up in the person of his Son in the womb of a Jewish teenage virgin seems preposterous.

Moreover, given our propensity to develop self-serving ideologies

---

15. J. L. Mackie pursues this line with respect to mere theism in *The Miracle of Theism* (Oxford: Clarendon, 1982).

16. A sympathetic summary of Celsus can be found in Henry Chadwick, *Early Christian Thought and the Classical Tradition* (Oxford: Clarendon, 1966), 22-30.

and our ignorance of the whole, it is natural to pit our own theories and speculations against the wisdom of God in the redemption of the world. We have our own well-developed diagnoses and prescriptions for fixing the universe or for standing by the status quo. Once these become internalized as an informal set of standards, the challenge of the gospel can be met with robust and even violent resistance. Thus, grasping the deep meaning, relevance, and truth about the world and ourselves is a hardwon intellectual achievement that is rightly treasured in the church. Mature believers do not abandon the faith because it is publicly and persistently attacked or because it is mocked and caricatured. This complex negative response is expected and treated with understanding and reserve, as well as with fear and trembling.

Furthermore, believers walk by faith rather than by sight. There is no test that is decisive in coming to believe. Informed believers do not subject God to some foreordained trial. They rest content with trusting in God, in his work in history and in the world, and in the media that transmit the full faith of the church and the action of grace. Final intellectual vindication rests in the future, in the life to come. Whatever the level of epistemic success here and now, there is more to come when faith culminates in sight.

It must also be noted that believers vary in the intensity of their commitment. They can readily stumble into unbelief; they can stray back into old vices and intellectual habits; they are engaged in a never ending struggle to remain faithful in love and obedience. Within the journey, there may be glimpses of the divine vouchsafed in personal experience. There may be a high level of assurance and conviction. There may also be stretches of spiritual darkness and loneliness. These matters are person-relative and are intimately tied to the providence of God.[17]

Moreover, coming to embrace the truth about God characteristically depends on obedience, humility, suffering, and purity of intention. Given our alienation from God and our propensity to evil, we readily develop insensitivity to the truth about ourselves in the created order.[18] Just as com-

17. Joseph Butler is one of the few perceptive philosophers to note that a life marked by doubt can be a divine vocation. See Joseph Butler, *The Analogy of Religion* (Philadelphia: Lippincott, 1876), 253. Carol Zaleski provides an illuminating comment on doubt in the lives of the saints in "The Dark Night of Mother Teresa," *First Things* 133 (May 2003): 24-27.

18. Alvin Plantinga's treatment of this theme in chapter 7 of *Warranted Christian Belief* is exceptionally good. It matches in sensitivity and acumen anything available in the history of theology.

ing to know other persons often depends on a readiness to set aside our agendas and to pay careful attention to the other before us, so coming to see the truth enshrined in the canonical heritage of the church involves self-examination, coming to terms with dark and hidden corners, and being radically open to painful self-discovery.[19] Our cognitive capacities, habits, and dispositions need repairing, and they can be healed in part only by appropriate exercises and practices that enable us to switch perspectives and deal forthrightly with the light.

This repair of our cognitive capacities is in turn made possible by the healing activity of the Holy Spirit, who searches and cleanses the soul of impurity and fear. Given the human alienation from God, given the ingenuity of human agents in finding ways to oppose the truth, there has to be effective divine grace that will open the eyes of the soul and enable us to see the truth. This is precisely what we find in the testimony of belief across the ages.

We note finally that at the core of the faith, as seen from an epistemic point of view, there is a special divine revelation that comes to us from without and brings the truth about God and ourselves to a burning focus. This too has been central in the testimony of believers as to why they believe as they do. Crucial to the truth of canonical theism is the claim that God has acted in history to disclose his purposes in creation and redemption. God has both spoken and acted to make known his nature and purposes; because of these we are warranted in accepting very robust claims about his character and intentions.

We might summarize our second nest of epistemic observations in this fashion. Canonical theism will not unnaturally appear initially absurd. Believers walk by faith and not by sight, and they vary in the intensity of their convictions. Coming to the truth about God and ourselves requires increase in virtue; such spiritual and moral progress is made possible by the healing work of the Holy Spirit. Finally, divine revelation is generally seen as playing a pivotal role for the highly ramified beliefs that emerge in the canonical faith of the church.

We now need to pause and dwell on the critical place of divine revelation in the justification of canonical theism. Of all the epistemic suggestions that lie buried in the canonical heritage of the church, this is the single

---

19. For this reason narrative form is not just decorative but may be cognitively significant. Narrative often helps to draw one out of one's own world into other possibilities.

most important component that has caught the attention of theologians and philosophers. While it has suffered neglect over the last generation, it rightly has a special place in the church's claim to know the truth about God.[20]

Once we put divine revelation in place, we shall find that it is not like adding one item to our list of epistemic comments. As we explore the place of divine revelation in the epistemology of theology, we will soon see that it has epistemic features that are intrinsically complex and unique. So much so that it has a role in enriching our commitment to the epistemic platitudes elaborated in chapter 2. By laying out its contours, its nature, and its effects, we hope also to provide a way of tackling the epistemic worth of canonical theism that can be laid out more clearly and systematically than we have achieved heretofore.

20. The topic has been quietly dropped from many of the best introductory text-books in philosophy of religion.

Chapter Four

Revelation, the *Oculus Contemplationis,* and Evidence

—⟨ɷɷɷ⟩—

The Polymorphous Nature of Divine Revelation

Discourse about God within the canonical heritage of the church is concerned to a great degree to bear witness to God's acts of redemption and to draw us into the life of the church. The primary interest is soteriological, that is, to bring about the healing of human agents and restore them to their proper dignity and destiny. However, to have access to God's acts is ipso facto to have access to the truth about God. Indeed, critical to the healing of human agents is that we come to know the truth about God and ourselves. Once we pursue what it is to have the truth about God and ourselves, we are naturally led to explore this in terms of a vision of divine revelation.

As with human agents, God is made known through what he does. Revelation is therefore a polymorphous rather than a monomorphous activity. It supervenes on those acts that disclose the character, nature, and purposes of the agent in question. Imagine for a moment asking someone to take five minutes and reveal herself. This is a very odd request compared, for example, to asking someone to take five minutes and read a book or pop round to the shop. We can make sense of this request only by imagining someone taking five minutes and telling us who she is, where she is from, and what she has done over the years. Some kind of narrative of action will be crucial in any attempt to secure something significant or revelatory of the person in question. Hence one reveals oneself in, with, and through the various acts one performs. In this sense "reveal" is akin to other polymorphous concepts like "teach" or "farm." One teaches by giving lectures, holding tutorials, setting papers, and requiring set texts to be read; one farms by plowing fields, planning what crops to plant, driving tractors, and cleaning out byres. Teaching and farming are not activities done after these activities have been performed; they are done in performing these other activities.

In coming to terms with divine revelation we need to attend to the great diversity of divine action represented. The starry sky above and the moral law within have both been seen as avenues into the divine mind. The natural order displays the wisdom and power of God, and the voice of conscience makes manifest the moral character and will of God. Within creation revelation is said to occur in a variety of situations. Revelation is found in God's word to prophets and apostles. It is enacted in the mighty acts of God in the history of Israel and in the life, death, and resurrection of Jesus of Nazareth. It also takes place in the human heart as the veil of ignorance and sin is removed through the activity of the Holy Spirit and people are enabled to behold the light of the glory of God in the face of Jesus Christ. Finally, revelation will take place at the end of time when the ultimate purposes of God for creation are consummated and fulfilled.

Once we begin to spell out the content of the particular revelatory acts attributed to God, we are in a position to make sense of a further feature of accounts of divine revelation that is very striking, namely, the tendency to gravitate toward the word of God and the incarnation of God in Christ as especially significant. In fact, these two themes merge in an interesting way when the revelatory significance of the incarnation is captured by stressing that Jesus is the Word of God par excellence.

We can begin focusing on the word of God by noting that some of the actions we perform cast extraordinary light on what we do and hence on what we truly are like as a person. Consider the case of Mr. Miser, who hoards all his money and steadfastly refuses to give away a penny to help the poor. He refuses all kinds of pleading made on their behalf. Then he dies and leaves all his money to the local Anglican priest, who is required by the terms of the miser's will to distribute it to the needy of the parish. This is accompanied by an explanation. Unbeknown to others, Mr. Miser had made a rash promise to his father on inheriting the family fortune that he would never give a penny to the poor so long as he lived. Moreover, he was honor-bound to keep this promise a secret during his lifetime. The final will and testament of the supposed miser totally alters our reading of his life and character. Precisely because of this we naturally want to say, "Well, I never thought old Miser had it in him. Fooled me, he did! What a revelation of the old fellow!" It is in situations like these that the concept of revelation takes root. By examining the network of a person's actions, it is immediately clear that some acts are revelatory while others are not. Some stand out as windows into the character of a person and are identified precisely by their capacity to illuminate otherwise dark or ambiguous tracks of action. This is surely the reason for the saying that actions speak louder than words.

The crucial issue at stake for understanding divine revelation here is that the emphasis on the speaking God is not accidental once we place it in the conceptual field of revelation. The action of speaking takes us into a class of actions that are characteristically revelatory. We often clear up queries about what people are doing and the rationale for their actions by asking them to tell us what is going on. Personal avowals and confessions are virtually essential for us to have any idea of what agents have done on various occasions. Indeed, in the case of God this is extremely important, for generally speaking we do not have the functional equivalent of bodily actions or bodily movements in our endeavors to discern God's action in history. The main point can be worked out here very simply by imagining living in a universe where all agents, including the embodied agents we know, are dumb. Speaking, whether human or divine, is characteristically revelatory. Which is one reason why we use "speaking" as a vivid metaphor when we say that actions speak louder than words.[1]

1. This important insight went badly astray in conservative theories of revelation and inspiration. The deep issue at stake here is the natural place God's word to prophet and apostle has in the unveiling of God's action in history. Given God's decisive action in Israel and in Jesus for the liberation of the cosmos, it is entirely fitting that this was accompanied by a form of verbal revelation that identified and articulated what God has done and is doing. Unfortunately this observation went awry. Protestant scholastics of the Reformation and their fundamentalist offspring translated this into a theory of divine dictation and divine inspiration that created enormous problems for the critical investigation of the Bible. Few have seen the ramifications of this conceptual confusion. David Brown is wide of the mark when he tries to see my own work as allowing fundamentalism back in again in the form of a new inner canon of ipsissima verba of God. See his *The Divine Trinity* (La Salle, Ill.: Open Court, 1985), 57. In my work on inspiration and revelation I

Of course, what we now want to know is how to cash out the claim that God spoke to the prophets and apostles. Did the airwaves change? Did they hear voices? Did they see visions? Were there a telepathic communication and an inward hearing of the message from God? Did God just bring it about that the prophet thought certain thoughts, and also bring it about that he thought of those thoughts as coming directly from God? The short answer to this is that we rarely know. This does not mean, however, that we cannot imagine all sorts of conceptual possibilities. After all, divine speaking is not something that simply stopped with the prophets and the apostles. There are legions of case studies in the history and phenomenology of religious experience that we can draw on. Think of Paul's experience on the road to Damascus, or Augustine's experience in the garden, or many instances of a divine call to the Christian ministry. To be sure, we face here exactly the blinders and blinkers that dismiss all references to divine intervention as mythological. The suppression of whole tracts of religious experience from the record of the church as enthusiasm, fanaticism, Pentecostalism, and the like, is the offspring of this prejudice or prejudgment, and we cannot pause to set that story straight here. What we must accept is the historical limitations that confront us. What we have are precious traditions within and without scripture in which the word of the Lord has come down to us in such a way as to save our souls and initiate us into the kingdom of God. Those who heard the word of God had more on their minds than recording the phenomenological features of their experience. What mattered was the content of what God had promised and demanded. It was more important to heed the summons of the Lord of hosts than to preserve the record of the material forms of God's word for posterity, even though we can at times catch a glimpse or two of these in the traditions of God's people.

---

have very deliberately steered clear of a comprehensive account of canon in Christian theology, so his inference at this point is invalid. Brown is also worried that I do not engage more fully with the biblical material. But this is also wide of the mark. I am well aware of the debates about the meaning of the biblical traditions, but one can often best get access to the conceptual considerations I think are crucial by bracketing out these matters for a time. Brown errs in the opposite direction. As noted above, he begs vital conceptual questions by identifying revelation with scripture and hence perpetuates the mistakes that have bedeviled the discussion.

The Incarnation

Moreover, the word to the prophet has a kind of ancillary purpose. The really crucial word from God has come not in the word to a prophet, or in the verbal content of some ancient book. The true Word has come in the person of a Jewish laborer, who was anointed of God, who died on Golgotha, and who was raised by God on the third day. The epistle to the Hebrews captures the matter succinctly: "In many and varied ways God spoke of old to our fathers by the prophets; but in these last days he has spoken to us by a Son, whom he appointed the heir of all things, through whom he also created the world. He reflects the glory of God and bears the very stamp of his nature, upholding the universe by the word of power. When he had made purification for sins, he sat down at the right hand of the Majesty on high, having become as superior to angels as the name he has obtained is more excellent than theirs."[2] It was this revelation of God in Jesus that caught everybody off guard, and that, when properly appreciated, became the center of the church's revelation. This is where the intellectual storm was let loose theologically, rather than on debates about the exact nature of the word to prophet and apostle. The insistence on this unique act of revelation put the very being of God at issue rather than the contingency of this or that way of God speaking to the Fathers. This is most fully reflected in the Nicene Creed, where considerable attention is given to the nature of Christ while the nature of God's speaking to the prophets is barely mentioned. Over time the church came to believe that it was here where the intellectual homework had to be done thoroughly. Ontological and metaphysical questions were and are inescapable.

We need to be candid here and record the offense of this kind of revelation to our minds. Many become uneasy if revelation is not cast in a form that is neat and tidy. It is difficult to tolerate a revelation that is transmitted in the life of a Jewish carpenter. It is hard to accept a revelation transmitted through human witnesses who enshrine it in a varied set of traditions that are so mundane and unspectacular. Moreover, the accompanying requirements about prayer and fasting, about repentance and faith, are easily dismissed as pious afterthoughts. Our problem, we assume, is an intellectual problem, and it must therefore have a conventional intellectual solution written down in an appropriate text that all can

2. Hebrews 1:1-4.

read and understand. Our quest for revelation, that is, tends to entail a set of assumptions about the human predicament that casts our ideas about the nature of revelation in a certain mold. Hence even if we think that Jesus is the Word of God, we assume that his work is that of a teacher, if not of ethics then of some prosaic scheme of salvation that will bring us happiness in the life to come. In the process we set aside the sheer intellectual audacity of the Christian claim about incarnation and run the risk of misreading the nature of God's action in Christ.

Our dilemma in this is very subtle. We are right to press the cognitive dimension of the issue. The canonical heritage informally claims that God has revealed himself uniquely in Christ; there is no going back on this cognitive claim; the determination with which Christian theologians have explored the background and ramifications of this claim is staggering and even appropriate in its proportions. Yet we must move circumspectly as we attempt to articulate how divine revelation in this instance is identified and justified. This is where our conceptual work becomes, once more, quite crucial.

Our actions, including our acts of revelation, are not performed in a vacuum. Even our speaking is done with certain people in view, and it is related intimately to the problems, dispositions, issues, and forms of life of those addressed. The Christian claim about revelation in Christ has to be understood, then, as part of a comprehensive vision of ourselves and our predicament that shapes the very form and character of that revelation.[3] God did not send a library of books for our enlightenment, even though we find the books of scripture indispensable in one way or another for maturity in the faith. Nor did God send his Son so that we might hold extended seminars on ontology and metaphysics, even though these may throw valuable light on what is at stake. God sent the Son to liberate the cosmos from sin and grant us eternal life. Hence the crucial first-order verbs that are deployed to describe God's action in Christ focus not so much on revelation as on salvation, redemption, healing, and restoration. It is in and through these actions that God is truly revealed and made known. To develop a vision of revelation independently of them is profoundly misleading and distorting. Reminding ourselves of the conceptual

---

3. This theme has been pursued with great sensitivity of late by Paul K. Moser in "Cognitive Idolatry and Divine Hiddenness," in *Divine Hiddenness,* ed. Daniel Howard-Snyder and Paul K. Moser (New York: Cambridge University Press, 2002), 120-48.

connections between our actions, our intentions, and our contexts brings this readily to mind.

We can pursue this further by noting that revelation is characteristically an achievement verb. In the case of speaking, for example, if we claim that someone revealed something through saying something, then someone has to grasp and pick up on what is said for there to be a revelation. At the very least, something could have been picked up or grasped. Otherwise all we have are certain locutionary acts, that is, the mere saying of something. So in the case of speaking, the agent needs to perform the illocutionary act of revealing himself or herself. For revelation to occur something has to be picked up and received, or could have been picked up and grasped. Hence revelation, to be revelation, has to be in principle subjectively effective. It has to be such that it can find its way into the life of the individuals and communities to which it is directed.

The implications of these observations for divine revelation are clear. Hearing God speak or being confronted by the incarnation is not a casual affair like reading the local newspaper or switching on the television. At one level we are in the long run inevitably confronted by our darkness and rebellion. Our initial natural reaction to divine revelation may not be one of welcome but one of awe and even terror; given our alienation from God, we invariably put into action a host of devices to keep the offense of the Word of God in Christ at bay. At another level we are confronted with the dignity and extraordinary significance of ourselves as human agents. This can easily be dismissed as wishful thinking or as romantic twaddle by those trapped in despair about themselves and the world as a whole. In this instance our alienation takes the form of a helpless sense of victimhood that has to be worked through to resolution.

Hence it is not surprising that classical Christian accounts of coming to faith and belief are concerned to stress the inner working of the Holy Spirit as part of the total process of revelation. We cannot come to see in a deep way what Christ has done, and thereby what God has revealed through him, without a profound immersion in the Holy Spirit. Such an immersion makes possible the kind of repentance and conversion that enables us to bear the full truth about ourselves without hopelessness and despair. It is surely no surprise, therefore, that accounts of divine revelation can easily collapse into a theory of inner illumination. Developing a fitting response is not something that comes easily or natural to us. We surely do need the veil of darkness about ourselves and the world to be removed by the Holy Spirit if we are to see what God has done for the healing of the world.[4]

At this point we return to the polymorphous nature of both the concept and nature of God's action in history. God is indeed revealed in, with, and through what God does; manifold and wondrous are the form and diversity thereof; and one ingredient in that diversity is the hidden work of the Holy Spirit in our hearts and minds. A Christian account of divine revelation will gather up all that God has done to reveal himself to the world and relate it in rich and surprising ways both to the means of grace that transmit divine revelation and to the tasks and projects of ecclesial and everyday existence. Having pressed home this point rather aggressively, we are now in a position to pursue why we might think that God really has revealed himself to the world as is suggested by our reading of the canonical heritage of the church.

Discernment

The core issue can be approached by thinking of the problem as one of discerning the action of God in creation, in history, and in one's own life. At stake is the recognition of God and his revelatory action. Once we express the issue this way, in terms of discernment and recognition, we do not have to take in the full stretch of God's activity all at once. We can, as it were, enter the circle of revelatory action at various points, selecting relevant revelatory actions, and then move on to explore the full range available to us.

The strategy of discernment and selection applies very clearly to the personal human agents that we know. We can start with people we meet where we are, fill in the pertinent background information as needed, and then continue to increase and grow in our knowledge of them. We can even begin without meeting people directly and start, say, with a communication from them. The communication itself constitutes evidence to us of their existence. We do not need to prove their existence independently of that communication. Indeed, our knowledge of lots of people is derived en-

---

4. Paul K. Moser develops this theme in a very interesting way in "Cognitive Inspiration and Knowledge of God," in *The Rationality of Theism*, ed. Paul Copan and Paul K. Moser (London and New York: Routledge, 2003), 55-71.

tirely from our access to the communication they have sent us. Insofar as we encounter their action or its effects, we are already in the business of coming to know them. Later on we can meet them in person and add that to our stock of experience, constantly reworking our image and knowledge of them. We do all this informally and not necessarily by way of inference from data. We bring to this recognition a basic ability to identify human agents. We have a sense of what it is to encounter other human agents and we learn how to read their actions and intentions off their behavior. However complex the prior concept formation and the prior learning involved, we find ourselves simply interpreting and reading the actions of others in our everyday lives. We rely on basic, bedrock human capacities to read the world as populated by other human agents and their actions.

The same can be said of our initial awareness of God of divine revelation. We do not need to have to hand some proof of the coherence of theism and then of the existence of God and then check out if God is really at work in the world revealing himself. We simply find ourselves aware of the reality of God in our inner experience and in our encountering the world. Thus we are aware of God in creation and in his speaking to us in our conscience. We experience God, as it were, straight off, as we perceive the world around us.[5] We have a sense, however vague, of God and his presence in the world and in our lives. We have, in the language of Hugh of St. Victor, an *oculus contemplationis*, a contemplative or spiritually discerning eye.[6] In this case our ability to perceive God's active presence in creation is

5. This point might also be made by appeal to a principle of initial credulity that states that things are as they appear to us to be, unless they appear otherwise. Thus we find that it appears to us that God is manifest in creation; unless we have good reason to think otherwise, we should go with our appearances. We could take the principle of initial credulity, as Richard Swinburne does, as a basic principle of rationality. For the exposition and defense of this principle see his *The Existence of God* (Oxford: Clarendon, 1979), chap. 13, and *Providence and Evil* (Oxford: Clarendon, 1998), 20-27. See also Caroline Franks Davis, *The Evidential Force of Religious Experience* (Oxford: Clarendon, 1989), chap. 4.

6. Hugh of St. Victor spoke of an *oculus contemplationis*, contrasted in turn with *oculus carnis* and *oculus rationis*. See Roderick M. Chisholm, *Theory of Knowledge* (Englewood Cliffs, N.J.: Prentice-Hall, 1966, 1977), 133-34. Clearly the idea of *oculus contemplationis* has affinities with the idea of *sensus divinitatis*. However, the latter has richer theological overtones than I deploy at this point; hence I prefer the former notion. What I am after is the idea of perception of the divine as a basic cognitive act; the difficulty we face is how to say this anthropologically without overcommitting ourselves theologically prior to deploying the resources of divine revelation that are brought into play. Another way to achieve this end would be to

basic and bedrock. We do not work up to God from a series of arguments, deductive or inductive, but already interpret ourselves and the world we inhabit within a theistic framework. We perceive God's general revelatory activity in creation. In seeing the world and various elements within it we naturally form the belief that God created it, that he is awesome in power, and the like. We are aware of the voice of God within registering approval or disapproval of our actions and thoughts and form the belief that God is our judge. We do not need to be argued into this; such beliefs arise spontaneously and naturally. Creation, as it were, acts as a sign or signal of the divine. We have to be argued out of the beliefs thus formed to become atheists. The default position is this: in the absence of good arguments to the contrary, we recognize straight off God's general revelatory activity in the world and within ourselves.

Reformed epistemologists are right to exploit this insight. We are entitled to believe in the general revelation of God in creation without first having to hand good arguments for the reality of God.[7] The world itself evokes in human agents generally a sense of God that should be taken seriously as it stands. We do not need first to establish that we have spiritual senses, check out how reliable they are, and then decide to trust them. As with our other senses, we work from an initial position of trust. We trust introspection, perception, memory, and the like as bedrock in our intellectual life. We see ourselves on reflection as complex truth-detecting organisms with extraordinarily complex sensors that transmit information to us we know not how or why. We find ourselves believing a host of things about ourselves and the world around us; beliefs appear in us accompanied by varying degrees of assent and commitment. We naturally find ourselves inhabiting a world of objects, properties, agents, and the like. We also find ourselves inhabiting a world already haunted by the di-

---

deploy something like William P. Alston's notion of a doxastic practice, but this too presupposes more than I want or need to at this stage of the argument. See his highly original and subtle account of Christian mystical practice in *Perceiving God* (New York: Cornell University Press, 1991), chap 5. There are moments in what follows when I shall sometimes revert to the language of *sensus divinitatis*, especially when I am in the neighborhood of positions that prefer this language.

7. It has been common to run together general revelation and natural theology, but this is clearly a mistake. The doctrine of general revelation involves an *assertion* that God is revealed generally in creation; natural theology involves an *argument* from general features of the universe to the proposition that God exists.

vine, pressing in upon us from many directions at once. We are entitled to see the world this way unless we have good reason to believe otherwise.

We may also find ourselves undergoing a variety of more particular experiences that we take to be the presence or activity of God in our lives. Here we go beyond a general sense of God in creation and find ourselves presented with the reality of God in such a way that we naturally form beliefs that God is manifest to us. Alternatively, we look back over our lives and see either particular events or a string of events as representing the providence of God. Again, we are not making inferences from data to the confirmation of a religious hypothesis; we perceive our experiences straight off in terms of God's presence, or we read what is happening straight off as God's providence.

Epistemologically we rightly interpret what is going on here as a form of perception of the divine. We assume in this a particular anthropology; that is, concomitantly with the interpretation we see ourselves as having the native capacity to perform basic cognitive acts of perceiving God.[8] If we need to, we can spell out this assumption as a capacity given to us in creation, but this is by no means necessary either psychologically or logically for us naturally to read our experiences as the self-presentation of God or various stretches of events as acts of providence. We simply begin with the acts of perception themselves in ourselves or as mediated through the testimony of other human agents we know. We either trust or do not trust these acts of perception. There is no independent way of certifying their reliability; we either go with the order and grain of nature, or we do not.

Of course, in articulating what is at stake I have left aside for the moment the place that communities have in supplying the conceptual repertoire deployed in speaking in this manner about ourselves and about God. As in the case of discerning human actions, we are initiated into a very subtle and complex body of concepts that we naturally pick up and put to work in our descriptions of the world and our experience. We do not start from some initial state of nature; we make our observations and develop our descriptions inside linguistic communities that supply networks of concepts that we deploy as a kind of second nature over time. The originating conditions and the learning that is at stake in the deployment of such complex notions as human and divine agency lie outside our ken for now. We simply have them to hand one way or another. I am assuming,

8. For a very illuminating discussion of this claim, see Davis, *Evidential Force*, 145-55.

that is, that for us to deploy the concept of human and divine agency, these concepts are already in place, logically speaking.

There is nothing startling about this observation, for it applies to the fundamental categories that are in place when we describe our experience of the world and ourselves. Thus I could not describe my car as green without already having to hand the concept of a car and the relevant concept of color. Equally, I could not describe the actions of my neighbor mowing the lawn if I did not have a rich concept of human action in place. Extending the analysis to include the concept of divine action — while involving a much richer potential ontology than one where we employ only those concepts that relate to the physical and human world — does not add anything radically new to the situation, philosophically speaking. In all these cases we invoke a whole network of complex concepts to articulate our experience. To advance the claims that we do, we assume as logically prior the relevant repertoire of concepts.

In the current discussion we are claiming to see in creation, in our lives, and in our experiences manifestations of divine action. We are also claiming that our ability to do this is a basic cognitive act. We have captured this by saying that we have spiritual as well as physical sensory capacities that are not reducible to other acts of cognition. Aside from being able to see the physical and human world and reliably describe activities that arise within it, we are also able to perceive a divine order in the universe and reliably able to describe the divine activities that arise within it. We capture this anthropologically and ontologically by noting, following the language of Hugh of St. Victor, that human agents come equipped with an *oculus contemplationis*.[9] This simply parallels our observation that human agents possess physical and moral senses, that is, they are able to discern events and actions in their experience straight off. For the sake of discussion, let us call this the *oculus contemplationis* theory.

Exploring the Evidentialist Alternative

There is, however, another way to think of the situation we are exploring. Two features of the theory in hand prompt us to do so, one negative and

---

9. Readers more at home with the language of *sensus divinitatis* may want to substitute this notion at this point.

one positive. First, it may appear luxurious and question begging to introduce talk of an *oculus contemplationis*. Thus we are introducing unwanted and superfluous anthropological elements to undergird the claim that we perceive God in the world and in our experience. It looks as if we are inventing an arbitrary epistemological theory to ground our epistemological proposals. Second, it is surely no accident, it will be said, that we claim to become aware of God when presented with certain general features of the universe, that is, with creation as a whole and with the order and beauty that is such a marked and pervasive feature of it. As Kant famously remarked, it is the starry sky above and the moral law within that prompt us to think of God. In Plantinga's terminology, certain recurring features of the universe trigger our awareness of God, and these characteristically reappear in the material that has been pivotal in the classical experience-oriented arguments for the existence of God. So why not think about the situation overall in this way? Rather than sensing the reality of God, we are in fact informally articulating arguments for the existence of God, arguments that are best knocked into shape in terms of the cosmological, teleological, and experiential arguments for the existence of God.

We can see how this might work by noting that ordinary theists, when quizzed about why they believe in God, often say something like: "Well, of course there is a God. How else can you explain the existence of the world? How else can you explain the order and beauty I see all around me? How else can I can make sense of my sense of right and wrong and my sense of God's presence in the world?" On this very different analysis we are to see this kind of discourse as involving the informal positing of a religious hypothesis in which the existence and ongoing agency of God are seen as the best explanation of a network of various features of the universe. In this scenario there is no need to think of some *oculus contemplationis*. All we need are our ordinary senses coupled with the capacity to frame theistic explanations for features of the universe already registered in our experience. If there is an additional sense, then we can posit an illative sense, that is, a capacity to perceive below the surface of our formal reasoning so as to frame and to test hypotheses informally. Of course, we can then attempt to work out more formal versions of these arguments, say, by use of probability theory, but the crucial point is that we have here a form of reasoning that does not posit a theistic, much less a Christian, anthropology. Let us call this the explanatory hypothesis theory.

Much hinges on how we proceed at this stage. My own inclination is to favor the first analysis — the *oculus contemplationis* theory. One reason for this choice is phenomenological. The language of the discerning or contemplative eye is not accidental; it captures a crucial feature of how things appear to many believers. Believers see God at work in creation and in their own lives; they do not initially argue themselves into believing that this is the case. So it is a stretch to think of the relevant cognitive activity as that of hypothesis formation and testing. Secondly, the primary claim of the tradition is captured by a claim about general revelation rather than a claim about natural theology. God's presence and power are manifest and revealed in creation as a whole. This is radically different from a claim about hypothesis formation and confirmation in experience. Thirdly, the *oculus contemplationis* theory fits naturally with the possibility that all have access to the divine in creation rather than the chosen few who can form and test hypotheses informally or formally. The latter makes access to God dependent on human ingenuity and intelligence. Fourthly, the explanatory hypothesis theory strikes me as much too intellectualist and rationalistic in orientation. I suspect it trades on the assumption that religious belief formation is fundamentally a matter of forming theories and then testing them by data and evidence. Intuitively I find the notion of seeing or perceiving God's presence in the universe and in our experience more natural and persuasive. The analogy with perceptual experience at this point is striking, even though the primary motivation for this move is not to argue from analogy. Rather, we are seeking to find a way to articulate how best to represent the judgments of those who see God at work in the world straight off, that is, without appeal to any formal argument.

Yet we need not choose rigidly between these alternatives. Indeed, if one favors the tradition of the *oculus contemplationis,* then one can take up the cause of natural theology, deploying the kinds of arguments that lie at the base of the second strategy. The epistemic payoff for favoring this logical order of business is not inconsiderable. To begin with, one is not dependent on arguments from natural theology to be entitled to believe in God. This entitlement is secured by the claim that we have here cognitive acts that are basic, and nonderivative. The second strategy taken clearly is so dependent. It hinges critically on the forming of good informal judgments or on the securing of the validity and soundness of the relevant arguments. One is entitled to believe only if one has made the relevant informal or formal calculations and gotten them right. Furthermore, the additional appeal to natural theology can surely be supplementary to the appeal to the *oculus contemplationis*. Natural theology, insofar as it succeeds, increases the strength of the appeal to the *oculus contemplationis* by providing additional reasons for reading the world and our experience as manifestations of divine action. Natural theology takes the form of confirmation of initial perceptions. Thus the confidence supplied by the *oculus contemplationis* may be increased by these additional arguments, yet the confidence can also survive their defeat. Thus the deep shape and structure of the theist's intellectual position is at stake in these deliberations. The best way to think of that deep structure is to see it as positing an initial *oculus contemplationis* complemented by an illative sense that does indeed form complex explanatory theories that are supported by the same experiences that trigger our initial beliefs about God.

The Case of Special Revelation

We can now extend this analysis to cover the recognition of acts of special divine revelation in history. In perceiving this or that prophet as a bearer of a message from God, the believer is not forming and testing a religious hypothesis. In seeing, say, Jeremiah or Paul as a recipient of divine revelation, the believer finds herself drawn to believe that God has called and commissioned Jeremiah and Paul to be bearers of special revelation. In seeing in Jesus Christ the incarnation of God, the believer in listening to the gospel about Jesus finds herself drawn to believe that he is the Son of God. In these instances of special and extraspecial revelation, the believer sees God speaking and acting in very particular ways. To deploy once more the language of the senses, one senses that God is here, in Jeremiah or in Jesus, speaking and revealing himself to the world.

This is not a matter of forming religious hypotheses and then testing them against the data in hand. We can imagine how this option might play out for a prophet. We posit that if God is to make a revelation to the world, then that revelation is to be identified, say, by accompanying miracles. Perhaps we extend this to draw up a set of credentials that pick out a true prophet. So the prophet must show evidence of an inward call, must teach what is consistent with prior divine revelation, must not lead folk astray to false gods, must deliver a message that is significant, must utter predictions that actually occur, and the like. So we check if the relevant credentials accompany the prophet. If they do, he is a genuine prophet, and we should believe what he says; if they do not, we reject him as a false prophet.

We can also imagine how this might be applied to a true messiah from God. We posit, say, that the true messiah must be accompanied by a very special miracle, say, his resurrection from the dead. We add in other kinds of credentials. Thus the putative messiah must fulfill earlier predictions about his life and ministry, must have a special kind of self-consciousness, must perform very special miracles, must show no traces of sin in his life, must teach in a very special way, and so on. We then check out if he has been raised from the dead, if he has supplied the relevant signs and wonders, if he shows no traces of sin, and the like. If he has met these criteria, we have a true messiah; if he has not, we have a false messiah.

There are at least three very serious problems with this kind of approach. This whole way of thinking provides far too intellectualist an account of how theists come by their convictions and commitments. They do not first work out theories like these and then apply them to the data. They find themselves drawn directly into believing in special revelation rather than forming and testing religious hypotheses like these. Moreover, believers do not give up their convictions about special revelation when this sort of position fails to pan out. Thus the purported argument is not really doing any intellectual work in the initial commitment. Finally, the schema of hypotheses and relevant confirmation turns out to be ad hoc and *post eventum*. The position developed turns out very conveniently to establish that special revelation is given in Israel and in Jesus Christ. The credentials turn out to be singular and particular; they do not really function as an independent source of access to the truth about God; they represent what is taken to be the case for prophets in the Jewish and Christian tradition. Thus the whole exercise turns out to be circular.

The insight that lies buried beneath the explanatory hypothesis theory is that there may indeed be corroboration of the initial belief, and this is often supplied by the kinds of data that are transposed into a list of criteria or credentials. Thus one's initial sense that God has spoken in a special way, say, through Jeremiah, may cohere with and thus be strengthened by his avowals about his call, by the way his message dovetails with earlier revelation, by the depth of his message, by the ensuing events, and the like. Equally, the initial sense of God being incarnate in Jesus may cohere with and thus be strengthened by the signs that accompany him, by the authority with which he speaks, by the depth of his analysis of the human condition exhibited in his teaching, by his resurrection from the dead, and the like. Indeed, the signs that accompany Jesus function as manifestations of intelligent design at work in and around Jesus. Thus the coherence of revelation and miracle is entirely natural. Miracles really do have epistemic freight, and it is important to recognize this.

The Potential Role of Miracle

To bring out the force of this point, consider the following scenario. Mr. Prophet approaches Mr. Skeptic and sensitively reports the following experience. "God spoke to me last night and told me to tell you that if you buy a single lottery ticket on Friday between the hours of five and six o'clock in the evening, you will win six million dollars. I cannot at this point fill you in on the phenomenology of the experience; indeed, I refuse to be drawn out on how God told me, for I am under orders from God to refuse to pursue questions of that nature at this time. If you want we can have a seminar later on the issues at stake."

Immediately, Mr. Skeptic laughs and makes fun of Mr. Prophet. Mr. Prophet then fills out the experience further. "I was expecting you to take this line. For God also told me that you would be skeptical. So he also told me to tell you this. On Thursday you will suddenly fall ill, with intense pain and internal bleeding in your stomach. The pain will be so bad that you will lose consciousness. However, at four o'clock the next morning, you will wake up feeling completely better."

It so happens that Mr. Skeptic falls suddenly ill on Thursday afternoon with intense pain, and he loses consciousness. His friends rush him to the hospital. There a set of relevant tests shows that he has developed an ulcer of the stomach. The experts tell him that the chances of any kind of immediate healing are very slim. At the very least it will take six months of dieting, medication, and rest before they can offer any hope of recovery. They keep Mr. Skeptic in hospital overnight to give them time to work out the relevant therapeutic measures.

Early on Friday morning Mr. Skeptic wakes up feeling completely better. The doctors take him in hand, perform the same set of relevant tests, and discover that the ulcer is gone. They shake their heads in wonder, discharge him immediately, and go about their work as usual.

The crucial question now is: Will Mr. Skeptic buy the lottery ticket? If he does, he has grasped intuitively that miracles operate as confirmation for claims to possess divine revelation. What lies below the surface of Mr. Skeptic's intuitions at this point?

We can readily discern what is at issue precisely because we have eliminated any appeal to the *oculus contemplationis*. I think that the intuition works off the logic of the argument from design. The content of the conversation and the events surrounding it exhibit intelligent design in a very striking manner. On the one hand, naturalistic explanations are logically available, but one has to stretch to make them fit. It could be that Mr. Prophet made up the story to make fun of Mr. Skeptic; it could be that the recovery was simply a matter of spontaneous remission covered by laws that we do not yet understand. Over against this Mr. Prophet insists that he is not making fun of Mr. Skeptic; and holding out for a revision of the laws of nature related to ulcers seems implausible. Mr. Skeptic might be more tempted to think that a big mistake was made in the initial diagnosis. But then the second tests would be questionable too, for they rest on the same kind of evidence. On the other hand, an explanation in terms of divine agency provides a smooth account of the network of events that have occurred. It ties together the prophet's report, the sudden sickness, and the surprising cure into a single explanation. The explanation is not complete, of course, for we still do not know why God would do all this at this time in Mr. Skeptic's life. However, incomplete personal explanations are still explanations, so much so that most folk confronted with this could barely wait until five o'clock on Friday to buy the ticket.

Note what is at stake here. Nothing here shows that miracles have happened, or that God has spoken, or that God speaks in this manner. The point is that miracles do have epistemic value, and the deep reason why they do is that they exhibit conspicuous design in the universe that in this instance dovetails with a word from God. Miracles are signs of God's presence in someone's life. They thus cohere with and corroborate the original claim to divine revelation. Yet they do not operate in isolation, nor can we require that all special divine revelation be accompanied by miracles. In this instance the miracle simply fits with other claims, rather than operating as some kind of religious hypothesis that could be predicted in advance independently of the precise claim on offer.

Overall, what I am tracking here is a parallel between the way our sense of God speaking through creation works epistemically and the way our sense that God has spoken through prophets and through Jesus Christ works epistemically. Once we allow claims to both general and special revelation to operate within the framework of an *oculus contemplationis*, then initially we can allow both kinds of claims to stand or fall together. We trust what we see, or we do not. We are entitled to hold the beliefs formed in our encounter with creation or with the lives of crucial religious figures in history. We are not here operating on the basis of hypothesis and confirmation. However, we may find that the original judgment formed as a matter of discernment coheres with and in some sense is strengthened by the data that begin to show up both in natural theology and in debates about the credentials of prophets. In both cases the latter phenomena and the accompanying explanation fit with the message presented. The accompanying miracles function as signs that bear additional witness to the special revelation. We are entitled to believe without the miracles, and yet the miracles do add weight to the initial beliefs that are allowed to stand in their absence.

A Note on Sin and Virtue

One more point deserves mention at this juncture. Once we operate with the fundamental idea of the *oculus contemplationis*, then we can understand that this sense can be impaired and healed. Just as our capacity to discern what other human agents are doing can be clogged by our fat, relentless egos; by our corrupt and cynical modes of thinking; by our despair and lack of confidence; by the burden of victimhood and oppression; and by our own narrow agendas, so can our capacity to discern rightly what God is doing in the universe and in history. It is not at all accidental on this reading that recognition of divine revelation is intimately related to repentance and commitment to virtue on the one hand, and to the internal work of the Holy Spirit in illumination and enlightenment on the other. Through the grace of God, spiritual exercises help to focus the attention and to purify the doors of perception, and thus to enable us to see God. This provides additional reason for accepting the deep structure of the life of the mind developed above. Moral and spiritual factors may be relevant to our ability to posit relevant explanatory hypotheses for our experiences and to finding ways of relevant confirmation, but surely moral and spiritual factors are far more relevant to the exercise of the kinds of basic cognitive acts we have posited here in terms of sensing and discerning the action of God in the universe and in history.

What is at issue is purity of heart rather than ingenuity in framing religious hypotheses. The former is open to all, given certain assumptions about creation and the universal operation of prevenient grace. The latter is restricted to those who have the relevant ingenuity and creativity. If commitment to divine revelation is pivotal for a robust spiritual life, then it would be odd indeed if God left us so dependent on such limited expertise. Yet the use of our minds in seeking and finding such additional understanding is not forbidden us. Faith is permitted to pursue such understanding both informally and formally even while it can stand secure without it. In some circumstances, our spiritual vocation requires that such work be pursued.

This adage applies to the overall proposals advanced in this chapter too. I have sought to analyze what is before us in claims to divine revelation as these show up informally in the canonical heritage of the church. I have tried to unpack the particular claims that can be extracted from a robust reading of that heritage and to show how they can be summarized in terms of the concept of revelation. I have drawn attention to important features of divine revelation in this arena, emphasizing its polymorphous nature, the natural place of speaking within it, and the very special place given to divine incarnation. In the second half of the chapter I took up the identification of divine revelation and developed an account that gives primary place to our *oculus contemplationis*. In addition, I have reworked the kinds of data that show up in natural theology and in theories of evidence for divine revelation so that they operate as corroborating evidence that coheres with and thus strengthens the initial beliefs legitimately formed independently of propositional evidence. None of these insights or proposals is essential for the exercise of proper faith in divine revelation. Faith permits us to pursue this kind of reflection without itself being dependent on such reflection. Just as we can perceive the world without having any theory of perception to hand, so we can perceive divine action in the world without any theory of spiritual senses in hand.

What we have done is increase our understanding of faith. We might also say that we have made progress in understanding what it is to come to terms with the claims to revelation that show up informally in the canonical heritage of the church. Hopefully, we have provided an illuminating account of how to come to terms with our initial epistemological queries that center on why someone might come to believe that the Christian church is right to claim possession of a special revelation of God in history. However, we have by no means come to terms with what it is to have such a revelation on our hands. To that we now turn. We shall see that there are epistemic features of the appeal to divine revelation that are rarely noted and that go a long way to meet some of the standard objections leveled against claims to possess a divine revelation.

Chapter Five

Crossing the Threshold
of Divine Revelation

—⟋⟋⟋—

Agents and Revelation

In the last chapter we saw that an appeal to divine revelation as central to the warrants for canonical theism is a natural development. The core concept governing its vision of God is that of God as a personal agent. God is primarily identified as the creator and redeemer of the world. Indeed, action predicates are constitutive of the divine reality encountered and worshiped in the canonical life of the church. This has immediate bearings on how we are to think of knowledge of God, for there are characteristic ways in which personal agents are made known and in the manner in which claims about them are adjudicated.

Agents are fundamentally made known by what they do. Thus we come to know personal agents by encountering them in our experience and by becoming acquainted with their actions. This applies especially to historical agents. We are utterly dependent on records, witnesses, and memories of what they have done if we are to get beyond mere names and faces and proceed to the level of their nature, achievements, significance, projects, purposes, and the like. Moreover, the justification of claims about agents invariably involves citing this or that action or achievement. Consider the critical role of references, character witnesses, gossip, personal anecdote, and the like when we are challenged about our claims about this or that person. Historians are trained to make graded assessment of the agents whose stories and actions they narrate, and invariably cite this or that action in justifying, say, the role and place of Pope Pius XII in events related to the persecution of Jews. These basic principles also apply to knowing persons in the present. Actions are pivotal in coming to know personal agents and in offering an account of our proposals about their nature.

Yet attributing actions to this or that agent is not generally a matter of framing hypotheses and then looking for confirming evidence. We have a bedrock capacity to describe our experiences in terms of human agency and action. We see straight off what is going on when we meet others; we have the capacity to understand their actions and to explain them in terms of the reasons or motives governing them. We can, of course, look for corroboration for our initial perceptions and for our understanding of what agents are doing. Thus our initial perception that Jones stole the car may be strengthened by all sorts of other considerations, but many of these will come by perceiving other actions of his as well as by, say, physical evidence.

I have suggested that our understanding of divine action follows the same general pattern. We come equipped with an original, native capacity to perceive God's general and special revelation in the world. This perception can then be found to cohere with other things we find out about the world or about the content and accompanying events related to special revelation.

The Offense of Divine Revelation

Yet there are features of the commitment to divine revelation that are not captured in this analysis. Consider in this context the startling remarks of Paul.

> I am astonished that you are so quickly deserting the one who called you in the grace of Christ and are turning to a different gospel — not that there is another gospel, but there are some who are confusing you and want to pervert the gospel of Christ. But even if we or an angel from heaven should proclaim to you a gospel contrary to what we proclaimed to you, let that one be accursed! As we have said before, so now I repeat, if anyone proclaims to you a gospel contrary to what

80

you have received, let that one be accursed! Am I now seeking human approval, or God's approval? Or am I trying to please people? If I were still pleasing people, I would not be a servant of Christ. For I want you to know, brothers and sisters, that the gospel that was proclaimed by me is not of human origin; for I did not receive it from a human source, nor was I taught it, but I received it through a revelation of Jesus Christ.[1]

This is an extraordinary passage. What is striking in the present context is the abruptness of the language and the complete absence of standard academic civility and convention. There is no reference to the degrees earned, to the dissertations completed, to the books written, to the intellectual breakthroughs made, to the original insights articulated, and the like. There is no survey of pertinent literature, no appeal to carefully constructed premises and relevant conclusions, no reference to publicly available evidence, no refutation of competing positions, and no rebuttal of pertinent objections. It would appear that we have to take Paul's word for it. We have a straight appeal to authority delivered in tones and terms that are intolerant and even abusive.

I am, of course, using Paul as a foil and a platform at this point; I leave it to others to track the issue in exegesis and the history of theology. I simply note that Paul's appeal to revelation is embedded in a wider context that makes much of the calling of grace and of the place of Jesus Christ in the overall revelation of God in history. What interests me is the logic or grammar of revelation as we see it played out here. Paul rejects any appeal to conventional human warrants. The gospel he expounds is not derived from human sources or origins; it is received through a revelation of Jesus Christ. The claim is clearly epistemological; it relates to the warrants for believing the gospel and accepting the implications that lie on the other side of belief. Let's look further below the surface and see what we can find.

One way into our journey is by contrast. The primary category at stake is that of a prophet or an apostle, rather than that of a scholar or a genius. We know how to delineate the latter two designations. A scholar is a trained expert who has been initiated into a field of learning with its own canons of discourse, modes of thought, patterns of explanation and evi-

---

1. Galatians 1:6-12.

dence, and the like. We can readily identify the academic pedigree, the list of publications, and the subjects mastered. A genius is a couple notches above this. The term "genius" picks out a thinker of extraordinary ability, insight, and originality, like Albert Einstein, who put together a truly original theory of relativity.[2]

A prophet or apostle occupies a radically different intellectual space.[3] The prophet may of course be a brilliant thinker or writer; consider what has been left behind in the traditions stemming from, say, Jeremiah or Ezekiel. We can certainly say this of Paul too. His writings are extraordinary in their intellectual power, construction, and content. However, this is not the critical factor one meets in a prophet. What sets a prophet apart is epistemology. The critical appeal is to divine encounter and divine speaking. The prophet is a recipient and mediator of divine revelation.[4] A sharp distinction is usually drawn between the ordinary word of the prophet and the word of God, or rather between the ordinary discourse of the prophet and the special word of the prophet whose content is either identical with or derived from the word of God. The relevant background narrative for a prophet is not one of educational attainment but one of spiritual pilgrimage in which the agent is confronted and called by God to speak in God's name.[5]

What also sets the prophet apart is a complex network of psychological states and dispositions. I would not make these in any way constitutive of the life of a prophet, but they are characteristic of the life of a prophet. Thus, on the one hand, the prophet is often found in a state of

2. It is interesting that a genius need not be the bearer of truth; we can readily identify a person as a genius without committing ourselves to the truth of what he or she has proposed. For example, we can readily identify Plato, or Marx, or Freud as exhibiting genius without being Platonists, or Marxists, or Freudians.

3. A classical treatment of this topic remains in Søren Kierkegaard, *Without Authority* (Princeton: Princeton University Press, 1997), 93-107. Kierkegaard appears to reject as unintelligible the crucial question of how prophets are to be identified and how one might argue for or against such claims, but his discussion, aside from its wittiness, is full of creative and fruitful comment.

4. It would be tempting to think in the wake of this that commitment to truth is constitutive of the concept of the prophet. Given that divine revelation is an epistemically positive process of belief formation like memory, it might look as if a prophet must speak the truth. However, if this were the case, we could not speak of false prophets.

5. The classical biblical passages that alert one to this are 1 Samuel 3, Isaiah 6, and Jeremiah 1.

fear and trembling. Have prophets really been called of God? Have they really heard what God is saying? Mixed with this is often a sense of burden and awesome responsibility. Have they really delivered what God has said to them? Have they been faithful? Have they resisted the temptation to cut the message to suit the hearers? On the other hand, there are amazing tenacity and confidence. The prophet will stand up to anyone, like Nathan to David.[6] They can be stern and resolute like John the Baptist in the Gospels[7] or like Paul here in his correspondence with the Galatians.

Philosophers and theologians are very nervous about this kind of behavior. There is, we might say, a natural aversion to the concept of divine revelation. The crucial components of this aversion can be located in at least four areas.

First, the appeal to divine revelation is thought to be subjective and arbitrary. It summons up a contact between the divine and the human that cannot be substantiated. The best we can hope for is the strong conviction that God has spoken; but this is entirely inward and personal. Hence the appeal to divine revelation destroys the life of the mind in its public manifestations and responsibilities. While claiming a privileged skyhook or private pipeline to the divine, it provides access only to the mental world of its advocates.

Second, the appeal is believed to be radically divisive. Its proponents set it above everything else, above reason, experience, intuition, testimony, imagination, and the like. They sit within the circle of faith and, of necessity, press for the outworking of divine revelation across the board in morality, culture, politics, and theology. Hence the appeal to revelation is naturally disruptive of the social order. It breeds fanaticism, and fanaticism, in turn, is the mother of abuse and violence. Hence revelation destroys inclusivism and pluralism, fostering instead a dangerous brew of exclusion and inquisition.

Third, it is thought to cut off reflection and reasoning. Any answer supplied in divine revelation is somehow delivered on a plate, the alternatives are shut down, and the life of the mind is suffocated and contracted. Revelation is a pious laborsaving device that stops us thinking for ourselves and makes us slaves of authority.

Fourth, the appeal to divine revelation is often seen as a disguised

6. 2 Samuel 12:7-14.
7. See, for example, Matthew 3.

and illegitimate bid for authority and power. It is a costume designed to establish its proponents in a privileged hierarchy; it is a weapon invented to intimidate and silence critics and challengers. As such, rather than accepted with trust, it should be received with suspicion and demythologized expeditiously.

The Grammar of Divine Revelation

To make progress on our topic, it is clear we need to deal with these worries as substantially as we can. Clearly some of these objections are weightier than others. The great value of enumerating them is that it forces us to look below the surface at the whole idea of divine revelation. We can respond to these objections only if we come to terms with the peculiar and unique features of revelation as an epistemic concept.

Revelation is an incredibly rich and complex concept. The core meaning is that of disclosure; something formerly hidden is now manifest. In revelation, as George Mavrodes has recently suggested, we have the following schema: m reveals a to n by means of k.[8] M represents the revealer or the agent of revelation; a represents the content of revelation; n represents the recipient of revelation; k represents the mode or means of revelation. The permutations on this schema are clearly manifold.[9] While the agent of revelation is restricted to God, the content can be the nature and purposes of God or the hidden depths of the human condition. The mode can be either by word or deed in all its variety; the recipients can be an individual, a community, or the whole known world. In the Christian tradition revelation can be general, that is, in creation and conscience; it can be special, that is, in the history of Israel; and it can be extraspecial, that is, in Jesus Christ. It can be internal in our hearts or external in human history. It is intimately related to the Bible and to the church; it is related to but different from divine inspiration.[10]

For our purposes the really pertinent point is that revelation is a piv-

8. George Mavrodes, *Revelation in Religious Belief* (Philadelphia: Temple University Press, 1988), 88.

9. Mavrodes draws an extremely helpful distinction between revelation as manifestation and revelation as communication. See *Revelation in Religious Belief*, 75-79.

10. I have argued this case in *The Divine Inspiration of Holy Scripture* (Oxford: Oxford University Press, 1981).

otal epistemological concept.[11] This is one reason why it is conceptually confused to look for a "biblical" conception of revelation. There is no biblical conception of revelation any more than there is a biblical conception of other crucial epistemic concepts. Indeed, to identify relevant material on revelation in scripture already presupposes that one is working with a concept of revelation brought to the text, for otherwise one would not know where or how to locate material on divine revelation in scripture. Bultmann very well brings out this point. Noting that the issue is not simply linguistic or philological, he writes: "[W]e have already presupposed that the New Testament speaks of something such as we ourselves mean when we speak of 'revelation.' Because of this our question is evidently guided by a certain understanding of the concept of revelation."[12]

Revelation belongs in that family of terms generally listed as reason, experience, intuition, conscience, testimony, and the like. Thus it serves as a warrant for other claims. It operates as a foundation, or ground, or reason, or basis for central theological claims about God.[13] The really critical point, however, is this: revelation is what we might call a threshold concept.[14] To be sure, in the case of, say, reason or experience, one relies on these immediately and directly. Revelation, like testimony and conscience, is a much more contested epistemic category. Their deployment generally presupposes a theistic metaphysics, but this does nothing to undermine their epistemic status, unless we already assume that theism is intellectually corrupting or poisonous. The crucial point to make here is this: once the term "revelation" is deployed, it is simply and totally applicable; and once revelation is accepted, one enters a whole new world where every-

---

11. See Rudolf Bultmann, "The Concept of Revelation in the New Testament," in *Existence and Faith* (New York: Meridian, 1966), 58. Of course, one's thinking about revelation can and should be informed by scripture, but this is another matter entirely. Moreover, note that "Bible," "scripture," and "canon" are not epistemological concepts. As I have already noted, these are better seen as notions that belong in the realm of soteriology; they are best seen as complex means of grace whose proper home is the church.

12. Bultmann, "Concept of Revelation," 58.

13. The term "foundation" here should be taken in its everyday sense without implying anything technical philosophically.

14. There are other ways to unpack the image of a threshold than the one I shall deploy shortly. For a helpful discussion of how this notion was used in the seventeenth and eighteenth century, see M. Jamie Ferreira, *Skepticism and Reasonable Doubt: The British Naturalist Tradition in Wilkins, Hume, Reid, and Newman* (Oxford: Clarendon, 1986), 23-26, 187-89, 228-30. Wilkins is especially interesting.

thing is liable to be seen in a whole new light. "Revelation" is what we might call a threshold concept. Compare the attribution of legal guilt. Once applied, it is applied simply and totally; moreover, once applied, it opens up a whole new realm of reality, depending on the particularities of the case.

The idea of a threshold is of course spatial or geographical. I am using it here metaphorically. Consider two examples where we naturally speak of crossing a threshold. Consider climbing a mountain. As one ascends, say, the back of the mountain, perhaps all one can see are some scattered fields, a delightful lake not much bigger than a pond, and a few lonely farmhouses. Then suddenly one reaches the top, and crossing over the threshold of the summit, one has an exquisite panoramic view of the whole countryside, a view that circles the full 360 degrees of the compass.[15] To cross that threshold is to enter a whole new field of vision that stretches miles and miles from every angle. My second analogy makes the same point. Consider crossing the threshold of a house. From the outside there is much to be seen externally; but far more remains totally hidden from sight. Step inside across the threshold, and a whole network of rooms, staircases, closets, basement, and kitchen is available. One has crossed into another world. In both cases one may or may not step across the threshold; however, the step across that threshold is singular and absolute; and once across, there is a new awareness of phenomena previously hidden from view. We might capture this insight by noting that the experience of revelation is a world-constituting experience.

Special revelation in the canonical heritage of the church, I propose, is like that. Unlike reason, experience, intuition, and the like, which simply happen naturally, we may or may not enter into revelation. To be sure, the original recipients of revelation, say, the prophets, may have had little or no choice in being the recipients of divine revelation.[16] However, whether they accept it, whether they explore it, whether they transmit it,

15. I develop this analogy from my own experience of climbing Topped Mountain near to Enniskillen County, Fermanagh, Northern Ireland.

16. As noted earlier (above, p. 64), my inclination in the past has been to say that revelation is indeed an achievement verb, so that we would refuse to designate an experience or phenomenon as revelation unless the recipient of the revelation recognized and acknowledged that there had been revelation. However we think of this inclination, we need to distinguish logically between the reception of revelation, the recognition of a revelation, the acknowledgment of a revelation, and the response to a revelation.

these are matters for decision and action. Once revelation is recognized, then the threshold has been crossed. Once one acknowledges the revelation, then everything may have to be rethought and redescribed in the light of what has been found. Moreover, the same basic pattern applies when the revelation becomes a mediated revelation in scripture and the church. Then, at this point too, once revelation is recognized, a threshold has been crossed. And again, once one acknowledges the revelation, then one enters a whole new world that requires extensive unpacking and intense reflection.[17]

Four features of the situation stand out. First, crossing over the threshold is often a matter of dramatic conversion. Accepting divine revelation is characteristically a profoundly self-involving experience that requires ample space, spiritual direction, and great patience.

Second, insofar as the divine revelation involves propositional content, that content has to be received as knowledge.[18] It cannot be treated as mere human opinion. Coming from God, the content is received as genuine knowledge. Hence it invariably generates a significant intellectual boldness that can easily be misread as arrogance.

Third, the response to divine revelation by necessity cannot be limited in its depth. It calls for a response of total and faithful allegiance, even to the point of death. Revelation naturally evokes a response of loyalty, trust, and persistence that must endure trial and testing.[19]

Fourth, when one crosses over into the world of divine revelation, then revelation will necessarily illuminate every aspect of one's existence, even though one does not know in advance where and how this illumination will make a difference.[20] The extent of illumination may be

17. I am well aware of the possible echoes this may evoke of Karl Barth's famous essay "The Strange New World of the Bible," in *The Word of God and the Word of Man* (London: Hodder and Stoughton, 1928). Barth renders invaluable service in helping us to see that there is another world on the other side of divine revelation. His detailed material proposals deserve close attention.

18. Divine revelation need not directly involve propositional content; in some cases of divine manifestation, the proper response may be total silence before the mystery and complexity of the divine.

19. This is a persistent theme of the epistle to the Hebrews.

20. It is sometimes thought that having propositional content precludes further exploration. Bultmann captures the issue nicely. "God the mysterious and hidden must at the same time be the God who is revealed. Not, of course, in a revelation that could be grasped in words and propositions, that would be limited to formula and book and to space and

such that divine revelation involves a loop-back effect leading to a reconceiving of the cognitive capacities that brought one to divine revelation in the first place. Descartes notes this perceptively in an oblique manner in the way he appeals to the veracity of God to secure the reliability of his senses. Descartes rightly said that once he had established the reality of God, he could then put this discovery to work in retrieving his commitment to the senses. This move is often thought to be viciously circular; a more careful reading will rescue Descartes from this charge.[21] More pertinent to our purposes, it is worth noting here that it is obvious that the notion of the *sensus divinitatis* makes very good sense on the other side of the threshold of divine revelation. In speaking of a *sensus divinitatis,* one is looking back and reconceiving one's initial capacity to see God in creation as a cognitive gift from God in creation. The same might be said for the idea of the *oculus contemplationis.* It should not surprise us in the least that in a secular culture these notions appear odd and question begging. They are neither odd nor question begging when relocated within a rich vision of divine revelation. Acceptance of divine revelation will also have profound and unexpected knock-on effects on how we see things around us, above us, within us, and before us. Speaking of the divine revelation in Jesus Christ, Abraham Kuyper captures this graphically when he notes that "there is not a square inch in the whole domain of our human existence over which Christ, who is sovereign over *all,* does not cry: 'Mine!'"[22]

Most if not all of these observations are borne out by the life of Paul. Revelation led to a dramatic conversion to Christ; it produced an astonishing boldness in mission, proclamation, and teaching; it evoked a persistent and tenacious commitment; and it led him to rethink his theological

---

time; but rather in a revelation that continually opens up new heights and depths and thus leads through darkness, from clarity to clarity" ("Concerning the Hidden and the Revealed God," in *Existence and Faith,* 30). On this analysis my second point might be thought incompatible with my fourth. However, Bultmann is mistaken to think that grasping a revelation in words and propositions is incompatible with a revelation opening up new heights and depths. These are not at all mutually exclusive.

21. For a splendid discussion of the relevant sources and issues, see George Dicker, *Descartes: An Analytical and Historical Introduction* (Oxford: Oxford University Press, 1993), 119-41.

22. James D. Bratt, ed., *Abraham Kuyper: A Centennial Reader* (Grand Rapids: Eerdmans, 1998), 48, emphasis in original.

worldview in new and unexpected ways. It is small wonder that he needed a lengthy sabbatical to come to terms with the gospel; and it is no surprise that he was prepared to face imprisonment and martyrdom rather than abandon it. A lot of people really did think he had lost his mind; many still do. Crossing the threshold of divine revelation is a massive cognitive and spiritual revolution.[23]

Overcoming Aversion to Divine Revelation

With this in mind, we can briefly respond to the standard sources of aversion to divine revelation. Let me work backward through the four problems I enumerated above.

Rather than a bid for power and authority, the proclamation of divine revelation is a marvelous gift to be shared with enthusiasm and flair. Its acceptance should evoke a spirit of service and humility of the kind long visible in the lives of the saints of the church.[24] Indeed, without appropriate love and humility the presentation of divine revelation will be hollow and inappropriate.

Rather than narrowing our options and suffocating the mind, divine revelation opens up a whole new world that calls for the straining of every intellectual nerve and muscle in order to fathom the treasures made available. Thus the careful and imaginative study of the canonical heritage of the church, the primary means of the mediation of revelation across the centuries, becomes a joyful necessity.[25] Moreover, the articulation of the

23. This is one reason why issues related to salvation and the Christian life have fascinated evangelicals; they have wanted to explore the full ramifications of life inside the world of revelation. It is also a reason why evangelicals have characteristically been interested in evangelism. The importance of the wing of evangelicalism that has focused on this dimension of the tradition is well brought out by Gary Dorrien, *The Remaking of Evangelical Theology* (Louisville: Westminster John Knox, 1998).

24. This surely provides one reason why the church developed a canon or list of saints; the community identified over time paradigmatic responses that would signal appropriate reception. Virtually every tradition does this informally. It comes as something of a shock to most Protestants to discover this. For the way this crops up as related to John Wesley, see my "The End of Wesleyan Theology," *Wesleyan Theological Journal* 40 (Spring 2005): 7-25.

25. Note here that rather than phrase the issue in the conventional terms of scripture and tradition, I want to redescribe the relevant media as the complex phenomena that are

riches of divine revelation across space and time becomes an enduring intellectual challenge.[26]

Rather than a source of division and bigotry, divine revelation can be the occasion for uniting Jew and Gentile in the service of God in the world. Paul got in trouble precisely because he insisted that divine revelation called for an enlargement of the borders of Israel rather than a narrow policy of exclusion. In our current cultural and political situation, it is imperative that we make room for claims to divine revelation, rather than settle for a narrow set of secularist or theological boundaries.[27]

Rather than an occasion for retreat to a mere confessional circle of faith, divine revelation calls for sophisticated public discussion that tackles rival claims to possession with sensitivity and thoroughness. Proponents of different and even contrasting traditions of divine revelation have as much to think through together as they do apart. Moreover, rather than restricting our epistemological endeavors and confining ourselves to the method of authority, revelation calls for a deepening of our epistemological reflection.[28] We are by no means confined to the standard range of

---

identified as the canon of scripture, the canon of truth, the canon of saints, canonical iconography, canonical liturgies, and the like. It is crucial that we not repeat the mistake of simply reducing these phenomena to divine revelation, as has happened again and again in the treatment of the canon of scripture. David Brown would appear to have fallen into this trap in his magnificently erudite and fascinating *Tradition and Imagination: Revelation and Change* (New York: Oxford University Press, 1999).

26. Hence there is need for the constant renewal of systematic theology in every generation.

27. The emergence of "postmodernism" has created space for a rich variety of voices in the current theological situation. However, particular claims to possess divine revelation invariably evoke profound epistemological debate and discussion. Simply positing a shift from modernity to postmodernity will not take care of the normative questions at stake. There are very tangled historical and constructive issues that have to be worked through from top to bottom. Moreover, it is naive to think that canonical theists will be readily welcomed to the postmodernist table; their hearty commitment to the truth of the Christian tradition will rightly evoke profound suspicion.

28. By method of authority, I have in mind the position contrasted with the method of tenacity, the a priori method, and the scientific method by Charles S. Peirce ("The Fixation of Belief," in *Charles S. Peirce: The Essential Writings*, ed. Edward C. Moore [New York: Harper and Row, 1972], 120-37). Although Peirce does not take this position, I think it likely that many have treated the appeal to revelation as a form of the method of authority. At the very least, and Peirce comes close to making this point, the method of authority has long been associated with certain kinds of theology that did make much of the appeal to divine revelation.

epistemic options, but are challenged to provide the conceptual horizons that will permit the full range of questions and resolution that fragile human agents pursue within and without the arena of religion.

What is needed is appropriate humility in the face of divine grace, imaginative and rigorous thinking in the wake of divine disclosure, supportive and collegial research in the midst of profound and contested differences, and deeper and richer epistemological inquiry in response to the complexity and subtlety of our intellectual commitments. Serious mistakes have been made in past explorations of the full contours of revelation. Facile solutions on the relation between revelation and history and on the relation between revelation and science have been offered and found wanting. The way to deal with these is to revisit the terrain, find out what went wrong, and go back to our intellectual labors.

In doing this we should take heart from Paul. Paul was no philosopher, but he tacitly possessed the kind of intellectual acuity that is the mark of fresh and original thinkers. We can see why he was so adamant in his writings when we unpack the kind of logic that lies beneath the surface in the appeal to revelation. We may not have to be as tough as Paul was with the ancient Celts in Galatia. He was fighting for the existence of the gospel and the church, seeking to bring the church into line with divine revelation as a radically inclusive body of Jews and Gentiles. We live in a much more complex universe of discourse and discussion. Canonical theists will stand with Paul in his commitment to divine revelation, bearing whatever offense, scandal, or stigma such commitment may evoke. More positively in following the logic of divine revelation, they might apply to themselves the suggestions of Charles Sanders Peirce.

> The genius of a man's logical method should be loved and reverenced as his bride, whom he has chosen from all the world. He need not condemn the others; on the contrary, he may honor them deeply, and in so doing he honors her the more. But she is the one he has chosen, and he knows that he was right in making that choice. And having made it, he will work and fight for her, and will not complain that there are blows to take, hoping that there may be as many and as hard to give, and will strive to be the worthy knight of her from the blaze of whose splendors he draws his inspiration and courage.[29]

29. Peirce, "The Fixation of Belief," 136-37.

Revelation and Criticism

In this chapter I have sought to explore the significance of divine revelation as an epistemic concept. Drawing on the apostle as an example, I have sought to make clear that the concept of revelation involves the crossing of an intellectual threshold that brings with it significant epistemic consequences. Philosophers and theologians are naturally worried about claims to divine revelation, but most of these worries stem from a failure to come to terms with the way revelation functions from an epistemic point of view. As a threshold concept, divine revelation, once accepted, has the potential to alter one's whole intellectual landscape. Coming to accept a divine revelation is not simply a matter of adding one more item to one's stock of beliefs. Once one steps inside the revelation, one has to rework one's identity and be open to the implications that lie on the other side of the threshold. My aim, in other words, has been to focus sharply on the way the acceptance of divine revelation constitutes a world-orienting event for the believer. More strongly, we might say that the acceptance of divine revelation is a world-constituting experience for the believer.

It might be thought that this observation is incompatible with the strategy I developed in the last chapter. There I was at pains to show that we can legitimately ask critical questions about the rightness of particular claims to possess a divine revelation. If we do this, are we not now standing in judgment over revelation when divine revelation, once adopted, stands in judgment over our reason and us? If we judge a claim to divine revelation by our reason, are we not ipso facto making our reason ultimate, when in fact revelation has to be acknowledged as ultimate? Are we not undermining our suggestion that crossing over the threshold of divine revelation is a world-orienting event in our lives? The straight answer to all these questions is no.

The crucial observation to make at this point is quite simple. It is one thing to come to believe we have divine revelation and challenge the content of that revelation. It is another thing entirely to challenge or ask questions about the claim that someone possesses a divine revelation. Adopting the former procedure would indeed seriously undermine the core of the argument to date; pursuing the latter does not.[30] Moreover, it is

30. Here Locke's insistence that it is right and proper to raise questions about the ac-

precisely because accepting a divine revelation involves the crossing of a threshold that we have the logical space to inquire whether in fact we have crossed into a new world of divine revelation or been taken for a ride by a false prophet or a bogus agent of God. Far too much is at stake in accepting a divine revelation to permit us to shut down critical questions about the human sources to any claim to divine revelation. The common notion of taking leaps in the dark or into the abyss much too readily overlooks the clear intellectual dangers of an overused metaphor.

It is all too common for proponents of divine revelation to use the privileged status of divine revelation as leverage for avoiding the hard questions about the original identity and legitimacy of the divine revelation espoused. They transfer the status that rightly belongs to God, to his Word, and to his claim upon our lives to their own claims to be bearers of the Word of God. In the worst-case scenario they resort to coercive strategies of persecution and violence to secure commitment to divine revelation, thinking to defend this by appealing to the transcendent character of God. On pain of death or the sword we are to believe what they say about God's Word, as if it is the Word we are opposing when we fail to be convinced by their claims.

The God of the revelation that surfaces in the canonical texts of the Christian tradition cannot be fitted into this scenario. It is a mark of the condescension of God in his revelation to us that he subjects himself to our critical scrutiny. In his appearance in the incarnation, God permits himself to be examined and questioned. God is not, as it were, nervous about his status in our midst. He dares to trust himself to us, knowing that his identity and action on our behalf can withstand our intellectual inquiry as much as our wickedness and folly. Indeed, anything else than this opens the door to idolatry and misplaced allegiance, for false identification of the sources of divine revelation leads us to false gods. Thus we were right to take up the issue of the proper identification of divine revelation, and the position we developed in the last chapter is entirely compatible with the observations we have made here. Indeed, the work we pursued in this chapter enriches what we need to say about the epistemic

---

tual possession of divine revelation is on target. Thus it is one thing to call into question the content of a revelation, given that it is divine; it is another matter entirely to question whether someone really has a divine revelation. We need not accept Locke's strictures on the content of reason to see the force of his crucial point. See John Locke, *An Essay concerning Human Understanding*, ed. Peter H. Nidditch (Oxford: Clarendon, 1975), 4.19.14.

moves we have been plotting throughout this volume. That work also gives us an angle of vision for examining how we might tackle the rationality of belief in the canonical doctrines of the church. To that we now turn.

Chapter Six

Divine Revelation and
Canonical Doctrine

—⟁⟁⟁—

Canonical Doctrine and *Sensus Divinitatis*

In the last chapter I argued that it is illuminating to think of the positive response to special divine revelation as akin to crossing a threshold. The acceptance of divine revelation is a world-constituting experience or a perspective-constituting event. We enter a new world of the divine where everything is now potentially transformed or baptized. In this chapter I want to explore the significance of this insight for understanding the rationality of accepting the canonical heritage of the church. More particularly, I want to explore the significance of this insight for the acceptance of the canonical doctrines adopted by the church.

Clearly, the exploration of the intellectual status of the adopted doctrines of the church is of great importance in securing the positive epistemic status of a robust form of theism rather than the mere theism that normally detains the philosopher of religion. I shall approach our quarry from an angle of vision that is familiar in the history of philosophy and theology. It has long been common to work toward, say, the content of the Nicene Creed, by seeking to derive it one way or another from special revelation. Thus by exploring how this strategy can be played out, we can further clarify more carefully and precisely the place of divine revelation in the epistemology of theology. We can also revisit some crucial connections between divine revelation and other important epistemic concepts such as religious experience, imagination, divine inspiration, reasoned argument, and the like. I shall proceed by examining a raft of standard ways of relating divine revelation to doctrine en route to developing my own position.

We need to clarify afresh what we mean by revelation and canonical doctrine. By revelation I mean here the polymorphous activity of God that was laid out in the first half of chapter 4. Thus I am assuming a rich vision of divine action that includes God's work in creation, the gracious unveiling of God in the covenant acts and deliverance of Israel from Egypt, the commissioning of chosen prophets, the sending of the Son, the coming of the Holy Spirit, and the appearance of apostolic teachers, like Paul. Divine revelation is an unfolding drama that took place over time, that created the Israel of God, and that came in an appropriate order. Its fullest expression is in Jesus Christ, the incarnate Son of God.

By canonical doctrine I mean here the official doctrine canonized by the church as a whole, operating self-consciously as a community with a robust sense of ecclesial self-consciousness and with a firm desire to be led by the Holy Spirit.[1] To keep the discussion to manageable proportions I shall focus on the doctrines of the incarnation and the Trinity, for these are clearly the core doctrinal materials of the tradition, even though in their creedal form they are inescapably tied to a substantial doctrine of salvation. Moreover, they are related in various ways to a vision of creation and of human nature that I shall draw on as necessary. While I am leaving the loose edges in the doctrinal content of the canonical heritage of the church unspecified, this flexibility in no way radically affects the core material at issue or the central questions I want to pursue.

As we move to explore the first set of options in our journey, I want to register the limitations of any appeal to the *sensus divinitatis* or to the internal witness of the Holy Spirit. The recovery of appeal to the *sensus divinitatis* and to the Spirit's internal witness is clearly a great advance in recent work in the epistemology of religious belief. We owe a great debt to the work of Alvin Plantinga in this arena. With uncommon skill, clarity, and depth he has virtually single-handedly rediscovered vital epistemic concepts that were set aside in the modern period. Yet we can surely ask how far these ideas will take us. Plantinga clearly thinks they give us pre-

---

1. This should not be taken as some kind of romantic vision of the church that ignores the rough-and-tumble of historical existence.

cisely the kind of robust theism that I am seeking to articulate. As I have already indicated, I am not persuaded of this conclusion.

Yet it is important to note where we differ at this point. To put the matter at its sharpest and simplest, Plantinga does not need a robust doctrine of divine revelation to secure the canonical doctrine of the Trinity. All he needs is for someone to utter the relevant teaching of the church and for this to be the occasion when the Holy Spirit brings it about directly or indirectly through the *sensus divinitatis* that a person believes the doctrine of the Trinity. We can go straight, as it were, from the working of the inner witness of the Holy Spirit to the doctrine of the Trinity. Plantinga does not need a doctrine of special revelation, and he does not rely on one. It is, moreover, not clear that he even needs a doctrine of general revelation in creation. All he needs for the production of mere theism is that when we encounter various characteristic elements in creation, God brings it about that our senses respond appropriately and that the mechanism of the *sensus divinitatis* triggers the belief that God created the universe. He does not need to speak of God being generally revealed in the world; from an epistemic point of view this latter claim is superfluous.

On the analysis I am developing, the *sensus divinitatis* (or the *oculus contemplationis*) simply does not take us that far. It takes us at best to belief in God and to the initial identification of divine revelation, but this deployment of the *sensus divinitatis* works within the context of a rich vision of general revelation. For the Trinity we also need additional steps to get us from the use of our *sensus divinitatis* (and any appeal to the inner witness) to this goal. One way to repair Plantinga's position at this point, and to bring it closer into line with what I have proposed to date, is simply to add in a robust account of special divine revelation and thereby make the requisite transition to the doctrine of the Trinity. In reworking Plantinga's vision in this manner, we would in fact be in the neighborhood of Calvin's version of the matter. However, I shall not wager any bets on that exegetical issue. Let's explore the possibilities schematically and identify the epistemological issues at stake. As needed, I shall add in other themes that are readily within reach of the theologian.

Some Well-Worn Dead Ends

One obvious move is to locate divine revelation in scripture or in the tradition of the church and then argue that the doctrine of divine revelation is warranted by scripture or by the combination of scripture and tradition. We can imagine a variety of ways in which this position can be spelled out, depending on which kinds of logical relations hold between the revelation and the relevant proposal about scripture. We have in reality two critical variables to consider: the relation between revelation, scripture, and tradition; and the relation between revelation and the canonical doctrines of the church. How might we think of the options available to us if we go down this road?[2]

First, we might think of scripture itself being dictated, spoken, or authored by God and then propose that the doctrine of the Trinity is simply one of the propositions uttered by God and contained in scripture. On this view we would accept the doctrine of the Trinity as itself directly revealed by God. It is not a matter of its being deduced from other utterances of God; it is itself an utterance of God, and thus it is secured precisely because it is spoken by God. A purist and economical Protestant might be very attracted to this position, if the relevant construal of scripture could be secured.

Second, a variation on this position that has had more appeal to premodern forms of Roman Catholicism is that divine revelation is given partly in scripture and partly in tradition. Both scripture and tradition are in fact conceived as dictated by God, and the doctrine of the Trinity is secured by its being directly given through propositional revelation in the tradition of the church. As with the first case, the doctrine of the Trinity is grounded by being uttered as a true proposition by God, given alongside but outside of scripture.

Third, we might keep the vision of scripture as spoken by God but treat the doctrine of the Trinity as deduced from various propositions within scripture. In this we assume that the laws of logic are secure, so that deduction need not itself be warranted by a reading of scripture. The cru-

2. In what follows, perceptive readers will have little difficulty identifying the particular theologians or theological traditions that lie within the boundaries of the positions I sketch. To avoid distraction about contested exegetical issues, and to keep clearly in view the logical structure of the positions I articulate, I shall refrain from noting their possible origins within the history of theology.

cial point is that the doctrine of the Trinity is deduced by valid inference from scripture.[3]

Fourth, we might keep the aforementioned doctrine of scripture intact but insist that the doctrine of the Trinity is secured by an appropriate reading of scripture as a whole. The doctrine of the Trinity is an exegetical or hermeneutical hypothesis about the nature of God as supplied by a rounded reading of the Bible. In this instance we assume the validity of notions like the reading of scripture as a whole, and we assume the ability to execute this practice reliably in the case of scripture. Moreover, we can build in whatever exegetical and historical expertise is essential to execute this task. So we can imagine two teams of biblical scholars with all the requisite skill encamped, say, for a year in the basements of Harvard and Princeton. On this view they should be able to arrive at the doctrine of the Trinity without undue difficulty.[4]

Fifth, we can think of another possibility that keeps the doctrine of scripture in place for the moment. Imagine this scenario. From the propositions of scripture the early Christian readers are given access to certain ideas or themes about the nature of God. Over time these ideas develop in such a way that the doctrine of the Trinity becomes an apt way of capturing the intellectual significance of these ideas and themes. Thus the doctrine of the Trinity is a work of synthesis that gathers up the human outworking over time of the ideas and themes that are originally derived from divine revelation.

We have constructed five very different ways of deriving the doctrine of the Trinity from special revelation. If we now rework the doctrine of scripture, we can readily construct other ways to achieve the same end. Thus, suppose we claim that rather than thinking of scripture as a direct revelation from God, we envision scripture as a witness to the original special revelation given in Israel and in Jesus. Let's see what options this alteration opens up for us.

Sixth, we might develop a theory where the doctrine of the Trinity arises when we recurrently immerse ourselves in the witness of scripture.

---

3. It would be pedantic to add in the variation of this position that would work off a combination of scripture and tradition.

4. Of course, if we insist that the teams of biblical scholars be committed to the requisite vision of scripture, we are likely to be shorthanded, but that is a separate point in this thought experiment. In any case, it is not clear that this position requires that the biblical scholar sign on to any particular theological construal of scripture.

That witness leads us again and again to affirm the doctrine of the Trinity. It simply so happens that, if we properly listen to scripture, the revelation to which it bears witness is made alive to us through the work of the Holy Spirit, and we find ourselves believing the doctrine of the Trinity. On this analysis the Nicene Creed is a fitting witness to the doctrine of the Trinity that keeps recurring in the history of the church. The creed at this point is subordinate to the witness of revelation through scripture and stands under its judgment. It simply so happens that this trinitarian vision of God constantly arises from our exposure to the divine revelation reactivated by God in generation after generation of believers.

Seventh, by changing the hermeneutical rules for reading scripture, we can develop a very different vision of the relation between divine revelation and the Nicene Creed. Reading scripture in a less Protestant fashion, we might insist that the divine revelation to which scripture bears witness can be properly interpreted only when received in faith in the life of the church, that is, in the sacramental and liturgical communion of the people of God. Divine revelation and the scripture that bears witness to it belong to the church. They will inevitably be mutilated and misread by the individual reader cut loose from the sacraments and liturgy of the church. Scripture, the point of access to special revelation, cannot be properly read outside of the church. When scripture is read inside the borders of the church, one will rightly and accurately see that the doctrine of the Trinity can be derived from its witness. Presumably we should be able to record the success of this move by investigation of the results of this kind of work by those who have studied scripture in this fashion.

Eighth, consider one more scenario. In this case we see scripture as either authored by God or bearing witness to special revelation, but we once again alter the hermeneutical rules related to the interpretation of scripture. All Christian doctrine, including the doctrine of the Trinity, is derived from divine revelation. Yet the doctrine of the Trinity does not lie on the surface of scripture. It is derived from scripture in the church as the church is assisted in its reading by the Holy Spirit. Over time various options emerge in the reception of divine revelation through scripture. Various teachers in the church try out different lines of inquiry. The danger then is that particular teachers in the church will misread their own scriptures, drawing false inferences, making false judgments, and the like. If allowed to persist, false and inadequate teaching would become injurious to the spiritual and moral welfare of the people of God, and salvation would be at risk. To remedy this potential problem, God provides privileged access to the truth of divine revelation bequeathed through scripture to those who stand in the historic Christian succession of the episcopate. God gives the truth contained in divine revelation to the whole church, but what is needed is an interpretative norm that would provide a way of sifting appropriate from inappropriate interpretations of scripture. This norm is supplied by the consensus worked out by the episcopate but reflecting the mind of the church as a whole.

One way to register this consensus is by ecumenical councils where the properly constituted hierarchy of the church expresses the mind of the church. Sometimes, however, the hierarchy may be divided on what constitutes the mind of the church as a whole, or the hierarchy may be too unwieldy an epistemic mechanism or institution to work effectively. Thus God appoints one figure in the hierarchy, the bishop of Rome, the successor of Peter, to be the ultimate arbiter of what constitutes the consensus of the church on matters critical for the morals and theology of the faithful. Thus the true interpretation of the original special revelation given in scripture can be identified only by the bishop of Rome, who is given the requisite divine assistance to determine what constitutes the true if still incomplete interpretation of that original revelation. In this way the certainty required for a robust life of faith is secured, not just as a gracious gift in the past, but as an ongoing possibility in the present.

This review of the options open to us for thinking of divine revelation as a warrant for the canonical doctrine of the church has of course an air of abstraction and unreality to it. However, it would not be difficult to find echoes if not instantiations of these options in both ancient and modern attempts to deploy divine revelation in securing belief in the doctrine of the Trinity. Indeed, we can see in our review of the possibilities the contours of the kinds of positions that have been common in Protestantism and Roman Catholicism over the centuries.[5] In all these examples, scrip-

---

5. Perceptive readers will note that I do not develop a schema in which the doctrine of the Trinity is presented as the grammar of scripture or tradition, a move much favored in circles inspired by the recent work of George Lindbeck and reaching back to Wittgenstein for inspiration. Frankly I find this whole trajectory thoroughly implausible. The doctrine of the Trinity, if it is anything serious, is a metaphysical vision rather than a grammar. The analogy of grammar is therefore most unhelpful ontologically. I suspect, moreover, that this vision gains much of its purchase from the fact that it leaves lots of freedom in future speech about God and thus provides lots of room for innovation. The views I have sketched

ture has been systematically epistemized; that is, it has been seen primarily as a criterion of truth in theology. Rather than seen more modestly as a list of books to be used in the church for spiritual direction, scripture has been seen as the critical warrant for theological construction. Its primary function is as a foundation and test of the church's teaching. To secure this end some theory of divine revelation has been indispensable. It is precisely because scripture is seen as authored by God, or as the exclusive witness to the special revelation of God, or as the indispensable medium for hearing God speak in the present, or as divinely appropriated discourse, that it has been able to function as a criterion in theology. Without some such background assumption, that is, without a doctrine of special revelation, the appeal to scripture collapses. The underlying epistemological commitments may be concealed, they may be idling, or they may be systematically ignored, but they are critical if the enterprises we have demarcated are to succeed.

It is crucial at this point to keep our eye on the quarry. It is very easy to be distracted and drawn into important debates about the nature of historical criticism, the characteristics of hermeneutics, the relation between the Old and New Testaments, the meaning of the doctrine of the Trinity, the nature of scripture, the nature of language, and so on. Our concern is more modest. We are interested in the place of divine revelation in the epistemology of theology. It is useful in this regard to limit the issues under discussion and to press the matter clearly, even at the price of oversimplification. The primary issue before us is clear: Do any of these positions secure the doctrine of the Trinity? Here I have to record a summary judgment: as I see it, they do not. No matter how we explain the relation between special revelation and scripture, there is always a significant gap between the vision of revelation embraced and the doctrines adopted. While I share the conviction that a robust vision of divine revelation is indeed at play in securing, say, the doctrine of the Trinity, we need much more epistemic material in play to be successful in our efforts.

Moreover, most of the epistemological strategies that have to be deployed to keep these options afloat are much too intellectually expensive. In particular, many of them involve doctrines of the infallibility of scripture or of the church that are not necessary for the acceptance of the ca-

---

here read the doctrine ontologically and are much more robust epistemologically in their efforts to secure its truth.

nonical faith of the church. Like virtually all epistemologies of theology in the West until the modern period, they rest on a theory of *sola scriptura* that has outlived its usefulness. On my reading of the history, the effort to hold this vision became so difficult that it required precisely the doctrine of papal infallibility to ensure its survival. Once Protestantism experimented with a chaste doctrine of *sola scriptura*, it soon found itself hopelessly divided in doctrinal commitments. Adding in tradition as a norm of interpretation proved to be every bit as divisive, for the tradition of the church is even larger and more diverse than the scriptures. There is even more room for divergence of interpretation for tradition than for scripture. Hence the urge to develop a teaching office and an epistemic mechanism that will infallibly secure the right interpretation of the original revelation in scripture was irresistible.[6] This is precisely why the doctrine of the infallibility of the pope is not some hangover from the past. It is indeed an old idea, invented for a network of reasons that are all too human, but it has been brilliantly reworked to solve the epistemological dilemmas thrown up by the brutal and complex history of theology in the West. Ironically, the doctrine of papal infallibility is intimately related to the adoption of the doctrine of *sola scriptura*. It is no accident that it was formally adopted in the late nineteenth century as a solution to a network of problems that became visible only after Protestantism had played out the appeal to scripture to its extreme and essential limits.

Current efforts to weave together bits and pieces of scripture, tradition, reason, and experience are ad hoc measures to shore up the tottering edifice that Protestantism has become. By the twentieth century Protestantism could no longer follow its own trajectory and stick to *sola scriptura;* nor could it follow Roman Catholicism and adopt the epistemological dogmas that are now constitutive of the life of faith in that ecclesial tradition. So modern Protestant theologians fell to bundling epistemic concepts together and rattling them around in their heads, like a gambler rattling around the dice in his hands in the hope that the numbers would come out just right on the next throw. The theological outcomes these elastic epistemic notions make possible are legion; they require a complex vision of ecclesiastical pluralism that is now threatening to disintegrate

---

6. It would take us too far afield to chase down the concept of a teaching office in the church. It is much too readily assumed that there cannot be a teaching office in the church without the charism of infallibility; this strikes me as simply false.

under pressure from within. Wandering from this epistemological pillar to that epistemological post, much of contemporary Protestantism is like a house swept clean of its resources. Changing metaphors, Protestantism has become like the penniless alcoholic; bereft of money but still addicted to the bottle, the alcoholic has nothing left but the bad smell of the empties piling up in the corner. Postmodernism offers a wobbly way forward beyond this grim state of affairs by adopting an ironic skepticism about epistemology and by reinstating this or that favored element of the faith as best it can.[7] What remains within much of Protestantism is a network of ecclesiastical interest groups and renewal movements fighting it out for control of the tradition. It is time for a recovery of nerve in every direction.[8]

A Better Way

Yet we seem to have backed ourselves into a corner. Having rejected so summarily the standard ways of deploying a theory of divine revelation to secure the faith of the church, have we not created an insuperable crisis for ourselves? There is indeed a way out. We can find it by using the epistemological resources already at hand. Some of them are assumed or deployed in the positions I have schematically depicted above; some have been secured in the vision of divine revelation already developed; and some have been laid out in the early chapters of our project.

We begin again with the vision of divine revelation already put in place and recall afresh that revelation is a world-constituting event. From the beginning, special revelation in Israel created a very special people.

7. A fascinating illustration can be found in the work of John Caputo. The religious turn within Continental philosophy that he charts and represents with such style and bravado is of particular interest. See, for example, James H. Olthuis, ed., *Religion without Religion: The Prayers and Tears of John D. Caputo* (London: Routledge, 2002).

8. It is worth noting that periods of epistemic crisis in the church are often accompanied by a turn within popular Christianity to pietistic and evangelical forms of the faith. Thus in the Middle Ages, when scholasticism foundered as an epistemological tradition, there was a turn to mysticism and a piety that centered on the crucified Christ. Likewise, when epistemic crisis was precipitated by the aftermath of the Reformation and the emergence of the Enlightenment, Methodism and other forms of pietism and revivalism flourished. Today the Western church is clearly in the midst of a fresh epistemological crisis and is awash with lively forms of evangelicalism and Pentecostalism.

The soteriological intention embedded in Israel worked itself out in the formation of a community with a long history that culminated in the renewal of Israel in and through the life, death, and resurrection of Jesus of Nazareth. The God of Israel established a covenant, and in the course of evoking deep trust in his promises and in his great acts of deliverance, God created a fragile and complex people who over time were tutored in the unique form of monotheism that became central to the Jewish people. In and around this there arose practices of devotion and worship; forms of leadership; a very rich, diverse canon of scripture; and the like. It was within this community that the extraspecial revelation made through Jesus of Nazareth was effected, recognized, and received. It was in the community created by Jesus that this revelation was treasured, recorded, preached, mulled over, and transmitted across the generations.

Jesus of Nazareth was not, however, just one more word from God; nor is he simply a word about God. He was the Word of God incarnate, who was raised from the dead, who sent the promised Holy Spirit to the people of God at Pentecost. Just as the early Israel was driven to work through to a deeply monotheistic vision of God in the light of special revelation and its experience of God, so too was the new Israel driven to stretch its initial commitments to accommodate the new world opened up in the arrival of its Savior and Lord. Thus the positions I traced earlier in this chapter are correct to seek out a place for the critical significance of divine revelation in the emergence and articulation of the doctrines of the incarnation and the Trinity. There is an ordered progression of divine revelation in Israel and in the church that operates as pivotal data in the very particular vision of God that emerges over time. At one level we can indeed say that God is triune because of the self-revelation of God as Father, Son, and Holy Spirit in creation, in Israel, in Jesus, and in the experience of the church.

However, this kind of summary statement is inadequate if it stands much too starkly or alone. Thus we have already argued that we cannot get to a robust commitment to divine revelation without appeal to the *oculus contemplationis*. We have also recorded the appropriate place that experience of God, that is, of the self-presentation of God to the believer, may have in coming to believe in God and in his presence in our lives. Furthermore, there is a genuine place for the appeal to reasoned argument, as seen in natural theology and in arguments from miracle, in strengthening the conviction of believers.

In addition, we note that none of these epistemic strategies can work without a prior dependence on the epistemic platitudes I laid out earlier. Thus we rightly assume reliance on the senses, memory, conscience, testimony, intuition, deduction, induction, judgment, and the like. None of these is left behind when we perceive God as manifest in our lives or in providence, or when we are exposed to divine revelation. Human agents are incredibly sophisticated cognitive organisms that have a host of doxastic practices at their disposal in recoding what is going on in the world and in adding to their stock of knowledge from a variety of primary sources. Special revelation, rather than canceling nature, corrects and enriches it.

On our side the data from special divine revelation are taken up and integrated into what has already been secured, so that fresh insights, conceptual changes, and new doctrinal vistas are opened up. The transformation of previously secured convictions is to be expected in these circumstances. If we must work with convenient slogans and summary statements, we might say that the doctrine of the Trinity arose over time out of the deep interaction of the special revelation of God in Israel, the extraspecial revelation of God in Jesus Christ, experience of God in the Holy Spirit, and sanctified creative imagination and reason. It is radically incomplete and inadequate to trace the kind of revolutionary change in the doctrine of God represented by the Nicene Creed merely to the divine revelation enshrined in scripture. We must also take into account the place of religious experience, imagination, and reason.

We must also provide ample space for the guidance of the Holy Spirit in leading the church into the truth about God. We can see this very readily, once we grant initially the following two assumptions. First, there really was a unique and special revelation given to the world through Israel in Jesus of Nazareth. Second, the reception and understanding of this divine revelation is not immediately apparent. Indeed, its initial significance requires the call and commission of Paul as a prophet. We can then see that it would be extremely odd for God to go to these lengths to make known his name and not provide critical assistance to the church as a whole in unpacking what this means. In thinking of the alternative to this, we are to imagine God going to great lengths to come to us in Christ and even to send the Holy Spirit, but then essentially announcing that we are entirely on our own in exploring the critical ramifications of his revelation to us. God, as it were, shrugs his shoulders and leaves us at the mercy of our human intellectual endeavors. From this angle we can surely see the deep significance of the ongoing work of the Holy Spirit in the church in coming to the truth about God enshrined in its canonical doctrines.

We might capture this move in terms of a vision of divine inspiration working in, with, and through the life of the church as a whole. Having given a once-for-all revelation in Jesus Christ, the Holy Spirit inspired the whole life of the community in its worship, in the choice and development of leadership, in the cultivation of sanctity, in its love and compassion for its members and for the world, in the writing of the scriptures and their collection into a canon, in its diverse ministries, and the like.[9] Within this the Holy Spirit also inspired and guided the church in its institutional developments. So when disagreements arose that affected the whole body, as happened when Jews and Gentiles mingled in one body, leaders and appropriate representatives of the church gathered to work through the issues.[10] In a real sense the church was a charismatic community, so that its assemblies and councils were genuine charismatic events where the participants trusted God to lead and direct them. Thus when disputes arose on how best to capture the truth about God as given in the economy of salvation, the Holy Spirit worked in, with, and through its teachers, leaders, and members to come to the truth.[11] And given the presence and

9. I am assuming here that the Holy Spirit played a pivotal role in the life of Christ.

10. The Jerusalem Council, as depicted in Acts 15, represents the paradigm case I have in mind.

11. Essential to this vision is a sense of the church as the body of Christ, equipped by the Holy Spirit with diverse gifts to fulfill Christ's ministry in the world. Note how St. Symeon the New Theologian describes the task of the teacher in the church. "If it is true that the saints become genuinely members of Christ Who is God of all, and if, as we said, they have as their duty remaining attached and united to His body so that He may be their Head and they — all the saints from the beginning of the world until the last Day — may be His members, and the many become one body of Christ, as it were a single Man, then it follows that some, for example, fulfil the role of His hands, working even now to accomplish His all-holy will, making worthy the unworthy and preserving them for Him. Others are the shoulders, bearing the burdens of others, or even carrying the lost sheep that they find wandering in the crags and the wild places abandoned by God. These too accomplish His will. Others fulfil the role of the breast, pouring out God's righteousness to those who hunger and thirst for it, providing them with the bread which nourishes the powers of heaven. Others still are the belly. They embrace everyone with love. They carry the Spirit of salvation in their bowels and possess the capacity to bear His ineffable and hidden mysteries. *Others, again, take the function of the thighs since they carry in themselves the fecundity of the concepts adequate to God of mystical theology. They engender the Spirit of Wisdom upon the earth, i.e., the fruit of the Spirit*

work of the Spirit within it, the church was able to recognize the outcome as the truth, however inadequate or incomplete its verbal expression may have been.[12]

Thus the journey from divine revelation to the doctrines of the Trinity and the incarnation took time. The relevant intellectual work was done in the church drawing on all the rich network of epistemic practices and resources at its disposal. While for the purposes of analysis we can distinguish the place of the Gospels,[13] the critical role of experience of God, the emergence of pivotal insights, judgments about this or that false trail, deductions from earlier commitments, the critical place of a creative teacher, and so on, there is no way to reduce this process to some formal calculus. Thus the relation between revelation and the doctrines of the incarnation and the Trinity is multidimensional, informal, and indirect. We could, of course, say that the doctrines express the cumulative effects of the church's experience of God, but that is a very compressed summary of a very complex process. From beginning to end there is an ineradicable element of trust, so that we either do or do not go with the judgment of the church as a whole.[14] We might even speak here of a sense of the body as a whole, of a communal as well as a personal *sensus divinitatis*.[15]

Note that it is a mistake to look here for proof, for demonstration,

---

and His seed in the hearts of men, through the word of their teaching. Finally there are those who act as the legs and feet. These last reveal courage and endurance in temptation, after the manner of Job, and their stability in the good is in no way shaken or weakened, but instead they bear up under the burden of the Spirit's gifts" (*On the Mystical Life: The Ethical Discourses*, Vol. 1: *The Church and the Last Things*, trans. Alexander Golitzen [Crestwood, N.Y.: St. Vladimir's Seminary Press, 1955], 43-44, emphasis added).

12. It should be noted that the work of the Holy Spirit is critical in the ongoing reception and understanding of the church's doctrine, on this analysis. The idea of passive reception is totally alien to the whole line of thought deployed here.

13. For a fine exploration of this theme see Francis Young, "The Gospels and Doctrine," in *The Cambridge Companion to the Gospels*, forthcoming.

14. The importance of trust in secular institutions is well brought out by Onora O'Neill, *A Question of Trust* (Cambridge: Cambridge University Press, 2002). About trust in the church, it strikes me that Protestants are simply skeptics who constantly operate with a hermeneutic of suspicion, while Roman Catholicism trusts only in the hierarchy and the bishop of Rome, casting around for an epistemology of infallibility to secure the relevant trust. An adequate theological, more especially pneumatological, reading of the life of the church will avoid both these alternatives.

15. Newman's insightful and controversial essay *On Consulting the Faithful* (London: Collins, 1961) remains an important text wrestling with this neglected topic.

for finalizing deductive arguments. It is equally a mistake to look for sure-fire guarantees. It was this quest that led to theories of infallibility, whether of scripture or of the church. One worry that drove this development was the feeling that without absolute foundations, without external guarantees, the alternative is subjectivism and arbitrary judgment. This still haunts the discussion in the West. The quest for absolute certainty, coupled with a drive toward simplicity, drove theologians to look for a quick fix in epistemology. Epistemic anxiety became the order of the day. Worries about making mistakes, fear of falling into error, observations about human fallibility, and a fundamental lack of trust in our cognitive capacities and practices fueled skepticism and the quest for supposedly objective, independent criteria of validation that would somehow save us from ourselves. We want an external authority either in a book or in an institution that will save the day.[16]

Consequently epistemic theories of scripture and the church were developed. In time they were asked to carry burdens that are exaggerated and superfluous. We can make no progress in epistemology without trust, and this dependence on trust is not canceled by the arrival of special revelation. Without trust in our own capacities, in testimony, and in the hard-won intellectual gains of communities, we will be hopelessly impoverished intellectually, or we will wobble back and forth between assertion and skepticism with nowhere to lay our heads. Our slogans and popular sayings are instructive at this point. We would like to get to the proverbial bottom line, or the last word, or the final analysis, or the end of the day, where we can eliminate the dependence on our native cognitive capacities and practices. These goals cannot be secured either in life generally or in theology; nor should we seek them or crave them; they are a snare and a

---

16. Consider in this context the startling comment of Aleksi Stephanovich Khomyakov: "[T]he Church is not an authority, just as God is not an authority and Christ is not an authority, since authority is something external to us. The Church is not an authority, I say, but the truth — and at the same time the inner life of the Christian, since God, Christ, the Church, live in him with a life more real than the heart which is beating in his breast or the blood flowing in his veins. But they are alive in him only insofar as he himself is living by the ecumenical life of love and unity, i.e. by the life of the Church" ("On the Western Confessions of Faith," in *Ultimate Questions*, ed. Alexander Schmemann [New York: Holt, Rinehart and Winston, 1965], 50). It is not entirely clear that Khomyakov, while making some extremely incisive epistemological comments, does not manage to avoid the epistemizing trap that so readily awaits us. See, for example, 55.

distraction. The better course is to reflect more carefully on the actual for-mation of our beliefs. On the other side of the skeptical abyss that is so readily foisted on us by the fearful and the disillusioned, we need to re-cover our nerve and regain our confidence both in ourselves and in the God who has led his people across the centuries.

Recovering the Canonical Heritage as a Means of Grace

In reworking our epistemic options we are also liberated to reclaim the soteriological value of the scripture and tradition of the church. We need to retrieve and redescribe scripture and tradition as the complex canoni-cal heritage of materials, persons, and practices given to the church over time by the Holy Spirit to bring us to God and to re-create us in his image. In their own way all of these mediate divine revelation, for God has made available the precious truth about himself not just in a book but in a rich network of media. This is the truth at the base of Roman Catholic concern to press home the importance of extrabiblical traditions and practices. Moreover, within the canonical heritage of the church there is indeed a special place and function for scripture in providing extraordinary access to Jesus, the Son of God. This is the truth enshrined in Protestantism. The mistake is to insist that these insights must be epistemically ordered so that one becomes the foundation for the other. Once we do this, we are en-snared in a wild-goose chase to derive one from the other. Before we know what has happened, we are then driven to develop a full-scale epistemol-ogy of theology that co-opts the rich and diverse canonical heritage of the church into service whether it will fit or not.

Over against this I propose that we receive the Nicene Creed and the great doctrines of the church it articulates as one more means of grace in the life of faith. This observation fits with the humble origins of the creed, where preachers, catechists, teachers, and bishops hammered out its con-tent in the evangelistic ministry of the early church. The primary place of the creed was in spiritual direction and in sustaining the life of the faithful. To be sure, the creed was also used to set boundaries and to make evalua-tions of right and healthy teaching, but we must be careful not to exagger-ate this role or to make it primary.

When called upon to explain why we think the creed is true, we can and should appeal to the place of divine revelation in Israel and in Jesus.

However, we should also draw attention to the place of religious experience, to the use of sanctified imagination and reason, and to the promise of God to grant the Holy Spirit to the church and lead it into the truth. We should without apology and embarrassment display our reliance on the *oculus contemplationis* as a bedrock capacity given us in creation to perceive the truth about God. We will, of course, have to speak of the great damage done to our cognitive capacities by sin. However, we can also lay claim to the illuminating and enlightening work of the Holy Spirit in our hearts and in the sacraments of the church.[17] In and around this we will have to come to terms with the place of repentance and virtue in coming to see the truth about God. We also need to take seriously an informed and tutored trust in the church to come to a right judgment historically in its hard-won convictions about Christ and about God.

Given this complexity, we will have to abandon our standard and simplistic ways of operating epistemologically. We will have to shake the temptation to look for a monothematic or relatively easy way to secure the positive epistemic status of the faith of the church. As I have sought to exhibit in this chapter, we have at our disposal a more complex and subtle network of concepts and practices to capture what is at stake. With this in place, we can now look for fresh ways to work through what this means for the rationality, justification, and warrant for our robust theological commitments. In doing so, it would be shortsighted to stop exploring the epistemic consequences of special revelation. As we have noted over and over again, revelation is a remarkable epistemic concept. To embrace it fully is a world-constituting experience and a perspective-constituting event in our lives. We shall bear this in mind as we turn in due course to a more formal pursuit of those central epistemic concepts that have been constantly cropping up in our discussion.

---

17. The importance of the effective work of the Holy Spirit is a theme too readily forgotten by Reformed thinkers who press hard on the intellectual consequences of sin in damaging the *sensus divinitatis*. If there is no antidote to the cognitive effects of sin in the work of sanctification, then the outcome will be despair and skepticism. If the *sensus divinitatis* is damaged all the way down without repair, it is hard to see how we would even know anything that really counted about God or about ourselves. Merold Westphal runs this risk in his very insightful essay. See his "Taking St. Paul Seriously: Sin as an Epistemological Category," in *Christian Philosophy*, ed. Thomas P. Flint (Notre Dame: University of Notre Dame Press, 1990), 200-226. We need to remember that epistemically as well as spiritually, where sin abounds, grace abounds all the more.

Chapter Seven

Conversion

———❧———

Keeping an Eye on Theory

In the last chapter I explored the relation between divine revelation and the canonical doctrine of the church. I argued that the church had at its disposal the epistemic resources to develop and adopt, for example, the doctrine of the Trinity as found in the Nicene Creed. This is not to say that the church was especially interested formally in laying out how it arrived at its canonical doctrinal commitments. Given the soteriological focus of its life, and given its primary interest in first-order theological convictions about God and about Christ, these matters were left in the bosom of the tradition. There was no need to descend formally to this metalevel of inquiry. Indeed, once we start down that road, we can quickly find ourselves either in an infinite regress or arguing in a circle. For if we insist on the church having an agreed right method in arriving at its beliefs, we can immediately ask if we have the right method for getting to that method, and so on. So we seem to have to go on forever, or circle back around to one of the earlier methods deployed, or just stop somewhere without any method at all. While this is of enormous interest to the epistemologist and shows up in debates between foundationalists and coherentists, it is entirely of secondary significance in the ordinary life of faith.

As is generally the case even in secular communities, folk can agree on a decision even though they would never agree on the reasons or underlying warrants for that decision. Imagine a modern university faculty or a diverse committee being restricted in this way. This is readily forgotten in discussions about the epistemology of theology. Contrary to common assumption, it is simply not the case that communities must have an agreed method to arrive at agreed conclusions. Indeed, people who agree on the same method disagree quite substantially on the conclusions it may yield on particular issues. There is good reason to bear this in mind as regards the central decisions of the church. What is striking is that Christians from very different backgrounds, with different personalities, with different styles of thinking, can come together and formally agree on matters of enormous theological substance.

My more general point here is that the Nicene Creed can be seen as the fruit of entering into the new world of divine revelation given in Jesus Christ. For the Western Christian tradition, theologians have been keen to track a tight connection between canonized doctrine and revelation. This strategy of explicitly grounding all doctrine in scripture has left them extremely vulnerable to the Protestant impulse to test everything again and again against scripture, construed in one way or another as the medium of divine revelation.[1] It is too readily forgotten that Deism and modern Unitarianism initially arose precisely as a radically conservative movement that took the Protestant theologians at their word and found to the latter's distress that they were very hard pressed to secure the doctrine of the Trinity.[2] Initially the potential loss of the Trinity in much of the West was forestalled in part by the mechanism of violent persecution and state action. However, once persecution became otiose, and once the support from the state withered away, the effects of the underlying problem were free to surface. The requirement that all Christian doctrine be derivable

---

1. It would be hard to improve on the starkness of the preamble to the Scots Confession (1560) in the calls to ground everything in scripture. "[I]f any man will note in our Confession any sentence or chapter contrary to God's Holy Word, that it would please him of his gentleness and for Christian charity's sake to inform us of it in writing; and we, upon our honour, do promise him that by God's grace we shall give him satisfaction from the mouth of God, that is, from Holy Scripture, or else we shall alter whatever he can prove to be wrong" (quoted in B. A. Gerrish, *Saving and Secular Faith* [Minneapolis: Fortress, 1999], 61).

2. This is often noted as a feature of the theology of Arius too. It is not at all uncommon for modern evangelicals to drift away from the trinitarian faith of the church, or to develop intellectually in such a way that the doctrine of the Trinity is a confusing puzzle or simply idling.

from divine revelation mediated through scripture has turned out to have surprise effects in the life of theology and the church.[3] It is tempting to see such a requirement as a millstone around the church's neck that constantly threatens to drown its children in waves of epistemological and theological speculation.

Over against this I am arguing for a very different configuration of the practices and materials that make up the internal life of the church. What we have is the new world of divine revelation opened up to us across the early centuries in the church and developed within a network of complementary media, not least the medium of its canonical creed. In this alternative vision we remain utterly committed to the critical place of scripture in the life of the church. Indeed, we free up the whole canonical heritage of the church to be used as indispensable and splendid means of grace in the initiation of new believers into the kingdom of God. The church is thereby freed from its captivity to restrictive and disputed epistemological theory.

Yet this does not mean that teachers in the church should abandon epistemology. On the contrary, this volume is an exercise in the epistemology of theology. Once we are freed from the old epistemological straitjackets, we can strike out afresh, revisiting the old topics that rightly detained us from a fresh angle of vision, and with genuine freedom. Thus I have shown how we might retrieve all sorts of splendid insights from the history of philosophy and theology and put them to work afresh in our own day. In particular I have argued that special revelation operates as a perspective-constituting event in the life of the church.

We noted on several occasions that coming to belief in a robust form of theism such as we find in the canonical heritage of the church is a complex process. Thus we have a ladder of assent to the truth about God rather than a simple decision about the truth or falsehood of single propo-

---

3. So radical is the shift away from an earlier Protestant position that there is a marked move to make the doctrine of the Trinity a condition of a right reading of scripture rather than an outcome of reading it. Consider this comment by Robert Jenson: "To read the Bible whole, that is to read it as Bible, demands that the questions we bring to any text or set of texts or tradition or redaction — manifold and changeable as these questions will be — must be Trinitarian questions. And to read the Bible whole, *we must presume in advance that the doctrine of the Trinity is true,* and that it must therefore also answer questions the Scripture raises for us" ("Hermeneutics and the Life of the Church," in *Reclaiming the Bible in the Church,* ed. Carl E. Braaten and Robert W. Jenson [Grand Rapids: Eerdmans, 1995], 99-100).

sitions. This ladder is something of a nuisance epistemologically. Life is so much easier if we can limit ourselves to this or that proposition and adjudicate its truth-value by inspection. With a single proposition we can see if we do or do not have to hand relevant evidence and make the requisite judgment. Or, if we happen to be foundationalists, we can check to see if the proposition is properly basic. Of course, we all know that all this is easier said than done; but at least we know where we are, and with effort we can resolve the issue before us.

Once we put revelation into the picture and note its salient features, we find ourselves thwarted by the conventional portrait of our cognitive endeavors. Useful as it is for certain purposes, this portrait does not fully capture what we need to note and articulate. More specifically, it does not do justice to the subtle differences that emerge depending on whether we have or have not crossed the threshold.

How do these initial observations relate to our proposals about the nature of divine revelation? To explore the epistemological significance of divine revelation further, I shall ignore that in coming to believe the faith of the church we rarely accumulate our beliefs one at a time. Conversion characteristically takes place through stages, and sometimes we can identify where and when we have consciously come to believe this or that proposition or come to accept a network of propositions. However, even the acceptance of single propositions often carries with it commitment to a cluster of associated or background beliefs that are tacitly below the surface. In exploring the terrain before us I shall simply set all this aside in order to clarify how commitment to divine revelation alters our epistemic convictions and perspective. Thus I shall abstract and simplify for the purpose of elucidation and illumination.

In this chapter I want to pick up two distinct areas of interest across the threshold of special revelation: the vision of our cognitive capacities and the perception of evidence and counterevidence. In the next chapter I shall explore the nature of belief and unbelief. As we shall see, these topics bleed into each other in very interesting ways. The obvious way into both these topics is to identify and examine the status of our cognitive capacities and the import of evidence and counterevidence before and after crossing over the threshold. My strategy in the chapter as a whole will take the form of a narrative of conversion laced with implicit and explicit epistemic commentary.

A Conversion Narrative

Consider Ms. Convert, a person who began her intellectual journey with a weak but genuine sense of the manifestation of God in creation and was tacitly committed to something like our list of epistemic platitudes. These were something given with nature, we might say. Moreover, insofar as she thought of her own capacities, she tacitly took them to be reliable. Thus she did not stop to worry about whether perception gave her access to the world, or whether memory gave her access to the past, or whether she should always test testimony by other criteria, and so on. To be sure, she knew these practices were far from infallible; she also honed their usage over time, noting, say, that she had a good memory for names but not for dates, and that some people's testimony could be trusted only under certain restricted circumstances.

She was also perturbed from time to time by skeptical worries. She was perplexed that sometimes her senses deceived her, and from time to time she was fascinated that she experienced the content of her dreams with much the same certainty as she experienced the world around her. These phenomena troubled her. However, while eavesdropping on what her philosophy friends pondered from time to time, she had never quite been able to worry that she might be a brain in a vat or that maybe she was being systematically deceived by a very powerful, evil demon. Of course, were she to know that a mad scientist in the local university had managed to put human brains in vats and to manipulate the inputs in such a way as to get their original owners to think they were living an entirely normal life, then she might worry about that option. However, she had not heard that there were any such scientists in her neighborhood, and she was pretty sure that contemporary science had not yet opened up this possibility. Moreover, she was sure that if there had been such a remarkable breakthrough, she would have heard about it from her usual sources of information. Alternatively, if she had been brought up in a fundamentalist Christian sect that constantly harped on about the possibility of demonic possession where the victims were totally deceived about the outcome of their ordinary cognitive practices, she might have worried about this option as well. However, she had no such upbringing, and she found the whole idea of the demonic artificial, superfluous, and silly. Her default position in epistemology placed confidence in her everyday cognitions and practices. She simply relied on memory, testimony, reason, perception, and the rest of her cognitive capacities.

Finding that she tacitly believed in God was, then, no great surprise to Ms. Convert. She had no more reason to reject this outcome of her cognitive operations than a host of other beliefs that she found herself possessing. Belief in God, while not exactly on a par with belief in the external world and in other minds, was more like these beliefs than like belief in subatomic particles or in black holes. The latter relied on evidence worked over by communities of scientific inquiry over time and accepted on the authority of experts; belief in God did not. However vaguely or uncertainly, then, she believed in God. Furthermore, she found confirmation for her belief in reviewing what she later found out to be a network of classical arguments for the existence of God. Thus she found the idea of creation a handy way of making sense both of the existence of the cosmos and of the order and beauty that was so pervasive within it. There was something deeply satisfying in seeing the world as brought about by God, for phenomena can clearly be explained in terms of the action of agents as well as by the laws of science. Indeed, as she saw it, the laws of science fitted into a schema of explanation that interprets them as the effects of God's orderly activity and even of his faithfulness to creation. The converse — that persons and their actions could be reduced to or explained in terms of material objects, their properties, and the laws that governed their behavior — was far more difficult to secure and sustain.

In addition, Ms. Convert at times had a strong sense of the presence of God in her own experience above and beyond her perception of the divine in creation. This led her to explore the testimony of the mystics; she found that her convictions were not nearly as strong as those reported in their writings, but through her reading of them her initial beliefs about God were strengthened and confirmed.

Furthermore, she found it natural to read some things that happened in her life as exhibiting divine providence. Her skeptical friends teasingly dismissed these readings as luck or happenstance, but while she understood this tendency, she was by no means persuaded by it. Her own sense was that God was somehow with her, helping and assisting her. This was readily confirmed by the testimony of others, especially by those with more robust and comprehensive convictions of God that they had picked up in the Christian communities to which they belonged.

These latter friends became over time extremely important in her life. They had a stronger sense of God than she did, and she wanted to know more about their convictions. At times they exhibited a sanctity that went way beyond her weak efforts in pursuing virtue. Their avowals about the source of this sanctity were thoroughly mystifying to her, because these same friends in moments of intimate self-revelation readily confessed their lack of virtue and spoke very freely of their utter dependence on the grace of God mediated in the life of the church. Thus Ms. Convert was at once attracted and repelled. She was attracted by their love, but she was thoroughly repelled by their somewhat glum vision of themselves and the world. Frankly, they sometimes left her feeling depressed and disconsolate, even though this was not at all their intention. In time, however, her views about human nature shifted and she began to share their rather grim vision of the human situation, and yet she was drawn by hope that maybe all this talk about the grace of God and its availability in the church was not a dream but a reality. Hence discourse about sin and regeneration, while somewhat odd and fleeting, came within her reach.

Several factors inhibited her journey at this point. First, she was deeply disappointed in the divisions and bickering she found among Christian believers. It pained her that the communities that made such bold claims about God and his love should have so many unloving people in charge. Second, she was very perplexed by the strange doctrines of the church. What she heard and read about God, especially about the incarnation and the Trinity, struck her as downright incoherent and self-contradictory. It was difficult enough for her to conceive of God in the first place. After all, God as an agent without a body was impossible for her to imagine, for her imagination fed off images of agents who were characteristically embodied. She was able to overcome the ensuing dissonance by recalling that one could conceive of all sorts of things without imagining them, but the additional claims about God in the Christian tradition still gave her an intellectual headache. Third, she was sometimes sorely distressed at the enormous amount of widespread, useless natural evil she observed all around her. It troubled her that God should have made human creatures that turned out to be so systematically wicked. The mere fact that God was associated with them, much less that he created them and then sustained them, as they conducted their nefarious campaigns of evil, troubled her. It was as if the government official responsible for creating, sustaining, and overseeing the agency that gave ample opportunity within its own walls for gross corruption was still responsible for what happened, even though he himself had always acted on the best of intentions and never for a moment thought of putting his hand in the till.

Worse still, natural evil really did tempt her to despair of making sense of the world in theistic terms. Maybe God was incompetent; or maybe God was cruel; or maybe the whole idea of God was something she invented as a kind of cosmic comforter. When she read sociological and psychological explanations of the origins of belief in God, she could see why people would develop these ideas, but she also found it difficult to go all the way and yield to agnosticism or to outright atheism. In part, this was because she found that agnostics and atheists rarely agreed among themselves on how to think about the universe as a whole. They were every bit as divided as the theists she knew, although this did not seem to bother them unduly.

At this point Ms. Convert began a serious exploration of the life of the church as mediated in its scriptures and in its public practices. In and through this search she came to terms with purported knowledge of God vouchsafed in special revelation. Divine revelation was a strange idea initially, but if God was an agent, then applying the language of revelation to the action of God was a natural extension of insights already in place. So, just as she sensed God's presence in creation, she now heard God speak in his Word. Her capacity to hear was an extension, as she saw it, of her capacity to perceive God in creation. The seeing and hearing were, of course, not a physical seeing or hearing but a spiritual exercise or practice of her whole person. This hearing was accompanied by a mixed sense of dread and hope, dread before the awesome Word of God in Christ, yet hope that God's love reached out to all in mercy and new life. Such dissonance was not unwelcome because it was correlated with a persistent urge to immerse herself in the Gospels and to find out all she could about Jesus of Nazareth. As she mulled over the content of the Gospels, she woke up one day and discovered that she was a believer. As she continued to work out what was happening, she found herself drawn into the life of faith and offered herself for baptism.

I have used the evasive passive to describe a transition in Ms. Convert's intellectual journey that is difficult to capture. Conventionally we might speak at this point of conversion, but this is such a hackneyed notion that it cannot begin to do justice to the deep way in which her intellect, her will, her heart, and her very soul were shaken and reconstituted. Her states of mind and cognitive appraisals were varied and complex.

She sometimes thought of it as having lingered on the porch of a wonderful old mansion she had only wistfully observed from afar, before suddenly stepping inside and entering the vast rooms and winding stair-ways. Rather than being old and terribly musty, as she had dreaded it might be, the mansion turned out to be surprisingly fresh and airy; there was a feel of springtime in the atmosphere. The owner of the mansion had come down himself to welcome her as she entered, to escort her to her own very specially prepared room, to set a feast for her, to introduce her to a whole new network of friends, and to give her beautifully designed lumi-nous candles to find her way around. Sometimes he wistfully whispered in her ear in a way that cut right to her heart but that left her to mull things over rather than reach for the obvious inference. Even the portraits of an-cient occupants and treasured leaders of the past helped her get oriented, speaking to her in a way that no words could effect. In an initial tour of the building the owner made available to her some of the original plans and identified the names of the great architects who had helped to develop it. He even appointed contemporary guides so she could get her bearings and begin to work through the consequences of her decision.

Yet even the language of decision was much too weak. It failed to register the pull of the older, more comfortable world on the other side of the porch, before she had stepped into her new home. Speaking of the change as one due to her decision did not begin to note the fear and trem-bling or the attraction and dread that came over her during her conver-sion. Such language did not come near to capturing the agony involved in giving up old ways of thinking and acting. It did not properly describe the torture of abandoning the old scripts, of giving up the old clothes and abandoning the old bit parts she had been playing back then. Nor did the language of decision do justice to the thrill of trying out a whole new iden-tity, or of coming to terms with the new wardrobe of things old and new she had inherited. There was a personal death and yet resurrection; there was a giving up and yet a gaining; there was a sacrifice of everything she was and had and yet a finding of her true self. There was a horror at how blind and stupid she had been and yet a delight at the mercy and compas-sion that immersed her very being; there was a total loss of words to de-scribe her experience and yet a bubbling assurance that she had met the living God; there was a terrible sense of intellectual disorientation and yet a sharp focus in her thinking. Water had been turned into wine, she knew not how, but the taste and smell were exhilarating.

Happily, her conversion was accompanied by the kind of friendship and intellectual care that gave her access to the full faith of the church in its creed, its scriptures, its practices, its worship, and the like. She had even found that exposure to the classical icons of the tradition had helped her see what she was hearing and reading. They had given her food for her imagination and somehow drew her into the narrative of creation and redemption in ways that entered deep into her consciousness. In the end she crossed the threshold of divine revelation and found herself in a whole new world of beauty, moral endeavor, intellectual richness, and spiritual nurture. In a way that was truly personal yet not divorced from communion with the faithful, she entered into a new network of experiences of God that were naturally identified as experiences of the Spirit of God.

Help from Philosophy

Ms. Convert was fortunate to have a philosophy friend who helped her sort through the epistemic consequences of the shift in perspective that had come about as a result of her conversion. This friend was sufficiently sensitive to help her work out what was at issue. To be sure, what emerged sounded more like a dull list of comments to some, but sometimes dull lists are essential to registering what is at issue intellectually; on this occasion she was more patient than usual.

First, she developed a much more robust vision of her ordinary cognitive capacities and practices, like intuition, perception, reason, memory, testimony, and the like. Accepting and entering into the world of divine revelation, she now saw these capacities as underwritten by the power and goodness of God. Her new convictions had a kind of loop-back effect, so that skepticism was even less an option than it had been before. The initial reliability she had tacitly adopted was now explicitly owned and strengthened by her newfound faith. Theologically she saw herself as an extraordinarily complex truth-detecting organism whose epistemic mechanisms and practices reflected her being made in the image of God. She was fascinated by philosophical efforts to become clear about these cognitive operations.

She was also intrigued by theological descriptions and explanations of cognition that saw cognition and its contents as the work of the eternal Son present as wisdom and reason in creation or as the illumination of the Holy Spirit in the mind. Before, these had always appeared as impossible mumbo jumbo, a relic of an impossible medieval imagination. Now they represented a spiritual and metaphysical vision of reason, truth, and knowledge that extended her ruminations in an eerie manner. It was as if she had found a new network of ancient and medieval friends whose intellectual fecundity was at times dazzling in its ingenuity and surprises. Sometimes she felt they were drifting off into an intellectual la-la land of nonsense, but she was smitten by their confidence, whatever her misgivings about the details of their exploration and conceptual creativity. They made it clear that there were all sorts of new intellectual challenges that called forth the straining and full use of her cognitive capacities.

Second, she found that she took her moral sense or conscience far more seriously. She had always been amazed by the way various courses of action were accompanied by a sense of good or evil, where she felt drawn to the good and repelled inwardly by evil, and where good was accompanied by approval and evil was correlated with judgment. She now naturally saw this as the voice of God within her. It was as if there was an inner light that acted as the candle of the Lord directing and drawing her to virtue. Moreover, this sense was not just deepened by these redescriptions, it was enriched by the content of divine revelation, so that what before seemed heroic and impossible was now inescapable and fitting. In fact, what she once thought of as very odd forms of human behavior or even as vice was transferred to the terrain of virtue. She was fascinated by philosophical theories that tried to work out general principles that governed the life of virtue, that sought to connect virtue with human happiness and natural human flourishing, and that organized virtues and vices into various interconnecting lists. Yet the very articulation of these complex theses depended on bedrock trust in various initial intuitions that stood on their own feet. Or rather, they now appeared to her as a dependent or a tutored sense of good and evil that struck deep into a vision of creation and redemption.

Third, equally she had much greater confidence in her sense of the presence of God in creation and in her ability to hear the Word of God. She always knew in her heart of hearts that she did not need a network of propositional evidence to secure the beliefs that emerged from these sources. She really did have the capacity to see and hear God, just as she had the capacity to see and hear what was going on around her in the world of natural objects and human agents. In this case her initial anthropological intuitions were filled out, enriched, and confirmed.

Fourth, she came to realize that she had access to truths that went beyond the truths of reason and experience. Hence, it would be going backward rather than forward to have to work to her new convictions by insisting that they be equally well secured by propositional inferences from the data of "secular" reason and experience. For her there was no longer merely "secular" reason and experience. To go back into and be restricted to the confines of that "secular" world struck her not as progress and Enlightenment but as a form of intellectual regress. It was like agreeing in advance to shut oneself off from crucial avenues of learning and arenas of data. It was like posting forbidding No Entry signs to wonderful new landscapes in the name of liberty. It represented an intellectual narrowness that pretended to be critical and honest when in reality it was prejudiced and shallow. To be sure, she loved to toy with how far she might be able to reach the new truths of revelation by means solely of reason and experience, but only the superficial and naive saw this as anything other than an interesting intellectual exercise and as a way of helping her unbelieving friends make progress on the journey of faith.

Fifth, she had developed a different perspective on the conceptual difficulties that confronted her in the great doctrines of the church. Before, she had only two categories at her disposal, namely, coherent propositions and incoherent propositions. Now, given a sharp sense of the otherness and transcendence of God, she realized that there were inherent limitations in her ability to understand the divine. Hence, she readily added the category of mystery to her stock of conceptual options. Before, the appeal to mystery had always been thoroughly irritating. It seemed to her entirely arbitrary or a convenient laborsaving device that was in essence a cop-out. Now it did not trouble her that God was beyond her comprehension, that she had to stretch her language to the limits to get at the truth about God, and that these conditions might well be ineradicable. Indeed, it struck her as entirely fitting. Somehow a God who could be fully understood, and whose nature and activity could be described in the same way that we describe the regular laundry list of objects we encounter in space and time, would not be God. While there were still plenty of soluble mysteries about the natural world that might one day be unraveled, say, by science, mysteries were simply ineradicable in theology.

Sixth, on the inside of divine revelation she found that a battery of supporting evidence confirmed her trust in divine revelation. This support reached all the way from answers to prayer, to new encounters with God, to deeper self-knowledge, to personal revelation and divine guidance, and to the strengthening of her moral life through the sacraments of the church. It also included manifestations of the Holy Spirit in her life over time, represented by that inner witness that spoke within her and told her that she could legitimately address God as "Abba," Father; by the fruit of the Spirit in her relationships with others; and by the experience of various gifts of the Spirit in the ministry of the church. Of course, this evidence was extended indefinitely, albeit in a weakened form, into a wealth of testimony reporting the very same phenomena in the lives of the saints and ordinary believers. All these, singly and together, confirmed her belief that she had indeed encountered a decisive revelation of God in Jesus Christ.

Seventh, her faith was also confirmed by the striking inner coherence of Christian doctrine as this was spelled out with flair and imagination. Thus she saw how a robust doctrine of sin fitted with various visions of atonement, and how discourse about new birth, justification, sanctification, and the like mapped, albeit fitfully, her own spiritual experiences and journey to God. The doctrine of the Trinity came alive as a fitting summary of a host of scattered data collected and sifted in the church. The doctrine of the incarnation made sense as an entirely appropriate means of healing the human condition and as an extraordinary disclosure of God.

Eighth, she also came to see the importance of the testimony of the church in coming to the truth about God. Where before she saw dependence on others as a denial of her autonomy and freedom, she now came to see the latter as enmeshed in a vision of persons that was much too atomistic and individualistic. Human beings cannot avoid networks of trust and radical dependence on others in both transmitting and securing knowledge. There was no need at this point to look for some kind of absolute certainty or infallibility. It was enough to take testimony seriously and to trust that God had secured all that was necessary for her spiritual welfare among his people over time. Moreover, while it was useful to be able to identify the network of media through which God continued his witness in the world, it was important not to be too uptight about exactly where and how all this was displayed. It was sufficient to be able to identify the central features of the canonical heritage of the church and rely on them without fuss or ultimate guarantees.

Ninth, she had also come to reflect deeply on the theme of divine hiddenness. In debates between theists and atheists she had noticed that atheists often drew attention in a brash way to the paucity of evidence to the reality of God. In their analysis of the issues they assumed that the recognition and evaluation of evidence would be a straightforward affair that could be conducted in a way that eliminated the role of inner disposition and attitude. Furthermore, coming to identify a revelation of God would not depend on moral considerations or on the attitude of the recipient. God would have to operate in a way that they deemed appropriate, regardless of God's purposes in reaching out to the world. Now she realized that responding to divine revelation was not a spectator sport under our control. It was entirely appropriate that God's friendship should be withheld on God's side from those who had no interest in or intention of taking it seriously. God truly remained hidden from the proud and the arrogant; he was revealed to those who were open to a radical change of direction in their lives.

Tenth, she also came to appreciate for the first time in her life the inner logic of the ontological argument. The cosmological and teleological arguments operated on the basis of informal arguments to the best explanation. The vision of God as creator and sustainer of the world, together with its order and beauty, acted as a personal explanation that posited the phenomena as brought into existence by God for various intentions and purposes. Of course, the explanation was still incomplete; outside a fleeting appeal to the sheer immensity of divine love bursting in its very essence to create and redeem, she did not have to hand an account of the specific reasons for creating precisely this world rather than one closely akin to it. She did not, therefore, have detailed reasons to hand as to exactly why God had created and redeemed as he had. However, this was not the problem. The problem was that, logically speaking, one could always look for an explanation for the reality of God. Even as a child, it had always made sense to her to ask, "Who made God?" Yet there was something very odd about this question, and she was never clear why this was the case. While in her thinking about God she rightly relied on the analogy of personal agency in her conception of God and of the pertinent explanatory arguments that supplemented her sense and experience of God, somehow it did not always make sense to look for an explanation of God's existence. One might forestall the move to further explanation by appeal to simplicity and economy of explanation, but interesting and even insightful as these explanations might be, they never quite satisfied. They made God too contingent, too much like any other medium-sized object or agent in the universe.

Now she felt she had a better handle on the problem. The ontological argument showed why it did not make sense to ask why God was the stopping place of explanation. From what she had come to see and know about God in the canonical heritage of the church, God was a superlative agent, an agent who was beautifully captured in Anselm's vision of God as that than which nothing greater can be conceived. Such a superlative God must surely exist not just in a limited number of possible worlds but also in all possible worlds. Hence his nonexistence was truly inconceivable, and it made no sense to ask if he came into existence or was dependent on something else for his existence. Thus the ontological argument, rather than standing on its own in isolation, was the final move that brought much of the disparate evidence in hand to a fitting conclusion. The necessary existence of God was the terminus, the capstone, and the final resting place of explanation.

Eleventh, her newfound faith also had knock-on effects on her original encounter with evil and on the acute problems it had precipitated from time to time. This turned out to be much more subtle and complex than she had anticipated.

In fact, initially she discovered what she could only describe as a new kind of counterevidence against the existence of God. Thus she came to a much deeper sense of the depths of evil in the world. In fact, it surprised her that she had far less difficulty with the conception of the demonic than she had previously. Rather than making her theism simpler, this addition to her ontology made it far more complex and ragged at the edges. Further, she now had great difficulty making sense of experiences of the absence of God in her own life and in the lives of the saints. She felt at times that she had been strung out to dry in the wilderness with nothing to sustain her but her naked faith in the Word of God given to her in the church. She could not depend on her sense of God or on her carefully formulated reasoned arguments. She had to rely on radical, naked trust in God. Furthermore, she found herself being tested and tempted in ways she had not known before, phenomena that did not fit with the rest of her convictions. She was also fitfully troubled by the extent to which the heavens sometimes seemed like brass and there was no answer to her prayers of petition. The suffering and persecution of the faithful were equally disconcerting.

Yet the varied forms of dissonance that arose were gently if not fully absorbed into a complex form of cognitive equilibrium. She found either that the dissonant phenomena turned out to be fitting features of the universe as seen in the light of divine revelation, or that they could be treated as problems and anomalies that did not begin to overturn her convictions as a whole.

The same logic applied to her new response to the standard objections to faith that had given her so much trouble earlier in her journey. There was indeed genuine human agency in the world that more than readily explained the moral evils she encountered. Both moral and natural evil were refigured in a vision that saw such events as permitted by God as forms of testing and trial. With her experiences of the absence of God as a believer, they were also seen as permitted by God to bring about holiness, that is, to deepen trust and to inhibit or eradicate pride, presumption, and false security. Before her conversion, these sorts of phenomena appeared to support an agnostic vision of the universe, or, with other background assumptions, they could readily be seen to license various forms of atheism. Now, while they indeed counted as evidence against her robust theism, they could either be seen as compatible with it or legitimately left as unresolved. In some circumstances evil evoked lament and spiritual distress rather than unbelief or atheism. Such lament and spiritual distress required rather than undermined deep trust in God. Equally, these phenomena helped her to understand why her unbelieving friends found her so intellectually exasperating. She could now understand why her robust beliefs seemed so absurd to them. She could see why they found it perverse that she relied on those same absurd beliefs and the wider network of conviction in which they were embedded as explanatory and illuminating. A robust faith really did look at times like utter foolishness; it all looked like radical cognitive malfunction to many of her friends; and she understood this.

In laying out the various strands of transformation, we can see afresh the radical difference divine revelation makes to our epistemic commitments. Beginning with the observation that the acceptance of divine revelation is a perspective-constituting experience, I have argued that divine revelation casts fresh light on the nature of our cognitive capacities and on how we exercise our reason on evidence and counterevidence. The standard portrait that sees coming to believe in God simply as a matter of using our cognitive capacities, or of weighing evidence for and against particular propositions, is inadequate.

The work that has gone into this standard portrait is a hard-won intellectual achievement. Even though we have given good reason for staking out a different vision than is customary, the position advanced here exploits the harvest of extraordinary work in the epistemology of religion of the last generation rather than rejects it. What I have done is to drop the idea of divine revelation into the debate much as leaven is used in cooking. Special revelation rises and spreads in its own way to transform everything it touches. We began with a host of epistemic comments that are common in philosophy, but we ended with a thoroughly transformed vision of the way different insights work together rather than in competition with each other. We also saw that once theological claims about divine revelation are initially secured and put to work epistemically, then the discoveries that arise, and the redescriptions that ensue, have their own way of strengthening and transforming our initial commitments. In this way we give further substance to the claim that divine revelation is indeed a world-constituting concept.

The cords that connect us to divine revelation initially look rather weak and frayed. It is easy to dismiss them as flimsy and ephemeral. Equally it is tempting to bolster them with miracles and other surefire guarantees. Thus we seesaw back and forth between suspicion and intellectual overreach. There is another way. We begin where we are, taking seriously the epistemic capacities and platitudes that lie to hand. In due course we discover that the weak and frayed cords that connect us to divine revelation are but the outward covering for a steel cable with many interconnecting strands that can more than support us. Or at least that is how it turns out for the mature believer who has crossed over the threshold of divine revelation.

Chapter Eight

Unbelief, Belief, and Loss of Faith

From Unbelief to Belief

In thinking of the nature of our cognitive capacities and the import of evidence and counterevidence, we can see throughout this analysis that it is important to work diachronically rather than only synchronically in epistemology.[1] When we work synchronically we think of belief, by way of a snapshot of the particular beliefs we are evaluating. When we work diachronically we look at beliefs as involving a journey across time. Thus thinking diachronically about belief helps us to see that believing is a form of intellectual commitment that stands on a sliding scale, that is, it can be instantiated in various forms of dissent and assent that can be weaker or

1. I find it very striking that Kierkegaard in his finest work focused sharply on the synchronic rather than the diachronic. In *Fear and Trembling* he provides fascinating commentary on the famous story of Abraham's sacrifice of Isaac without any attention to the wider narrative. Despite his intention to focus on the psychology and passion of faith, his observations as a result turn out to be much too narrow. To be sure, his comments are ingeniously illuminating in certain ways, and they are presented with magnificent drama, but they are also profoundly inadequate. They are not sufficiently sensitive in their delineation of the diachronic elements in epistemology. Perhaps Kierkegaard rectifies the situation in his *Training in Christianity*, but I am not sure if this is the case. Newman overall in his writings strikes me as a much more astute thinker at this point. At the very least, we need the labors of both a Kierkegaard and a Newman to help us get through the thicket of issues involved.

stronger. Thus, as we have suggested schematically for Ms. Convert, we can imagine her beginning at one end of a spectrum where belief, say, that Jesus is the Son of God and Savior of the world, may be impossible simply because she thinks this proposition is incoherent, and yet ending up believing this proposition so firmly that she is prepared to die for it rather than publicly deny it. There are all sorts of points in between.

So we can think of the state of mind of someone rejecting the faith and being in a state of unbelief. We might also imagine someone fearing or even dreading that the faith is true. This person inclines toward believing the great truths of the faith but does so in such a way that in entertaining them there is an aversion to their being true. Further along the spectrum toward belief we can envisage someone suspecting Christianity to be true. The person is clearly on the brink of actually believing it to be true, but the dissent is extremely mild and unstable. Thus prior to believing, a person may have a very weak form of dissent that has within it flickering moments of assent. We might imagine someone wishing episodically that Christianity be true. Further along we can think of someone desiring it to be true. In the neighborhood we can imagine someone hoping that the great truths of the faith are true. Perhaps he finds the faith altogether incredible; it is much too good to be true; but he would love it to be true, and even at times hopes it is true. We can also think of someone holding or entertaining the great truths of the faith for the sake of further exploration and investigation. A person might well try on the faith for cognitive fit, so to speak. This is clearly stronger than doubting the faith, but it is much weaker than believing it. He is able to accept the faith without believing it.

On the belief side of the spectrum we can think of someone assenting very weakly to the faith; she is subject to times of intellectual depression and doubt. Further along the scale of assent we can imagine someone strongly affirming rather than just merely believing the faith of the church. Thus he believes with a natural assurance that carries him aloft even in the tough seasons of commitment. Moving yet further along, we can think of a person who resolutely holds the faith to be true. It pains her that people do not see the truth about God, and it fills her with passion to find ways to share it with good sense and enthusiasm. She has a faith so strong that it can move mountains. Again this is much, much stronger than merely believing.

As to the actual believing itself, there has been extended discussion of late on how far belief is a matter of will, of whether one can will directly to believe. I have little if anything new to add to this discussion other than to make two simple points. First, it is surely right to claim that one can influence the outcomes of one's beliefs indirectly by attending to the relevant data that rightly affect how and what we believe. Paul claims that faith comes by hearing the gospel message,[2] and the Gospels make much of the quality of our hearing.[3] This much clearly is under our control. This observation fits with believing as a diachronic process that works itself out over time and is causally touched by various factors. Second, there may well be a subtle and complex place for the will in coming to believe in divine revelation. The reason for this is that while faith indeed arises from various causes, faith also involves trust. Given the place of trust, there would appear to be space for genuine action on the part of the believer; there is a voluntary component in trust; there is a real sense in which the believer places his life in the hands of God. Hence believing the truths of divine revelation is not best captured by assimilating it to believing ordinary truths like two plus two equals four, or the grass in front of me is green. In these examples it makes no sense saying our beliefs are voluntary; with believing the truths or promises of divine revelation, the situation strikes me as much more subtle; there is very likely a voluntary component.

Forms of Belief

We now turn to develop a more general portrait of belief and unbelief across the threshold of divine revelation. I propose that we think of no fewer than nine forms or modes of belief and unbelief across the threshold. As we proceed, I shall work both synchronically and diachronically. Hence I shall work through a scale of belief and unbelief on the other side of the threshold of divine revelation, pausing to provide snapshots of belief and unbelief. There are very porous lines between belief and unbelief at times, but we shall not pause to worry overmuch about these lines.

First, there is the phenomenon of the nominal believer or nominal belief. The person holds to the faith of the church, but for all intents and

---

2. Romans 10:14.
3. This is well brought out in the parable of the sower. See Mark 4.

purposes refuses to act on it or to let it make any deep difference to her basic orientation in life. She may well exhibit a readiness to take part in the liturgical life of the church and to make use of the rites of passage publicly available in the culture. But her fundamental orientation is one of intellectual indifference; the basic direction and intention is to allow the faith of the church to lie idle. Sometimes this disposition is accompanied by real resistance to the faith; at other times indifference flows toward real faith. Whatever the ebb and flow, the prevailing cognitive state is one of minimal inward commitment.

Second, there is the phenomenon of the unformed or ignorant believer. This believer is never really initiated into the faith of the church in a serious way. He picks up bits and pieces of the faith and comes to believe, but there is no significant formation. He barely knows what he believes, much less why he believes. He cannot discern the difference between a meaty and relatively accurate presentation of the faith and an exotic and superficial version of the faith. Believers of this kind are exceptionally vulnerable to the charlatan evangelist who knows how to exploit their innocence and their ignorance. Equally they are liable to meander hither and yon without stability or depth.

Third, there is what we might call simply the ordinary or normal believer. This is the person who is baptized, say, at an early age, comes to believe in special divine revelation, is converted to a life of faith, and seeks to live a life coordinated with divine revelation and its divinely inspired reception. The crucial feature is that the believer acts on the newfound knowledge of God in a host of ways. Of course, the believer may have all sorts of doubts, may have bouts of weakness of will, may sin grievously and not just in ignorance, and so on. However, the direction of life has been set through the grace of God, and there is a clear intention to live a life of commitment and obedience.

Fourth, we can also think of a mature believer and mature belief. The believer in this instance has come to terms with the complexity of faith. She has moved to a second naïveté, so that she has explicitly reckoned with the nature of faith, the grounds of faith, the standard objections and obstacles to faith, and the like. While much of what she believes remains implicit and tacit, she can either articulate her convictions and their grounds when challenged or she can readily discern when others more skilled and knowledgeable can do so. She has a sense of the difficulties of belief and can sympathize with those who are opposed to robust forms of faith. Her faith is accompanied by a humble assurance that is both firm and meek. Above all else, her faith is a gateway to love for God and neighbor rather than a speculative intellectual exercise. Her greatest joy is to see the kingdom of God come with power and to witness the church recover her first love in the service of God and the world.

Fifth, there is the phenomenon of the heretical believer and of heretical belief. The believer in question is committed to divine revelation and is serious about working through its meaning. However, he sees divine revelation not as a gift to the people of God that is accompanied by a divinely inspired response, but as his own private possession. Moreover, he sees himself as fully authorized to interpret it on his own in isolation from the church. Thus he sees himself either at liberty or even duty-bound to make what he will of divine revelation. We can imagine here a scale in which at one end he respects the faith of the church but sees it as strictly advisory, and at the other end he is hostile to the faith and considers it systematically poisonous.

Note that we are not just speaking of a person who has his own well-worked-out opinions about the meaning and significance of divine revelation. Every mature believer who thinks seriously about divine revelation will have all sorts of such opinions. What we have is a person who insists on making his personal opinions the critical and real truth about God over against the judgment of the church as a whole. Thus he insists that his access to the central truths about God is better than the access claimed by the recipients of revelation, that is, the historic community of the faithful. Within this context he may lay claim to special intellectual and professional expertise and may be tempted now and then to harangue the church for not paying enough attention to his special services. He may even consider it a duty of the church to pay his salary, and he may quickly pick up the mantle of victim if the church raises questions about the impact of his ideas on the ordinary believer. If he is more sanguine, he will be sad and sorrowful that the church is so dense and backward in its orientation. Not surprisingly, the heretic makes much in these circumstances of the cognitive malfunction of the church, of his own proper cognitive functioning and expertise, of his duty to truth, and of his right to freedom.

Sixth is the schismatic believer and schismatic belief. Here is a person who accepts the faith of the church but, for whatever reason, insists on operating outside and in opposition to the body of the faithful. The crucial distinction in this case is the rejection of communion with other believers, often accompanied by determination to set up a rival community of faith. This clearly harms the cognitive life of the church in that it undermines the practice of virtue and thereby hurts the proper perception of God and the proper hearing of the Word of God. Schismatic believers deeply undermine the unity of the church; their actions and the response to them tend to create alienation; and the divisions that ensue prevent cooperation in the quest for truth. Thus the world finds it very hard to believe in the claims to divine revelation advanced by the church. Rather than affection and love, there are disharmony and bickering; rather than a delicate balance of unity and diversity, there are bitter division and name-calling; rather than common service and mutual edification, there are competition and rivalry. The truth of divine revelation is scattered and dissolved, and the church suffers severe cognitive malfunction. The testimony of the church is thus significantly impaired.

Seventh, there is the revisionist believer and revisionist belief. This person ceases to believe in divine revelation and in the inspired response worked out in the church. For one reason or another she comes effectively to hold that the church got it wrong on the identity and content of divine revelation. Perhaps, it will be said, certain kinds of religious experiences were misidentified as special revelation. Religious experiences are in turn seen as subject to radically different interpretations, so there cannot be the kind of closure associated with divine revelation. Alternatively the threshold of divine revelation has been eroded by, say, a vision of the results of modern biblical criticism, or the correlative interpretation has been undermined by contemporary insights and analysis. Yet it is still maintained that in some fundamental sense the Christian faith is correct about God, creation, the human condition, and the like.

Christianity on this analysis supplies us, say, with a network of symbols, insights, myths, themes, and values that is worth preserving for the sake of truth and for the healing of the world. Thus the faith needs to be constantly reinterpreted and revised to fit the contemporary situation. Faith itself is recast as something quite different from response to special revelation; it is seen as faith in God evoked by Jesus, or as faith in transcendence mediated through Jesus, or as basic trust in life itself that is represented in the story about Jesus. The intellectual content of the Christian faith must then be reconstructed in every new generation. In aiming at this, the modern or postmodern believer is free to use philosophical theory, echoes of the great doctrines of the past, populist mythologies, other religious traditions, ethnic and cultural traditions, and the like. In this way Christianity reconstitutes itself across the generations and survives the vicissitudes of cultural change.

It has been common in popular circles to see this sort of change in belief as a form of heresy. Clearly there are affinities and analogies with heresy, but the differences are sufficiently striking to call for the invention of a new category. The crucial difference between the revisionist and the heretic is that the revisionist professes to be faithful to the canonical tradition of the church in a way the heretic does not. The heretic thinks the church received divine revelation but got it wrong; he is convinced that his own personal judgment is a much better guide to its interpretation. The revisionist believer is a friendlier critic, insisting that in its day the canonical faith of the church was indeed a fitting rendering of the Christian tradition. Thus to say that the canonical faith was wrong is much too abrupt and vulgar. What is wrong is to keep repeating the tradition when we now find ourselves in a radically changed intellectual and social context. At this level the revisionist believer is much more radical than the heretic, for she is prepared to jettison divine revelation as well as the canonical doctrines that have emerged in its wake.[4] The fundamental issue for the revisionist is that we need a more progressive version of the faith that will speak to a new generation. The fundamental issue for the heretic is that we adopt his opinion about the meaning and significance of divine revelation over against that of the church.

Eighth, there is the phenomenon of apostasy. Here we can more readily talk of the apostate believer than of apostate belief. The apostate believes there was indeed a divine revelation, accepts it for a time, but then decides to reject the God of revelation who has come to liberate the world, and goes back over the threshold of divine revelation into the world of unbelief. What is critical here is that the person does this intentionally and voluntarily without initially giving up the conviction that God has indeed revealed himself to the world. Moreover, we can no longer quite speak of apostate belief precisely because of the crossing back over into the world of unbelief. Yet we can speak of an apostate believer. In this instance there is, as it were, the residue of the former beliefs still at work in the mind of the apostate.

---

4. In the eyes of the mature believer the revisionist believer is, in the name of enlightenment, giving an invitation to step back into the old world of darkness.

Here we enter a murky cognitive condition in the neighborhood of self-deception. At one level the apostate accepts divine revelation, but at another level he rebels against it and casts around for ideologies and substitutes that will serve his desires, his agendas, and his self-image. It was perhaps for this reason that Calvin described the human mind that rejected general divine revelation as a factory for the making of idols. This is an extremely astute epistemological comment. It serves to delineate a cognitive state that has received next to no serious investigation in epistemology.

Ninth, close to apostasy but different from it in tone and content is what we might call sublimated unbelief. In this case we have instances of unbelief that are clearly indebted either personally or culturally to earlier forms of belief. The old forms or content of belief may show up in the new beliefs. Thus much of classical foundationalism in modern epistemology may well be a transposition of doctrines of scripture in the Western tradition, where the commitment to a single, infallible ground for true belief is transferred to beliefs derived from intuition or experience. To take a different example, Marxism is often rightly seen as a transposition of Christian eschatological convictions to immanent forces of history that ineluctably lead to an earthly utopia. Some forms of modern humanism may well be a transfer of earlier Christian hopes for salvation to science, education, and technology. John Gray nicely captures the latter possibility.

> Positivism is a doctrine of redemption in the guise of theory of history. The Positivists inherited the Christian view of history, but — suppressing Christianity's insight that human nature is ineradicably flawed — they announced that by the use of technology humanity could make a new world. When they suggested that in the third and final stage of history there would be no politics, only rational administration, they imagined they were being scientific; but the belief that science can enable humanity to transcend its historic conflicts and create a universal civilization is not a product of empirical inquiry. It is a remnant of monotheism.[5]

---

5. John Gray, *Al Qaeda and What It Meant to Be Modern* (London: Faber and Faber, 2003), 105.

Loss of Faith

It is very important to distinguish these latter forms or modes of belief, that is, revisionist belief, apostasy, and sublimated unbelief, from periods of systematic doubt or from loss of faith due to the unbeliever being bombarded with objections against faith or with defeaters of faith. In the case of sustained doubt, the believer suffers from a bad bout of intellectual measles, where there are serious reservations about the truth of the faith that eventually are overcome. This is a common feature of life for many believers.

In the case of loss of faith, the person goes back over the threshold, but for what she takes to be good reason. She simply ceases to be convinced that she has access to divine revelation. She does so because she thinks she made a false identification of divine revelation, or because she believes she misread its proper significance. In both cases the original resources and the epistemic significance of special revelation are clearly recognized. Indeed, the consequences of loss of faith may be intellectually devastating and painful. Having come to an enriched conception of her cognitive capacities, the epistemic platitudes, her moral sense, and the like, the person suffering from loss of faith may fall into a period of skepticism, nihilism, and terrible despair. Even truth itself may seem to have gone under. It may take time to sort through the consequences of loss of faith and work through to the adoption of a fresh vision of the universe.

Kierkegaard's description of the consequences of loss of faith is especially memorable.

> If there were not eternal consciousness in a man, if at the foundation of all there lay only a wildly seething power which with obscure passions produced everything that is great and everything that is significant, if a bottomless void never satiated lay hidden beneath all — what then would life be but despair? If such were the case, if there were no sacred bond that united mankind, if one generation arose after another like the leafage in the forest, if the one generation replaced the other like the song of birds in the forest, if the human race passed through the world as the ship goes through the sea, like the winds through the desert, a thoughtless and fruitless activity, if an eternal oblivion were always lurking hungrily for its prey and there was no

power strong enough to wrest from its maw — how empty then and comfortless life would be![6]

It is tempting to see this observation as a form of intellectual scaremongering or bullying. If we sense that Kierkegaard is too grim at this point, then E. D. Klemke's robust way of coming to terms with the same bleak horizon is worth recording as an antidote.

I shall conclude with an ancient story: "Once a man from Syria led a camel through the desert; but when he came to a dark abyss, the camel suddenly, with teeth showing and eyes protruding, pushed the unsuspecting paragon of the camel-driving profession into the pit. The clothes of the Syrian were caught by a rosebush, and he was held suspended over the pit, at the bottom of which an enormous dragon was waiting to swallow him. Moreover, two mice were busily engaged in chewing away the roots of the already sagging plant. Yet in his desperate condition, the Syrian was thrilled to the point of utmost contentment by a rose which adorned the bush and wafted its fragrance into his face." . . . I know that I am that Syrian and that I am hanging over the pit. My doom is inevitable and swiftly approaching. If, in these few moments that are yet mine, I can find no rose to respond to, or rather if I have lost the ability to respond, then I shall moan and curse my fate with a howl of bitter agony. But *if* I can, in these last few moments, respond to a rose — or to a philosophical argument or theory of physics, or to a Scarlatti Sonata, or to the touch of a human hand — I say, if I can so respond and can thereby transform an external and fatal event into a moment of conscious insight and significance, then I shall go down *without hope or appeal yet passionately and with joy.*[7]

---

6. Soren Kierkegaard, *"Fear and Trembling" and "The Sickness unto Death"* (Garden City, N.Y.: Doubleday, 1954), 30.

7. Klemke, "Life without Appeal: An Affirmative Philosophy of Life," in *The Meaning of Life*, ed. E. D. Klemke (New York: Oxford University Press, 1981), 174, emphasis in original. The evolutionary biologist W. D. Hamilton supplies a nice expression of the joy noted by Klemke in a characteristically English way without the existentialist angst. Hamilton left instructions that he be buried among the beetles of the forests where he had conducted so much of his professional life. "I will leave a sum in my last will for my body to be carried to Brazil and to these forests. It will be laid out in a manner secure against the possums and the vultures just as we make our chickens secure; and this great *Coprophanaeus* beetle will bury

Given that many believers will find cold comfort in Klemke's bravado, it is not surprising that some have wanted to deny that there can in fact be any loss of genuine faith. There are at least three ways in which someone who believes in divine revelation might resist the whole idea of loss of faith. First, loss of faith underestimates the reach and security of the grace of God in the life of the true believer. Second, loss of faith does not reckon with the nature of faith as a form of loyalty to God. Third, loss of faith does not take the full measure of crossing the threshold and the deep intellectual consequences of believing in divine revelation. Let's call the first argument the argument from security in grace, the second argument the argument from loyalty, and the third argument the threshold argument.

The first argument proposes that the elect simply cannot fall from grace, and thus they cannot lose their faith. Indeed, God has revealed that faith is a gift from God, given irrevocably to those chosen by God to receive it, and hence God will ensure that they are kept secure forever. Believers may suffer from loss of confidence, and they may be subject to the discipline of God in their personal lives because of their sin, but in the end, if they have genuine faith, they will remain secure and cannot lose it.

A stronger version of this argument would press deeper into a doctrine of double, unconditional predestination. On the weaker version just outlined, God has simply determined or predestined that once faith is given, God always sustains it. Once faith has been given and received, the future outcome is totally outside the control of the believer. On this analysis, the initial faith does involve genuine human freedom and choice; folk can really say no to God; once on board, they are kept secure by divine discipline and grace. In this new enriched scenario, God predestines unconditionally who will be among the elect, ensures that the elect have true faith, and then guarantees that true faith will be sustained. Divine predetermination of the number and identity of the elect and divine predeter-

---

me. They will enter, will bury, will live on my flesh; and in the shape of their children and mine, I will escape death. No worm for me nor sordid fly, I will buzz in the dusk like a huge bumble bee. I will be many, buzz even as a swarm of motorbikes, be borne, body by flying body out into the Brazilian wilderness beneath the stars, lofted into those beautiful and unfused elytra which we all hold over our backs. So finally I too will shine like a violet ground beetle under a stone" (quoted in Andrew Berry, "Reasons for Being Nice and Having Sex," *London Review of Books* 25, no. 3 [6 February 2003]: 36). Because of government requirements Hamilton was actually buried in Oxfordshire.

mination of the causal conditions of their coming to believe are generally held to be compatible with genuine human freedom. Thus the elect believe voluntarily, but this does not mean their choosing to believe is uncaused. Faith is brought about by a network of causes that are all under the control of God and subject to divine determination. Faith is both voluntary and fully caused. Thereby it is totally secure, and a true believer cannot lose his faith.

It is important to be clear on where this first argument, either in its weaker or stronger version, goes wrong. The deep trouble with the security-in-grace argument is not that it presupposes a particular reading of divine revelation and scripture. The claims presented here about the nature of faith can certainly be challenged from within commitment to divine revelation as a misreading of the tradition. Thus they do not, for example, adequately come to terms with admonitions on the danger of falling away. Nor is the deep trouble with this argument that it cannot provide a coherent account of paradigm cases of apostasy without all sorts of ad hoc additions. Thus it is stretched and artificial to say that temporary believers were predestined by God to believe for a while but not for eternity. Nor is the deep trouble that this position does nothing to help a person in the midst of a crisis of faith when the core of the crisis is whether the person has true faith or is among the elect. Many sincere believers who belong in this tradition of thought fall into periods when they wonder whether they have true faith or not, or are unsure whether they stand among the elect or not. Being told that true believers are secure offers no help because precisely the point at issue is whether they are true believers. Thus any doctrine that says loss of faith is impossible at that point is useless in resolving the agony involved.

The really serious problem with this argument is that it misses the central, epistemic issues at stake; it fails to reckon with the fact that convictions about one's security belong within the circle of divine revelation. Thus this first argument fails to reckon with objections and defeaters that are lodged against the epistemic resources and practices that brought one to divine revelation in the first place. Once the steel cable is secured, it will hold; but the issue now is whether one really does have a steel cable at all; given the undercutting effects of new evidence, the cable begins to look like a fraying rope. In coming to believe in special divine revelation in the first place, the believer rests on prior epistemic practices that can be called in question, or she relies to some extent, as far as strength of faith is concerned, on various kinds of evidence that can be challenged. While, logically speaking, there are a crossing of an intellectual divide and subsequent epistemic reorientation after coming to believe in divine revelation, genuine loss of faith is still possible because the originating commitment can be genuinely undermined.

Similar considerations apply to the argument from loyalty to God. In this second argument, the primary concern is rightly to draw out the consequences of coming to believe in the God of the church. The God of the canonical faith of the church is worthy of total and complete surrender. One does not abandon the faith because one is subjected to suffering, or ridiculed intellectually in the academy, or imprisoned by the government. One rightly believes that God will sustain one through hell and high water; given such confidence, one rightly takes steps to develop a faith that is resistant to pressure and to cultivate a faith that sees betrayal with horror. Thus the very idea of loss of faith is disconcerting. Faith in God is unconditional; one trusts in God no matter what happens. To give up the faith is to engage in an act of betrayal that is unthinkable to the mature believer.

However, while total trust in God is the only appropriate response to God on the other side of divine revelation, the initial and ongoing grounds of trust can legitimately be undermined by new information or by good argument. Again, so long as the steel cable is secured, then the confidence and loyalty hold; what is at issue in loss of faith is whether the steel cable remains secured.

To be sure, the believer does not give up the faith at the first sign of trouble. So long as the originating and original commitment to divine revelation is secure, there will be and should be tenacity in believing. Moreover, the believer knows it is not always easy to distinguish between betrayal and looking for significant excuses for abandoning divine revelation so that life will be easier and less disconcerting. Thus the mature believer will proceed with caution and circumspection. However, there can in principle come a time when the whole house, so to speak, comes crashing down, and faith simply evaporates or withers away.[8]

The third argument, the threshold argument, operates from a different angle. Surely, if we do have divine revelation, the argument goes, then

8. Basil Mitchell's treatment of these sorts of issues is exemplary. See Basil Mitchell, *Faith and Criticism* (Oxford: Oxford University Press, 1994).

it follows that we have access to divine knowledge. Divine knowledge is more secure than human knowledge. Therefore we know in advance that any argument brought against divine knowledge must be either unsound or invalid or otherwise defective. Suppose someone says some item of divine revelation is incoherent or leads to a contradiction. We know in advance that this cannot be so, because divine revelation cannot involve a contradiction or lead to a contradiction. Either we have misinterpreted the divine revelation and need to backtrack and rework the interpretation, or there is something wrong with the argument that led us to posit incoherence or a contradiction, and we must now go back and figure out where we got that argument wrong.

This is a fascinating argument. It has cropped up in and around defenses of the doctrine of the Trinity and in and around theories of the divine inspiration and the inerrancy of scripture. Consider how the argument has been deployed for the doctrine of the Trinity. If the doctrine is either contained in or deduced from divine revelation, any argument that shows it to be incoherent must be mistaken, or the argument only shows that we have misinterpreted the doctrine. Equally, if divine inspiration secures the inerrancy of scripture, then any argument that appears to show errors in scripture must be false, or the argument merely shows that we have misunderstood the text of scripture. These considerations introduce a dynamic element into the situation that has interesting consequences for our reading of the history of theology that, happily, need not detain us here.[9]

The critical issue for us is that this third argument assumes there are only two ways to resolve the intellectual disequilibrium introduced into the debate by defeaters and objections. It posits that we must find a problem down the line in the human chain of argument that led us to think of revelation as involving incoherence or led to a contradiction, or we must revise our interpretation of divine revelation. However, there is a third possibility: one can also resolve the dilemma by withdrawing the original commitment to divine revelation. This too is a live option because the original acceptance of divine revelation depended on an initial, condi-

9. For a fascinating discussion of some of the issues in the neighborhood of this issue, see Eleonore Stump, "Revelation and Biblical Exegesis: Augustine, Aquinas, and Swinburne," in *Reason and the Christian Religion: Essays in Honour of Richard Swinburne*, ed. Alan G. Padgett (Oxford: Clarendon, 1994), 161-97.

tional commitment. What was thought to be genuine divine revelation, it might now be judged, has turned out in the light of further considerations not to be divine revelation at all. There are, then, three and not just two options. One can revise the standing interpretation of divine revelation; one can say the argument against revelation must be flawed somewhere; one can consider that one had misidentified divine revelation in the first place. It is this latter option that creates the space for genuine loss of faith.

Once we grant that genuine loss of faith is possible, another topic looms immediately on the horizon. Commitment to divine revelation is not at all unconditional or indefeasible. Claims to divine revelation can be undermined and falsified; they can be subjected to strain; they can be overturned by a review of the status of our cognitive capacities; they can be challenged by the undercutting of the evidence advanced in their favor, or by new evidence. These considerations are relevant to any advanced account of the rationality or justification of the robust theism that has detained us thus far. To these and other such matters we now turn.

Before we do, it is important not to exaggerate the significance of loss of faith. Our primary aim in this chapter has been to highlight yet once more that revelation is a world-constituting concept. Once it is added to the intellectual mix, the epistemic consequences are fascinating. It shatters once and for all the claim that belief is an all-or-nothing affair. To be sure, there are complex levels of assent in believing that apply whether divine revelation is or is not in place. As we have seen, there is a sliding scale of unbelief and belief that has many distinguishable points along its twists and turns. In the previous chapter we noted how divine revelation alters the picture diachronically by introducing changing conceptions of our cognitive capacities and of the way we weigh evidence. What revelation adds synchronically to our picture of belief and unbelief is no less interesting and weighty. In particular, our inquiries have thrown fresh light on various forms of belief and unbelief that are readily overlooked, not least the forgotten notions of heresy and apostasy. These ideas are not simply war cries to be thrown around lightly or unadvisedly; they are not merely polemical constructs to be dismissed as tools of power; they have epistemic overtones that deserve our considered attention and analysis.

Chapter Nine

Defeaters and Objections

—∽∿∿∾—

The Illusion of Global Defeaters

In the last chapter I worked through the significance of divine revelation for our vision of belief and unbelief. Toward the end of our analysis it became clear that commitment to divine revelation is conditional and defeasible; the original claim to have identified a genuine divine revelation can be undermined. In the light of this I proposed that it was genuinely possible for someone to give up the faith without lapsing into apostasy or revisionism. In this chapter I want to explore the epistemic insights that arise in and around the phenomenon of loss of faith. More specifically, I shall investigate what is at stake in having defeaters, that is, objections that overturn commitment to divine revelation. I shall make some general comments about defeaters, explore afresh the need to attend to particular claims and arguments, and then sketch out the precise kinds of objections that need to be made against canonical theism, if those objections are to be effective defeaters.

It is tempting to think that it is relatively easy to defeat all claims to divine revelation. Consider, in turn, two popular global defeaters, defeaters that, if successful, would overturn all claims to possess divine revelation.

All claims to divine revelation are undermined, it might be said, by the fact that the claims of one tradition cancel out the claims of another.

Given the contradictions that clearly arise in the competing traditions, the best epistemic policy is simply to set them all aside. The fact that Jewish revelation is incompatible with Christian revelation, and that Islamic revelation is incompatible with Christian revelation, tends to show that there is no revelation.

This is an extremely weak argument, and I shall not spend much time on it. For one thing, the conclusion does not follow from the premises. It is possible that within a series of incompatible claims, one may well turn out to be true and the others false. Thus three people may offer incompatible reports of what was said to them in a conversation, but this does not show that there are no true reports at all. To be sure, all may be false, but equally well, one may be true and the others false. More importantly, this whole line of reasoning short-circuits the kind of careful engagement that can and should arise between advocates of competing claims to divine revelation. Thus it begs the question as to how one may resolve the interesting possibilities that may be taken up and pursued. In fact, one of the fascinating issues arising for any mature believer in divine revelation is precisely how to think through the pertinent issues with patience and care. It is superficial to opt for a rejection of all divine revelation when one comes across incompatible visions of divine revelation.

Consider the remarkable observation of Franz Rosenzweig, standing in this instance inside the particularities of his Jewish tradition.

> Where there is something to see, God has an eye on it. Where man calls, God opens an ear. Where man hearkens upwards, or otherwise, where man closes his ear, the voice of the divine mouth can fill his ear. Where he stretches out his hand praying for help, God's hand can touch it. Where he would like to draw near in yearning or seeks to draw afar in defiance, God will step down to meet him halfway or to confront the fleeing one at the end of his flight. And where a human community seeks to please Him with fragrances or a sacrifice in an honest belief (not in a magical forcing of will that wants to buy itself free from another, closer duty) there He will — forgive the daring word! — not be so lacking in humor as not to smell it.[1]

1. See Franz Rosenzweig, *God, Man, and the World* (Syracuse: Syracuse University Press, 1998), 140.

Rosenzweig here offers a reading of other religious traditions taken from within the counters of his own commitment to divine revelation within the Jewish tradition. Each tradition must be permitted to speak in its own voice on other claims to divine revelation. The global defeater we are rejecting misses this point completely by deploying a superficial reading of the way competing revelations may legitimately be handled.

A somewhat more interesting global defeater runs something like this. Given all the false prophets that are out there fooling and fleecing us, if we let in one, we have to let them all in. The generalization deployed here is that all claims to divine revelation we have encountered of late are motivated by evil purposes. So the best epistemic policy, it is claimed, is to reject them all forthwith.

Note that the defeater is an inductive argument built on recent encounters with claims to possess divine revelation. Given that we know that all recent and current claims to possess divine revelation are motivated, say, by greed, we can dismiss all such claims as false. The obvious problem with this objection is that the generalization is extremely weak. The argument rests on our having tested recent claims to divine revelation and our having reached the generalization that they are impostors motivated by greed. We must have good evidence that recent claims to divine revelation are inauthentic, for we get to the required generalization only from particular cases. To be sure, if we had established our restricted generalization, we would have a probability argument against other claims to divine revelation, but we cannot pluck this generalization a priori out of thin air. Moreover, given its very small base, it provides only very weak evidence against past claims to divine revelation.

There is, of course, an air of unreality in the argument for the second global defeater. It is rare to find serious arguments for or against claims to divine revelation in the recent past not just among secularists and naturalists but also among even those who take revelation seriously. When we do come across arguments, they tend to be elliptical and informal. Indeed, we must acknowledge an interesting feature of our intellectual landscape that is in the neighborhood. First, it is in fact relatively easy to make claims to have received messages from God and gain a following. Second, it is also relatively easy to rebut claims to possess divine revelation. We can read these observations in one of two ways. We can see them as indicating that arguments about divine revelation are extremely flimsy, or we can see them as suggesting that ordinary people, when confronted with claims to divine revelation, can readily pick out the relevant arguments that need to be deployed for and against them. My own inclination is to accept the second option. The best way to support this interpretation is to look at an example from the recent past.

Exploring a Paradigm Case

Consider this case. Within days of the space shuttle *Columbia* falling out of the sky over Texas in early February 2003, a Mr. Abu Hamza al-Mazasri claimed in London that Allah had destroyed the shuttle because it was a trinity of evil against Islam.[2] Speaking on behalf of Allah, he said God had destroyed the *Columbia* because it was carrying Christians, and an Indian-born Hindu, and an Israeli Jew. Indeed, the explosion itself was a message from God because the first Israeli in space, Ilan Ramon, a former fighter pilot, was killed over an area of Texas called Palestine. *The Times* report continued: "Mr. Hamza, 44, said: 'The Muslim people see these pilots as criminals. By going into space they would have sharpened the accuracy of their bombs through satellites. These missions would increase the number of satellites for military purposes. It would increase the slavery of governance of other countries by America. It is a punishment from God. Muslims see it that way. It is a trinity of evil because it carried Americans, an Israeli and a Hindu, a trinity of evil against Islam.'"[3]

In response to these remarks, leading politicians and Muslims accused Mr. Hamza of inciting religious hatred and reveling in the deaths of innocent people. The reaction from the Muslim Council of Great Britain was dismissive. "The vast majority of Muslims are now quite disgusted by (Mr. Hamza's) sentiments." The Labour member of Parliament for Hendon, Andrew Dismore, added: "There is sufficient evidence to prosecute Mr. Hamza from the things that he has said." Meanwhile Whitehall officials were looking at the possibility of deporting the former imam of Finsbury Park Mosque in North London on the grounds that his citizenship was based on a bigamous marriage. The reporter from *The Times*, Steve Bird, tellingly finished his article with this piece of information: "The

2. I am using the nomenclature used in the report cited.

3. I picked this instance almost randomly from the press, in this case, *The Times* (London), February 4, 2003. The following quotations are from the same issue.

row over Mr. Hamza's comments came as NASA disclosed that damage to the shuttle during its launch has emerged as the leading theory for its break-up. It said the official investigation was concentrating on a piece of foam insulation that fell from the shuttle during its lift-off, striking thermal plates on its wing."

It is instructive to analyze the possible arguments in and around this case. My aim is not to refute Mr. Hamza's claim, nor to take up the issue of revelation in Islam, but to see initially how the claims and counterclaims might legitimately proceed. Indeed, if we can see how the arguments go to and fro in this dramatic and unusual case, we have all the more reason to think that arguments can be deployed in less dramatic and conventional cases. What are the ingredients in Mr. Hamza's reading of this event?

(1) There is a claim to have discovered a message from God. God had destroyed the *Columbia*, and through its destruction had sent a message to the world that God was punishing America. (2) There is an explanation of divine action. God was punishing America because of her military aggression and prowess, because she was seeking to increase her enslavement of other nations, and because she was in league with a Jew and a Hindu in opposing Islam. (3) There was a clear sign of the rightness of this reading of the event, namely, the fact that the disaster happened over an area called Palestine. By having the debris fall in Palestine, Texas, rather than, say, Dallas, God was signaling that he was sending a message to the world. It was not accidental that the debris came down in Palestine, Texas; this was in fact a sign from God that there was a message in the explosion.

Consider now the battery of defeaters that are clearly visible in the public remarks assembled against Mr. Hamza's claims. (1) Mr. Hamza's moral status is clearly questioned on several fronts. He is inciting people to racial hatred, and he is gloating over the deaths of innocent people. Moreover, he has broken the laws of the United Kingdom by committing bigamy and by engaging in acts of deception. Rather than having the capacity to see a message of God in the sky, Mr. Hamza is more likely reading the event in ways that suit his political aspirations and goals and that are intended to gain a following for his military commitments. (2) His views are not in keeping with mainstream Muslim sentiment and conviction. More generally, they do not fit into the theology that many mainstream Muslims hold on the basis of earlier divine revelation. In that theology, so the argument will go, God does not engage in acts that endorse deceitful bigamy. Nor does God provide warrant for inciting religious hatred or for gloating over the death of innocent people. Hence there is further reason to question Mr. Hamza's claim to be a recipient of a message from God. His proposal does not fit well with the community's general reception of the message of Muhammad. (3) There is a better explanation of the events; namely, there is a more parsimonious explanation in terms of falling foam insulation. This explanation in turn is backed up by trusted official investigations that are likely to be correct in their initial proposals. (4) The shuttle falling over Palestine, Texas, is entirely contingent. It is not, as Mr. Hamza suggested, a sign from God that he has sent a message in the explosion over Texas. Things just happened to fall that way; the debris could just as easily have missed Palestine, Texas.

We can easily construct the rebuttal to these moves by apologists for Mr. Hamza. (1) Bigamy is permitted under Islamic revelation. Further, there are extenuating circumstances governing the deception and the breaking of British law. If the United Kingdom were run under divine law, as it ought, there would be no need for deception. As it is, there is no other way to stay in Britain to carry out the legitimate missionary goals of Islam. Further, it is false that Mr. Hamza is inciting religious hatred; this is a misleading description of his praiseworthy efforts to stand up for Islam and the rights of Muslims. Equally, it is wrong to describe Mr. Hamza as gloating over the death of innocents. Those who died were not at all innocent; they were criminal agents of an imperial power intent on taking over the world, and they were enemies of God deserving of his righteous punishment. Thus Mr. Hamza is not morally delegitimized; on the contrary, his moral zeal puts him in a position to bring a message from God. (2) Whatever the views of mainstream Muslim leaders, they do not represent the proper interpretation of the theology of Islam. On the contrary, the true interpretation of Islam is given in that stream of Islam represented by Mr. Hamza. Thus there is no inconsistency with the tradition properly interpreted. (3) The alternative explanation of the events over Texas is not in fact incompatible with the claim that God is punishing America. Indeed, we can think of God working through whatever mistakes may have been made by the human and natural agents involved to bring about the explosion and thus to punish America. In this instance we need not even call into question the trustworthiness of the official investigation, even though there is ample evidence that official investigations can be flawed, and this one is in fact tainted because it is carried out by officials appointed by a government that is committed to the enslavement of weaker nations. But we do not even have to rely on this assumption to attain consistency and coherence with the relevant theological tradition. The compatibility between a scientific account of the explosion and an Islamic theological position is secure. (4) Thus the fact that the shuttle exploded over Palestine, Texas, remains intact. As such the positioning over Palestine points to the ongoing suffering of God's people in the Middle East and thus acts as a sign to them that God has indeed spoken to the world on Saturday, February 1, 2003.

It is worth noting that we could in fact insulate Mr. Hamza from criticism relatively easily. So we can imagine Mr. Hamza simply saying he has a message from God and insisting we take his word for it. His testimony is enough to carry the day; we are to believe simply on his say-so, as a matter of testimony; that is the end of the matter. Alternatively, we can well imagine a theologian from Mr. Hamza's former mosque insisting that we cannot question the content of Mr. Hamza's message because that would pit our finite minds and their sinfully oriented capacities against the truth of God. We can equally well imagine a philosopher in Mr. Hamza's circle appealing exclusively to Mr. Hamza's *oculus contemplationis* as a warrant for Mr. Hamza's seeing God at work in the explosion. Indeed, in this case it is fascinating that while we are told of a message from God, there is in fact no divine speaking and no human hearing. There is a message that is *seen* in the explosion over Texas. Alternatively, we can imagine someone suggesting that the original claim by Mr. Hamza should be seen as a control belief, or as an absolute presupposition of all thought, that is, a belief that provides the ultimate horizons within which the concept of reason operates and, therefore, a belief that only needs to be coherent with other beliefs to be secure in itself.

These moves are weak in the extreme in securing Mr. Hamza's claim to possess divine revelation. To rest on his word alone is a very fragile foundation indeed. In challenging his claim, we are not pitting our finite minds against God; we are pitting our finite minds against Mr. Hamza's finite mind. To rely on his *oculus contemplationis* alone without additional support is to be at much the same epistemic level as resting on his word alone. To construe the claim to divine revelation as a control belief or as an absolute presupposition of all thought seems on first sight to be an act of arbitrary faith. Hence these various strategies of defense in the face of criticism strike one as vain attempts to protect the claim from censure, to insulate it from scrutiny. Given the deadly consequences of Mr. Hamza's claim to divine revelation, these kinds of strategies are bogus and self-serving. Like the global defeaters we mentioned above, they represent an effort to provide a very general argument that will somehow give quick and easy victory to the protagonist.

This air of victory quickly collapses, however, as soon as we attend to a particular proposal that is seriously made and that has critical consequences for our lives. As we have just seen, particular claims to revelation cannot simply be advanced in this take-it-or-leave-it manner. Indeed, this is not how the informal discussion about Mr. Hamza's claims was actually conducted in public. Even though the debate can go back and forth in such a way as to exasperate the impatient and confound those in search of clinching proofs or finalizing philosophical theory, the arguments are genuine and draw on agreed epistemic practices. While it is theoretically possible to retreat into a position of isolation, the actual debate quickly moved outside these narrow boundaries. Proponents of particular divine revelation have to face legitimate objections and counterarguments. What our analysis makes clear is that there are serious arguments to be made for and against claims to be the recipient of messages from God. Once they are made, serious counterarguments are in order. Ordinary people operate informally in working through the relevant issues, and they are not easily fooled once their welfare is at stake.[4]

Radical Particularity

There is an obvious moral to be drawn from this excursus. Not surprisingly, given what I have argued heretofore and the case I have presented here, the crucial observation is that we need to be ruthless in attending to the particularities of the claims in hand. What we have, and what we must eventually get to in our deliberations, are very specific claims and counterclaims about particular claims to divine revelation that deploy appropriate sorts of epistemic considerations at the relevant points in the exchange. It is misleading to try to win the day by constructing make-believe scenarios that work off the general epistemic practices deployed in real-life cases. Thus, in response to a particular claim to divine revelation, we can easily

---

4. To be sure, if ordinary people are subject to coercion and persecution by the state, they may well be reluctant to challenge the prevailing option and let sleeping dogs lie.

invent a parallel but empty case that mirrors it at every step. We simply take the claim and invent an imaginary competing claim that mimics the grounds or arguments cited. More persuasively, we take the claim and then describe one of its competitors in terms of the ground or arguments offered. We too readily try to shoehorn other claims to divine revelation into the relevant epistemic vision in abstraction from the actual claims advanced by other religious traditions.

This is a mistake. Over against such abstract possibilities we need particular claims, worked up with specific phenomenological experiences, outlining a determinate message from God in either word or deed, coupled with accompanying phenomena, and pressed home with the relevant historical narrative. We need more than armchair possibilities and thought experiments; we need actual claims advanced in some detail and with some care.[5]

Generalizations about claims to divine revelation across the religious traditions of the world are in fact precarious. We are often misled in this arena by gravitating to revelations that are supposedly tied to particular books or scriptures. Given the tendency of theologians over the years to think of divine revelation as given in and through a canon or a book, we reach for a sacred book as the key to understanding revelation across the board in the leading world religions and then try to construct a general theory.[6] In our articulation of a vision of divine revelation informally available in the church, we have seen how misleading this reduction of revelation to a book is in the case of Christianity. Moreover, once we allow generalizations about books, we can readily see how impostors abound. Given the complexity of claims to divine revelation, given the epistemic significance to claims to divine revelation, and given the temptation for quick resolution of the issues in hand, it is easy to deceive the world by

5. The same applies to claims about doxastic practices or the *oculus contemplationis* as applied to competing religious traditions. It is not enough to claim that these notions can be used across the board in religion; we need carefully constructed arguments at this point. We might say that we need the functional equivalents of a William P. Alston and Alvin Plantinga that come forth from the competing religious alternatives and deliver the relevant and particular epistemic goods.

6. This is essentially the strategy deployed in Keith Ward, *Religion and Revelation* (Oxford: Clarendon, 1994). For my evaluation of Ward's position, see my "Keith Ward on Religion and Revelation," in *Comparative Theology: Essays for Keith Ward*, ed. T. W. Bartel (London: SPCK, 2003), 2-11.

bringing out the relevant book and then making what appear to be the right kinds of general epistemic moves. There are great material and social gains to be made from exploiting human cognitive fragility and gullibility at this point. The generalizations only aid and abet the impostors and charlatans. The antidote to this strategy is simple. Proponents of divine revelation need to advance in some detail the particular claims they think are secured, the relevant epistemic considerations they deem appropriate, the precise arguments they think strengthen their case, and the way they propose to handle standard defeaters and objections.

How much of this pattern is to be followed or deployed by advocates of a particular revelation cannot be decided in advance. We leave that to their proponents. It is not the task of believers of one set of claims to special divine revelation to do this for neighboring and competing believers. Thus it is up to Moslems to advance the claims of Muhammad; it is up to Mormons to argue the case for Joseph Smith; it is up to the local prophet in the Christian sect in East Texas to explain his proposals to the world; it is up to fundamentalist Christians to make their case; and it is up to canonical and other Christian theists to make their case for final revelation in Jesus Christ. Indeed, it is the mark of a serious theological tradition derived from divine revelation to own up to this responsibility and explain itself in public. There is no epistemological testing machine for telling us how these positions are to be developed, laid out, and rebutted. Let each tradition speak for itself and say its piece. In turn, let critics be free to develop whatever objections they deem relevant.

This policy clearly means abandoning the standard picture of objectivity that restricts discussion to publicly agreed forms of evidence, to academic neutrality, to independently measurable or quantitative data, and the like. These have their place where pertinent in critical inquiry; they are critical aids to reflection, but they cannot begin to capture the aesthetic dimensions of our cognitive endeavors, nor can they do justice to the richness and complexity of the issues at stake in each particular case. The idea that there is some sort of grand morality or ethics of inquiry at this point is deeply misleading and inaccurate. David Tracy's description of this option undoubtedly represents the views of many theologians.

> In principle, the fundamental loyalty of the theologian *qua* theologian is to that morality of scientific knowledge which he shares with his colleagues, the philosopher, historians, and the social scientists. No

more than they, can he allow his own — or his tradition's — beliefs to serve as warrants for his arguments. In fact, in all properly theological inquiry, the analysis should be characterized by the same ethical stances of autonomous judgment, critical reflection and properly skeptical hard-mindedness that characterize analysis in other fields.[7]

Aside from appealing to a vision of epistemic unity across disciplines that does not exist, and aside from failing to note that to appeal to divine revelation is not *simplicter* to appeal to the beliefs of one's own tradition, Tracy simply fails to reckon with the way claims to divine revelation should be approached. What matters in each case is accurate engagement, genuine sensitivity to all the issues in hand, and ability to comprehend alien sources of argument and data. These standards of intellectual excellence apply to the case to be made for defeaters, objections, and any rebuttals that are lodged. Relevant defeaters and objections against this or that particular claim must be laid out and argued in detail.[8]

On How to Become an Enemy or Friend of Canonical Theism

It remains in this chapter to work through the application of this strategy to the debate about the merits of canonical theism. Given the case I have sought to sketch out for canonical theism, we can see where the critical objections should be lodged. We can immediately pinpoint where the necessary pressure needs to be applied, if it is to work effectively.

First, we can undermine the claim to possess the relevant epistemic capacities that identify the original site of divine revelation. Thus, following Marx, we might for example try to undermine the whole idea of human agents as made in the image of God and possessing an *oculus contemplationis*. Thus we would construe this and all other theological claims to be the inventions of class designed to keep the proletariat from

7. David Tracy, *Blessed Rage for Order* (New York: Seabury Press, 1975), 7. Tracy may have revised this vision somewhat in his later work.

8. This policy also means abandoning the epistemic privileging of secular interpretations of religion so prevalent in departments of religion and in many schools of theology in the United States and elsewhere over the last generation. Note that I am not here excluding secular interpretations; I am simply insisting that all interpretation be subject to critical scrutiny.

challenging the social and political status quo. We would try, that is, to offer a competing and better-supported vision of human agents; we would seek to challenge the anthropology that operates as one element in the case for canonical theism. We can well imagine how a Freudian alternative might also be deployed to the same effect.

Second, we can try to cut away the ancillary arguments from natural theology, religious experience, and the like. Thus we might try to show that, say, cumulative case arguments in favor of canonical theism are faulty in some way or another. Equally, we might try to show that the appeal to perception of the divine in varied experiences of God is really a form of an argument from an analogy to ordinary perception of the physical universe and that the analogy simply does not hold.

Third, we can try to falsify the historical claims that are central to canonical theism. Thus we might attempt to show that the "Jesus of history," as developed by proper historical investigation, completely undermines the vision of Jesus developed in the canonical heritage of the church.

Fourth, we can seek to undermine the capacity of the people of God to reliably interpret or transmit the content of divine revelation. Thus we might argue that the "church of faith" is as much a construct as is the "Christ of faith," and that the "church of history" is in fact morally, spiritually, or intellectually incapable of arriving at the truth of God as it is in Jesus.

Fifth, we can try to damage the appeal to the new evidence that emerges on the other side of divine revelation. Here we might try to show that, say, the so-called experiences of the Spirit are much better explained as manifestations of emotion, that they are a misreading of other phenomena, that deploying language about the Holy Spirit is an inaccurate interpretation of religious experiences that are better explained in other ways. Or we might try to undermine the coherence or fit that the mature believer detects in the beauty and symmetry of Christian doctrine, and so on.

My aim here is to indicate the kind of argument that must be made if it is to be on target. The aim is not to be comprehensive, nor to rule out the possibility of new kinds of arguments in the future, but to map the terrain to be covered. The aim is also to indicate that we need very specific objections directed at very particular elements of the case presented here.

When we stand back and look at this picture as a whole, it may seem that we have let ourselves in for an excess of intellectual vulnerability. It immediately looks as if our position is so exposed from so many different angles that it can be hit from many different directions. Perhaps one good missile fired from long range will destroy the whole house of faith in an instant. This is a telling response, for it highlights again how we are gripped by an epistemic vision in which we think we can have one decisive disproof, and in which we fall back into the assumption that it is enough to take a single synchronic snapshot of the argument on offer. The analogy of a faith as occupying a building is helpful at this juncture. As we have seen, the journey to faith is less like constructing a little tin hut that the individual builds by his own single-handed labor and that can be knocked over by one good shove. The journey of faith is much more like coming to occupy a sturdy castle that has been hit often, and hit hard, and survived intact across the centuries. Moreover, while there are all sorts of vulnerable openings, there are plenty of skilled sentries on duty to help with the defense.

More formally, we should observe the following.

First, it is unrealistic and inappropriate to require that the mature believer be able to deal with all the objections that show up. It is appropriate that believers recognize objections when they are pertinent, that they do not pretend that they do not exist, and that they do what they can to fulfill their obligations to the truth. Moreover, it is entirely in order to rely on expert authority and the good judgment of others. This is inescapable in many areas of our intellectual life; it is misplaced to expect higher standards here than elsewhere.

Second, there is an entirely proper tenacity in believing. This stems not just from the sense of loyalty to God or from the danger of being intellectually hyperscrupulous. It is rooted in the fact that one should not abandon a vision of the universe that makes a radical difference to one's life, and that one has heretofore found intellectually and spiritually satisfying. Giving up a cherished faith is not like casting aside a set of old clothes, or like abandoning some recent ideas that have casually been picked up; it is to give up a precious heritage of faith and practice, and only a superficial and ignorant believer would do this lightly.

Third, many of the objections lodged are not as straightforward as they might at first appear. Rather than depending on totally independent considerations, many objections represent rival metaphysical visions of the universe. Thus a Marxist objection against, say, the *oculus contemplationis* represents a rival ontological and epistemological proposal that often presupposes the falsehood of a Christian anthropology rather than establishes it. It is not as if objections are always independent and fully secured; sometimes they rest on all sorts of weak or controversial assumptions.

This consideration applies especially to various proposals on the Jesus of history that are offered as neutral, objective, historical investigation or that lay claim to expert application of, say, "the method of historical criticism." The notion of historical criticism is much too easily wielded as a kind of sacred scientific exercise, when in reality it is deeply formed by presuppositions that are not at all the result of either historical or scientific investigation. There is in fact no historical investigation without prior ontological and epistemological assumptions. Even the distinction between literal and metaphorical tropes is utterly dependent on our beliefs about the world and our vision of the causal networks that operate.[9] Hence the effort to chart the relation between faith and historical inquiry is more complex than much of the current debate will allow. My aim here is not to ward off these objections and worries but to make sure they are not oversimplified or trivialized.[10]

Fourth, and most important, it is pivotal to note the direction of the argument at this point and what is at stake in a successful rebuttal. The kind of mature believer I have depicted here has very good grounds for believing as she does. It is not as if she goes into the discussion from a position of neutrality. She is fixed firmly in her position because she has won her way through to a thoroughly positive epistemic assessment of her assets in canonical theism. She has gained the high ground; her default position needs only a successful rebuttal to stay where she is. She does not need to produce new evidence for her position; all she needs to do is rebut the pertinent objection. She need not make or produce new missiles and fire them to continue in the faith; all she needs to do is knock down or defuse the incoming missiles.

My overall aim in this chapter has been to show that loss of faith is a genuine possibility and that loss of faith brings into view some important

---

9. If I say it is raining cats and dogs, we know immediately that this is a metaphorical expression because cats and dogs do not come this way out of the sky. It is clear that we necessarily draw on our background beliefs about the world when we make distinctions between literal and figurative discourse. This has important implications for the hermeneutics of divine revelation that cannot be pursued in any detail here.

10. I have pursued this thesis at length in *Divine Revelation and the Limits of Historical Criticism* (Oxford: Oxford University Press, 1982, 2000).

epistemological insights. We should resist the temptation to look for global defeaters. We should patiently unpack the logic at work in arguments for and against a revelation. Insulating our claims from criticism is tempting but unacceptable. We should work with particular claims to possess divine revelation, expecting proponents and opponents to take seriously the duty to provide specific argument or backing for their particular claims and counterclaims. We should resist the temptation to privilege this or that position in the academy by setting up standards of operation and success that have a pretense of neutrality but that spuriously smuggle in contested claims under the banner of proper scholarship or analysis.

Furthermore, it is relatively easy to identify where objections can be lodged against the claim to divine revelation that I have developed. In dealing with these, the mature believer should be aware of the dynamics of debate. More specifically, everyone should note that for the mature believer the default position is one where all that is needed to sustain the attained position is to rebut the pertinent objection under review. As we have noted, the objections come from radically diverse directions and are aimed at different elements in the overall vision. Rebuttals, if developed, will have to be tailored to meet them. It will help to flesh out what is at stake if we take a specific set of objections and see if there are adequate rebuttals. To that I now turn.

Chapter Ten

Revelation and Language

—==∞∞∞==—

Pressure on Claims to Possess a Divine Revelation

In the last chapter I pursued the topic of loss of faith in such a way as to show that specific claims to possess particular divine revelation are rightly the subject of discussion and argument. More generally I sketched how efforts to defeat the claims of revelation laid out in the body of this book should be directed. One of my aims within this was to persuade the reader that defeaters need to be quite specific; to be successful they should be focused and targeted in nature. We can illustrate the importance of this attention to particularity by taking up a fascinating cluster of worries that is likely to have occurred to readers who have become sensitized to questions about the nature of theological language over the last generation. So rather than tackle objections, say, from historical investigation or from recent observations about religious pluralism and diversity, I want to illustrate what I am recommending by diving straight into that fertile arena. There is a nest of concerns that are intimately interrelated and that can in fact be pursued together. We shall ease our way into the topic by some preparatory comments.

Contemporary theologians are under enormous pressure from ancillary fields devoted to the development of theories about the nature of language. The two really big camps in contemporary philosophy, that is, Anglo-American analytical philosophy and Franco-American postmodernism, are both extremely interested in the nature and significance of language.[1] In and around these philosophical developments are other intellectual trends that readily cast suspicion on claims to revelation in the Christian tradition. I have in mind critical theory, rhetorical criticism, poststructuralism, postcolonial theory, and the like. We should expect, therefore, that theologians who encounter the kind of substantial vision of divine revelation I am proposing here will have nagging doubts that it has not taken the measure of developments in these arenas.

I take it that some of these reservations are very general ones that apply to any and all forms of theological discourse and hence crop up with respect to revelation as the application of a more general network of problems. In the last generation within analytical philosophy, one very general worry centered in the coherence of all claims to think and speak of divine revelation. It was thought that there are contradictions buried in the very notion of divine revelation, so that the concept does not hang together logically.[2] Here the general appeal was to assumptions supposedly built into assertions about agents and their activity.

Two such assumptions were pertinent, and both involved the necessity of a body in order to secure any talk about agents and their actions, including their revelatory activity or actions. First, it was claimed that bodies are needed to pick out agents; second, it was claimed that all actions involve bodily movement. Neither assumption holds. Agents are often identified without reference to bodies. Thus God can be identified by uniquely referring expressions like "the one and only creator of the universe" or "the one and only Father of our Lord Jesus Christ." Equally, not all actions require reference to bodily movements. Thus mental acts like counting, or remembering, or thinking about politics do not necessarily involve as a matter of meaning reference to bodily movements.

Contemporary theologians are not really interested in these kinds of problems. Indeed, they are very quickly bored by them, suspecting that they represent a continued covert commitment to positivistic canons of

1. The deep historical connections between Anglo-American analytical philosophy and the European Continental tradition in recent philosophy are well brought out by Simon Critchley, *Continental Philosophy: A Very Short Introduction* (Oxford: Oxford University Press, 2001).

2. See Anthony Flew, *God and Philosophy* (London: Hutchinson, 1966), chap. 2. For a thorough discussion see Richard Swinburne, *The Coherence of Theism* (Oxford: Clarendon, 1977).

meaning discredited since the 1950s. Yet it is far from easy to identify what is at issue for contemporary theologians who appeal, whether directly or indirectly, to the nature of language to raise objections to divine revelation, or perhaps more accurately, to the particular conception and material vision of divine revelation I am proposing. Presumably what is at stake is that the claims about revelation I have advanced somehow contravene some general requirement about theological discourse. They violate some general rule of meaning in theology.

A Cluster of Worries

Consider four logically distinct objections.

One fear is that the claims I have advanced contravene the principle that theological discourse is essentially about the meaning and significance of human existence. Theological discourse is not factual or explanatory; it has its own language game and grammar. To make the sort of move I am making is simply to ignore this crucial feature of religious discourse. It wrongly treats talk of divine agency and action as factual and explanatory. This is surely much too crude and unsophisticated a vision of theological discourse; theological discourse has its own unique function.

A second concern is that all theological discourse is essentially metaphorical, symbolic, and analogical in nature, whereas I seem to be taking revelation literally. I am claiming that God really did speak to the prophets, or that he really did become incarnate in Jesus Christ. The sentences that express these claims should be taken as metaphorical, or symbolic, or analogical.

A third worry has arisen with particular force in the last generation. Is not this whole enterprise essentially oppressive? Does it not keep intact and perpetuate the kind of traditional and patriarchal discourse that has been so poisonous in its consequences, especially for women and minorities? Are we not saddled with the kind of hegemonic discourse that modern Christians should now abandon?

A fourth objection takes its cue from the inherently *apophatic* nature of theology and theological discourse. Surely, it will be said, we are systematically ignoring the *via negativa*, the fact that we are only permitted negative propositions, like God is not embodied, or God is unlimited, and the like. Do not the views espoused involve a much too robust and positive account of what God has done and what God is like? How can this be? Is this not some kind of unacceptable positivism of revelation? Where is the place of silence in this analysis?

Interpretation and Language

How are we to reply to these four concerns? As we proceed, it is worth registering that while they may be general in character, they are directed very specifically at the very particular network of claims I have advanced. Hence they deserve a considered response.

Let's begin by thinking more generally about the nature of language. Interpretation of a text, or of a spoken language, or of a divine revelation, is indeed a complex undertaking. However, if there are any acts of interpretation, there must be some basic acts of interpretation. There must, that is, be acts of interpretation that do not rely on some other acts of interpretation. It is relatively easy to see why this is so. If we cannot stop somewhere and trust our acts of interpretation, we are into an infinite regress of interpretation where one interpretation depends on another, prior act of interpretation back forever in time. To put the matter more practically, if someone suggests that we can understand what is said only after we have heard or read what he or she has said or written theory-wise, it must be the case that we are able to understand what he or she has said or written theory-wise. Unless that act of reading and hearing in turn depends on some other theory, we must be able to understand this second body of speech or writing on which the first is supposedly dependent. Hence there must at some point be a basic act of interpretation that is not dependent on another. Given that we do indeed manage to understand, I assume that this must be the case. There are basic acts of interpretation. Any antecedent argument that denies this must be rejected as pragmatically self-refuting.

This does not mean that there is not more to say about the nature of interpretation. Indeed, it is clear that we can genuinely be helped in reaching a deeper comprehension of what we already understand by attending to illuminating theories of interpretation. Thus it would be a mistake to infer from what I am claiming about basic acts of interpretation that our understanding of interpretation cannot be enhanced, enriched, improved, and the like. This is patently false, and it is clearly undercut by our actual experience of interpretation.[3] Our initial basic acts of interpretation can be vastly improved by exploring theories of interpretation.

Furthermore, it is clear that the possession of a language is an extraordinary gift and achievement. In my judgment it is one of the wonders of wonders. The complexity boggles the mind once one reflects on this at length. There are puzzles galore here that are well known in philosophy of language and philosophy of mind. I do not say this to throw dust in our eyes, but to urge caution in our judgments. As I mentioned above, we can make all sorts of claims without necessarily having to hand some theory of meaning that explains how we can say what we say. On this matter, as in epistemology, I am a particularist. We test our general theories by what we implicitly or tacitly know in our practices of speaking and meaning making. It is not that we learn some grand theory and then apply it in action. Rather we learn to speak, and in speaking we learn to do multiple things with words. The job of good theory of language is to make sense of all this as best we can. This is one reason for being relatively relaxed about meaning. Our theories of meaning are tested against tacit practice.

A further reason for being relaxed is that many theories that have ruled out all sorts of language, including theological language, have come and gone in time. After sailing from port with great fanfares blaring, they have sunk on the high seas. This has clearly happened to the old positivist strictures about verification as a necessary condition of cognitive discourse.[4] It is not too exaggerated to say that only in the twentieth century did we begin to think deeply about the nature of language. Thus to read someone like Horace Bushnell on language is to feel that one has wandered into a world of self-confident illusion. Once one has gotten a feel for the work of, say, Wittgenstein and Austin, one has the sinking sense that Bushnell does not know what he is talking about. This is not a cheap shot at Bushnell, a truly remarkable and delightful theologian; it is a measure of the difficulty of the terrain and the progress that has been made. Even then, we can succeed in securing meaning when we have bad theo-

---

3. Consider, by analogy, the odd request to read a book on how to read a book. If we cannot read a book already, why read a book on how to read a book? Books on reading books already assume we can read a book; they are really intended to improve our understanding and ability in reading a book.

4. For a recent revisiting of the debate about verification, see William P. Alston, "Religious Language and Verification," in *The Rationality of Theism*, ed. Paul Copan and Paul K. Moser (London and New York: Routledge, 2003), 17-34.

ries as to how we succeed, or no theory at all. There is a parallel here with epistemology. We can and do know all sorts of things about ourselves and the world without knowing how we know all these things. This applies to animals, to small children, and to countless adults. As in epistemology, it is important to think as clearly and systematically as we can about language.

To understand the fundamentals of meaning making, we need to attend to agents and their speech acts in particular situations and contexts. One of the greatest exponents, if not the discoverer, of this insight was the Oxford philosopher J. L. Austin.[5] There has been much work since him, and many have labored in the vineyard he planted, but we do not need to harvest all that work here. What are needed are the fundamentals of the matter.

When we speak we can distinguish immediately between three radically distinct dimensions of the act of speaking. There is, first, the *locutionary* act or event. For example, we utter certain sounds that are heard. Some kind of medium is used to communicate. There is, second, the *illocutionary* act. In and through, say, the sounds we utter, we perform certain acts. We make assertions, raise a question, curse, make promises, give a command, tell a joke, and so on. There is, third, the *perlocutionary* effect or act. In doing what we do our speech actions may have certain effects or consequences. Thus in making a certain assertion or in making a promise, we may have the effect of making some of our hearers feel sad, or elated, or jealous, and the like.

Now let's apply this to a particular claim about divine revelation. To stay focused I shall take a particular case where God reveals himself to a prophet, say, Jeremiah or Paul.[6]

First, consider the *locutionary* act. We do not know for sure the relevant locutionary acts on God's part, but we can easily imagine various possibilities. Unlike human agents, God has a whole range of possibilities at his disposal. Maybe he spoke telepathically or directly, mind to mind, with Jeremiah.[7] Maybe he caused Jeremiah to have a dream and at

5. Most famously in his *How to Do Things with Words* (Cambridge: Harvard University Press, 1962).

6. For the purposes of what follows I am going to treat Paul as among the prophets.

7. Note that Pannenberg misunderstood this in his discussion of some earlier comments along these lines in my *Divine Revelation and the Limits of Historical Criticism.* See Wolfhart Pannenberg, *Systematic Theology* (Grand Rapids: Eerdmans, 1988), 1:234-35.

the same time caused him to believe this dream was from God. Maybe God led Jeremiah to believe that some thoughts he was having were exactly God's thoughts, and he further caused him to tell the content of those thoughts to the people around him as being God's thoughts. We might think of Paul having certain visions of the risen Lord and then God addressing him through the words of the risen Lord. We can think of many possibilities, then, which would fit the bill for the locutionary act.

Second, consider the *illocutionary* act involved. At stake here are acts of promising and warning, of call and commission. In speaking to and through Jeremiah, God gave certain warnings and promises to the people of Israel. In speaking to Paul God called and commissioned him to be an apostle to the Gentiles.

Third, we can imagine certain *perlocutionary* effects or acts that accompany the locutionary acts. Jeremiah becomes uneasy; he wants to run away and hide; in his heart he shifts from elation to sadness. We can think of other effects down the line. Jeremiah is ridiculed and opposed; he is accused of being a false prophet; he is thrown in jail and dragged into exile. These are not part of the meaning of the speech acts of God; they are the contingent consequences of God speaking in and through Jeremiah. Equally the perlocutionary effect for Paul was to render him docile, to bring it about that he was prepared to receive instruction in the faith, be baptized, and the like.

Where, more precisely, does revelation fit into this? An obvious way to think of revelation in these instances is to say that it supervenes on the illocutionary acts performed. It supervenes on the promises and warnings of God given to Jeremiah, or on the call and commission given to Paul. In and through the acts of promising and warning, in and through these quite particular acts with their own particular content, God reveals his will and mind to Jeremiah and thereby to the people Israel. Likewise, in and through the call and commission God reveals to Paul what he wants him to do with his life. As I argued earlier, if we have access to these speech acts of God, then we know something about God.[8]

---

8. We can also say that revelation, where it is relevant to say so, can supervene on the nonspeech acts of God. Thus the act of God becoming incarnate is both an act of redemption and an act of divine revelation.

165

Dissolving the Cluster of Worries

Consider now our first worry. It is perfectly fitting and proper to speak of the claims of revelation advanced here as both factual and explanatory. When we say that God spoke to Jeremiah or Paul, we are making an assertion. We are saying that in the past God spoke to Jeremiah or to Paul. Moreover, the event of God speaking explains other events, so it is explanatory. It is legitimate to say that the act of God speaking brings about other events and actions; thus it explains the behavior, dispositions, and actions of Jeremiah. Jeremiah reacted as he did and spoke as he did because God spoke to him. Equally, it explains the acts and missionary labor of Paul.

Of course, the explanation is not a scientific explanation. It is not secured by predicting certain happenings in the light of a conjunction of general laws hooked to relevant states of affairs. However, there is no law of logic or inquiry that says all explanations must be scientific in form. We can also explain events by describing them as actions carried out by an agent for certain intentions and purposes. What we have here is a standard teleological explanation that cites the relevant motives, reasons, and beliefs that make various actions, dispositions, and behavior intelligible.[9]

The corollary of this is that it is not very helpful to say that canonical theism or even Christianity is a language game. We might, for certain very limited purposes, speak of Christianity being a language game, for example to bring out how doctrines, convictions, and practices hang together to shape and form a whole way of life in community. However, it is better to stress that what we have is a plethora of language games within the version of theism on offer. Within Christianity we use language in a whole variety of jobs, like making assertions, explaining happenings in history, giving promises, praying, baptizing, and so on. So we can use language, including the language of revelation, to convey information or to explain various events in history.

Now consider the second concern. When we say that God spoke to Jeremiah or Paul and thereby revealed certain things to Jeremiah or Paul, is the language we use literal, analogical, metaphorical, or symbolic? We can surely rule out the last two immediately — our claims are not felicitously described as metaphorical or symbolic. Take the sentences "God spoke to

---

9. It would take us too far afield to explore what other kinds of explanations are available to us, for explanation is by no means confined to the types identified here.

Jeremiah" and "God revealed certain things in speaking in and through Jeremiah." As I am using them here, these are not to be taken as a way of saying something else. "God spoke to Jeremiah," as used here, is not a metaphorical way of saying that Jeremiah had deep insight into the secret events of Israel's history, which he may or may not have possessed. It does not stand as a symbol for, say, divine seriousness about the moral and political behavior of Israel. On the contrary, it is to be taken as a depiction of the actual actions and events that transpired between God and Jeremiah. Equally, when we say "God called and commissioned Paul," this is not a poetic or roundabout way of claiming that Paul had a vocational crisis and resolved it by becoming a Christian missionary. This way of speaking is to be taken as an actual record of what God did in the life of Paul.

It is important to be clear here. In speaking to Jeremiah and to Israel through Jeremiah, God may well have deployed various metaphorical tropes or may have used various symbols. So in the course of communicating with Jeremiah, God may have caused Jeremiah to think of Israel as a pot in the hand of the potter, or to view the divine as a king, warrior, shepherd, or the like. God may have transmitted his promises by getting Jeremiah to envision their content in terms of a myriad of metaphorical expressions. All this is beside the point. What is at issue is how to understand the claim that God spoke to Jeremiah and to Israel. This is not a piece of metaphorical or symbolic discourse. Similar considerations apply to Paul.

Is our discourse then literal or analogical? The obvious thing to say is that it is better construed as analogical. What we are doing is drawing on the meaning of what it is to speak in the human situation and applying or stretching it appropriately to fit the events and experiences here attributed to Jeremiah and to Paul.[10] Such a move is entirely compatible with the earlier claim that the assertions involved are both factual and explanatory.

What about the third worry? Is not the language of revelation inherently oppressive and poisonous? Note that the issue here is not whether claims to revelation may be a cover for oppression, violence, discrimination, and the like. Clearly they can be, and they have been. We would be

---

10. We must be careful not to generalize too grandly here. Consider God becoming incarnate in Christ. It is often the case that this is the base for metaphor, as when we say, for example, that Hitler was the devil incarnate. How far predicates may be applied literally and univocally to God lies outside the scope of our inquiries here.

foolish to think that this will cease in the future. It is precisely because divine revelation involves the epistemic privileges it does that we can always expect folk in every generation to exploit it in all sorts of ways. Warnings about false prophets are always important. The issue at hand is that somehow the very use or appearance of the language of revelation is oppressive and poisonous.

I cannot see how we could begin to show that this is the case. To be sure, when God spoke through Jeremiah, the perlocutionary effect may have been that some of the hearers felt trapped, oppressed, and the like. However, this would not necessarily be part of the content of the revelation or divine speaking involved. It would not alter or be inherent in the illocutionary acts performed. It would simply be a contingent consequence, a contingent perlocutionary effect. On the contrary, the Word of God to Jeremiah might well be received not as an oppressive work but as a liberating word for obvious reasons. It would signal God's continued care for Israel and his utter faithfulness to his covenant. We can envisage a similar reaction from Paul. Perhaps he felt imposed upon, deeply distressed, or even violated. However, these effects are not constitutive of what God told him. They are not part of the content or meaning of divine revelation. This effect would have been entirely contingent. The very same speech act may have left Paul, if somewhat shaken in his boots, exhilarated and full of sober reflection.

It is worth pausing to apply this to the revelation of God as, say, father or king. It is surely the case that canonical theists see God as "Father" in the light of the revelation of God in Israel and in Jesus Christ. Indeed, Jesus, as Son of God, initiates the believer into a relation to God as "Father" that mirrors his own relation to God.[11] The view I have advanced throughout this volume sustains this perception. So am I not endorsing the view that males are superior to females, or that God must be envisaged exclusively in patriarchal categories, and hence contributing to the oppression of women? The distinction between illocutionary and perlocutionary acts is once more pertinent at this point. It is indeed the case that for some women, when they hear in reports of divine revelation that God is spoken of as father, the perlocutionary effect is a sense of oppression, moral indig-

---

11. Most famously stated by Paul in Romans 8:15. For a fine discussion of "Abba" as used by Jesus, see James Barr, "'Abba' Isn't 'Daddy,'" *Journal of Theological Studies* 39 (1992): 28-47.

nation, and the like. The very mention of the word "Father," whatever the illocutionary act involved, is enough to cause various negative reactions. This is a fact about the world that needs to be heeded and worked through pastorally and politically.[12] However, this in no way undermines the relevant meaning of the illocutionary act involved. If we claim that God has spoken to us in Christ and that in that he has called us to address God as "Father," the perlocutionary effect, good or bad, does not tell us one way or another what this means. Over the years in the Christian tradition the proposition that God is our Father has rightly been taken to mean that we should understand that God relates to us as a good father relates to his children. For millions of men and women this claim has been profoundly liberating when taken to heart and explored with all the other myriad analogies — male, female, and gender-neutral — that are applied to God. Read this way, it has equally acted to level all before God, male and female, calling into question various social hierarchies and categories. Whether and to what extent this is so has little or nothing to do with the language of revelation. It is rooted in the actual illocutionary acts performed by the speaker.

It is crucial to bear in mind that language in itself does not do anything good, bad, or indifferent. Speaking colloquially, it is true that we say that words hurt. Words do indeed hurt, but it is always particular words spoken by various agents on specific occasions. We must attend carefully not just to the surface of what is said, that is, the locutions; we must get beyond the surface to the illocutionary acts involved. Otherwise we will simply fail to understand what is said.

This takes us to our last objection. In what I have claimed about revelation, have I not set aside the crucial requirement that all language about God be seen as *apophatic,* as leading to a profound silence before the mystery of God? The answer is both yes and no.

The no is found in this. In the end we find ourselves at a loss for words both in describing the God we encounter in revelation and in understanding the wonder revelation inspires within us in contemplating what God has done in revelation. Crossing over into the world of revelation enhances the sense of awe and mystery at the heart of faith. That God

---

12. The negative effect may be tied to certain beliefs about the relation between language, society, and oppression; or it may be psychologically related to past experiences of abuse or victimization.

should do what he has done is a matter of staggering grace. Moreover, we are stretched to the limit both intellectually and spiritually in any attempt to depict the mystery involved. There is a genuine silence before God, and this is rightly recognized in stretches of complete and utter silence before the ineffable reality of God in worship.

We might even go further and say that the end of the journey to God is precisely such silence. Thus we are dealing here not simply with stretches of silence but with a silence that becomes a necessary feature of our very knowledge of God in and through divine revelation. We can think of at least three ways in which this claim might be fleshed out. First, we might see it as following from certain characteristic experiences of God in which the believer finds it simply impossible to put into language what he or she is aware of in the encounter with God. The failure to speak is here tied to the psychological or spiritual inability to speak given the sheer immensity of the reality that one has come to experience. Maybe with extended experience or in a different setting, say, in heaven as opposed to earth, human agents might be able to find words to describe their experience.

Second, we might develop this thesis in terms of the utter inadequacy of human language to depict the divine when encountered. Here the failure stems from the inadequacy of the medium of language to do the job required. Perhaps with improved linguistic resources, some believers would find words after all; maybe some of the saints are especially gifted in this domain.

Third, we might explain the failure in metaphysical or theological categories as stemming from the drastic distinction between the finite and the infinite, the creature and the Creator, the human and the divine. In this instance neither greater familiarity with God over time nor enhanced linguistic resources would make a whit of difference. Somehow in the very act of encounter with God, one grasps a critical metaphysical distinction between the creature and the Creator that rules out the very possibility of anything but silence.

There is no need here to take sides on these options. For the moment we leave them standing as they are. However, whatever line we take at this point, and here we come to the yes, it is a mistake to claim that nothing positive can be said about God. On the contrary, divine revelation dispels our ignorance, sheds light in our darkness, and gives genuine knowledge of God within the contours of human history. The giving and receiving of divine revelation are of course a matter of grace. We need divine assistance all down the line, from identification to reception, appropriation, and exploration by way of the intellect; from the first moments of belief to hope, trust, and obedience by way of the will; and from the beginnings of wonder to love, joy, and enthusiasm by way of the heart. However, the richness of response by way of intellect, will, and heart takes place in a world of genuine light and illumination where God is rightly perceived and understood. Hence the *apophatic* must be balanced by the *cataphatic*, that is, by appropriate diction and depiction in which God is accurately and richly displayed in all the resources of language at our disposal.

It is important to bear in mind what we have been doing in this chapter. My initial concern was to highlight afresh the fact that claims to possess a divine revelation are subject to intellectual scrutiny. Defeaters of such claims should be taken with the utmost seriousness. To illustrate what is at issue I have explored one cluster of objections in and around theories of language that arise against the vision of divine revelation I have worked out. Hopefully I have also given some indication of a vision of language that brings out how robust and substantial our claims about divine revelation are. While my response has been altogether too brief, I trust that it at least has been on target and now puts the ball, if not in the backcourt of the critic, at least well and truly over the net.

Perhaps this makes the whole exercise look very much like an irrelevant game for experts and academics. Unfortunately this is often the impression in debates about divine revelation and theology. However, if we yield to this temptation, we are mistaken. The task of working through complex epistemological theories, of providing arguments, defeaters, rebuttals, and the like, is not to play games but to get at the truth as best we can. Indeed, advancing claims in such a way that they meet the requirements of rationality, justification, knowledge, and the like is a critical human practice that is important for peace and human flourishing. Thus when someone insists that he sees messages from God in explosions in the sky, it is precisely time to raise questions about rationality, justification, and knowledge. We are no longer dabbling in irrelevant games that may be intrinsically interesting to eggheads. We are postponing the reach for the bomb and the gun. It is time we turned to these concepts as a fitting climax to our overall journey.

Chapter Eleven

Rationality, Justification, and Knowledge

—⟨ℯℓℯ⟩—

The Flourishing of Religion

The last thirty years have witnessed a remarkable turnaround in the fortunes of religious commitment. Expected to wither away in the corrosive and suffocating context of secularism and modernity, religion refuses to lie down and die. Contemporary culture is, as I mentioned at the beginning of our journey, awash in claims to possess divine revelation. It remains fashionable in parts of Europe to predict that the situation in North America is anomalous. North America, it is thought, will go the way of all flesh and, like Europe, abandon religion. This prediction has rattled around long enough now to be thoroughly discredited. Modernity, secularism, and religion have all flourished in North America; no sign of the end of religion is presently in sight; if anything, it is Europe that is the anomaly.[1] The challenge now is not the absence of religion but its virulent presence. In many ways our contemporary culture is ill prepared to deal with the questions thrown up by religion. In many intellectual and academic circles we have banished the art of the rational assessment of religion from all forms of public education, or we have essentially given all religions a free ride, or we have handed out blank

1. David Martin makes this case in his *Pentecostalism: The World Their Parish* (Oxford: Blackwell, 2002).

172

checks to entirely secular evaluations of religion. This is not a happy state of affairs.

A canonical theist with the kind of robust vision of divine revelation I have developed so far welcomes the quest for rationality and justification as that applies to religious commitment. Theologically she sees such a quest as not just compatible with her position but as required by it. Canonical theists owe it to other theists and nontheists to explain why they are committed to this version of theism. Furthermore, the quest for rationality and justification is intimately related to a vision of human excellence or of intellectual virtue that is part of that vision of perfection to which the canonical theist is naturally committed. More generally, there are very good reasons for taking seriously the quest for rationality and justification. Rationality and justification are linked to practices that have a pivotal role in human welfare. They are part of a wider network of interrelated concepts that we neglect at our peril.

As we proceed I make one assumption. I shall not here provide an extended analysis of truth. I take truth in fact to be a primitive concept that is tacitly available to us. Thus, while it is extremely useful to think of true propositions as those that correspond to reality, I am not tied to that notion in any strict sense.[2] The canonical theist is resolutely committed to a vision of theology as delivering true propositions about God, creation, the human condition, and the like. Thus theological discourse is not a disguised form of emotional or moral utterance; nor is it empty of cognitive content; the clear intention in confessing the creed, for example, is to commit to a very particular vision of the universe that is taken to be true; the intention is to make assertions, to make claims about the way things are. Yet in making this specific confession, I shall assume that we already have a handle on what it is to claim that the faith is true. The quarry here initially is to explore how far we can claim that the confession of the faith is rational and justified.

Rationality

Rationality applies first and foremost to persons and only secondarily to the beliefs professed or confessed. Thus "rational" is a predicate that be-

2. For a splendid collection of essays on truth, see Michael P. Lynch, *The Nature of Truth: Classical and Contemporary Perspectives* (Cambridge, Mass., and London: MIT Press, 2001).

longs to a family of important evaluative concepts that includes such notions as intelligent, lucid, open to evidence, articulate, honest, prepared to address objections where appropriate, reasonable, persuasive, compelling, and the like. It belongs, that is, in the world of intellectual virtue. I shall first sketch the contours of this world and then provide an analysis of rationality, justification, and knowledge. En route I shall indicate how the canonical theist fares in this arena. I shall round off the discussion by briefly exploring the difference, if any, divine revelation makes to the epistemic commitments of the canonical theist with respect to intellectual virtue and the status of knowledge.

Intellectual virtues are directed to the proper formation, maintenance, communication, application, and revision of our beliefs. Taken together, they provide a portrait of a vigorous, well-rounded cognitive agent. They arise out of the motivation to lead a healthy intellectual existence. In some visions of the intellectual virtues they are seen in terms of a means-end relationship to human flourishing. It just so happens on this view that intellectual virtue characteristically leads to human welfare. In more purist visions of the intellectual virtues, they are seen as intrinsically worthwhile; they constitute what it is to be an intellectually flourishing person rather than operate as exterior means to that end.

The intellectual virtues transcend our natural abilities, faculties, and skills, while they build on and foster them. In recent years, following the lead of Ernest Sosa, there has been a tendency to include the faculties of perception, intuition, memory, reason, and the like as instantiations of intellectual virtue.[3] Thus reliabilist epistemologies and epistemologies of proper functioning have commonly been classified as forms of virtue epistemology. This issue is somewhat verbal in the end, but it is important to distinguish this kind of epistemology from more responsibilist conceptions of virtue epistemology. In the latter case, rather than being constituted by intellectual capacities or abilities initially received or given over time due to natural endowments, development, and maturation, intellectual virtues involve traits of character that are gained over time due to voluntary training and exercise.

---

3. See Ernest Sosa, "The Raft and the Pyramid: Coherence versus Foundations in the Theory of Knowledge," in *Studies in Epistemology: Midwest Studies in Philosophy*, ed. Peter A. French, Theodore E. Uehling, Jr., and Howard K. Wettstein (Minneapolis: University of Minnesota Press, 1980), 5:3-26.

Intellectual virtues are such that they cannot be reduced to exercising skills or following rules. To be sure, intellectually virtuous persons will deploy all sorts of skills, and these often relate to particular intellectual virtues in a particular area of inquiry. Thus the skills essential to being a historian may be quite different from those essential to being a physicist. Equally, they will deploy a host of formal and informal rules as needed. However, the intellectual virtues transcend these rules. Furthermore, intellectual virtues are intimately connected to pertinent emotions and passions like empathy, delight, annoyance, repose, and outrage. Emotions often function as the engine of the intellectual virtues. Thus a person of intellectual virtue will care passionately about truth and will have an aversion to intellectual vice. Most importantly, intellectual virtues aim at cognitive contact with reality and are marked by success in gaining such access. Thus they are identified because they are governed by the quest for knowledge and because acting in accordance with them has actually been effective in getting us to truth.[4]

It is very odd that philosophers singled out rationality as privileged in their vision of intellectual virtue.[5] In everyday usage "rational" is but one predicate in a long list of intellectual virtues that can be assembled. The list given here is by no means complete: wisdom, prudence, foresight, good judgment, intellectual carefulness, fair-mindedness, flexibility, thoroughness, intellectual candor, courage, apt doubt, elegance, teachability, perseverance, understanding, truthfulness, intellectual humility, open-mindedness, sincerity, studiousness, originality, appropriate trust, and the like. It would be equally odd to single out "irrational" as the only important item in a list of intellectual vices. Interestingly, the lists of vices tend to be shorter than those of virtues; honey is clearly more effective than vinegar in fostering virtue and inhibiting vice. Any comprehensive list of vices would include the following: folly, obtuseness, gullibility, intellectual arrogance, insensitivity to detail, party spirit, wishful thinking, stubbornness, conformity, dishonesty, cowardice, willful naïveté, vicious curiosity, intellectual laziness, and the like.

---

4. I am deeply indebted to W. Jay Wood, *Epistemology: Becoming Intellectually Virtuous* (Downers Grove, Ill.: InterVarsity, 1998), and to Linda Trinkaus Zagzebski, *Virtues of the Mind* (Cambridge: Cambridge University Press, 1996), for my analysis of intellectual virtue.

5. The whole drive to reduce epistemology to a study of rationality, justification, and knowledge may be a very interesting development in the field. This reduction neglects a whole network of epistemic concepts and cognitive activities that play a pivotal role in everyday life.

Regarding the network of concerns in this project, it is clear that a canonical theist can readily and without prejudice be considered thoroughly rational in her intellectual commitments. This in part follows from the fact that the rationality is not predicated first and foremost of particular beliefs or networks of beliefs but of the agent who believes. Thus we cannot by mere inspection discover if this or that belief is rational. To be sure, it is common practice to break this wise policy. It is not at all unusual for even educated individuals to dismiss this or that religious belief as irrational in and of itself. There may indeed be specific religious beliefs that in context we would naturally describe as irrational. Thus if someone said that his dog was God, or that the color purple was God, we would indeed evaluate such beliefs negatively. However, it would be more felicitous to describe them as silly, incoherent, uninformed, ridiculous, rather than simply irrational. Moreover, we engage in this kind of appraisal because we assume in the current context that a person who seriously looked into the claims of religion would not count these as living options. We bring to our appraisal a background of relevant discussion, debate, serious argument, onus of proof, and the like.

What is at stake in claiming that the canonical theist, or by derivation canonical theism, is rational, is that the agent has considered what is at issue, is open to argument, has given some thought to alternatives, and the like. Our appraisals of rationality fit on a graded scale. We can think of a very minimal sense of rational in which the agent is simply permitted to believe the great truths of the faith. He or she has not flouted any obvious epistemic obligations. Thus, believing is not merely a matter of wishful thinking, or gaining fame among one's peers, or opting for the most self-serving set of beliefs possible, or manipulating oneself into belief despite the contrary evidence, or accepting a position because it resounds with the most popular slogans, and so on. Further along the scale, we can think of the agent being more rational than this. She takes the trouble to find out what is at stake in believing canonical theism, exploring pertinent objections, attending to relevant evidence from religious experience, and the like. Perhaps at the top of the scale of rationality we can think of an agent who has gone even further and thought through the deep epistemological issues that circle around commitment to canonical theism. These considerations show that theists as cognitive agents do not receive blanket appraisals; each has to be evaluated on merit. Rationality is not an all-or-nothing concept; it is relative rather than absolute; it clearly comes in degrees. Whether and to what degree a canonical theist is rational is a matter for contingent judgment related to the relevant target beliefs of the agent in question.

We can, in fact, readily correlate degrees of rationality with the different kinds of believers we identified earlier on the other side of the threshold of divine revelation. We identified a nominal believer, an uninformed or ignorant believer, an ordinary believer, and a mature believer. We can readily correlate these distinctions with various degrees of rationality. Thus it is a stretch to predicate rationality of the uninformed or ignorant believer; the ordinary believer is broadly rational; and the mature believer is robustly rational.

Justification

We might also capture the more positive ascriptions of rationality in terms of a "justified" cognitive agent. At this point we return to the more general landscape before looking at the situation of the canonical theist. There is a perfectly good sense of the term "justified" wherein we mean a person is justified in believing if, at a minimum, the person relies on the standard practices of perception, memory, testimony, and the like. We might refer to this as nonpropositional justification. Thus if a child reports that the cat is on the mat, he is justified in doing so if he has come to believe as a result of the use of his sight. What sits in the background is a tacit reliance on a significant range of reliable belief-producing mechanisms. In this case justification is tacitly tied to wider background beliefs about human nature. Human beings are conceived as cognitive agents with a range of intellectual sensors that pick up what is going on in the world; there is a causal tracking system between eyesight and the way things are. Just as a good thermometer registers accurate temperature, good eyesight registers accurate surface depictions of the world.

I have already argued that this kind of move is of limited value in arguing for the justification of canonical theism. On the best-case scenario, the *oculus comtemplationis* provides some warrant for believing in God and in divine revelation, but it can only take us a limited distance; it clearly does not have the agreed or consensual status we normally attribute to perception, memory, testimony, and the like. Moreover, there is a gap between what is available through the *oculus contemplationis* and the robust version of theism that is our quarry.

We can also think of "justified" as meaning that it is possible for persons to provide an account of why they believe. They can provide evidence for their belief; they could do so if challenged. We might also use "justified" to include the person who, although perhaps unable to provide a justification for her beliefs there and then, is morally certain that such a justification could be given if she had the time to think about it carefully or to research the topic. I think we can also use the term to refer to a person who, although he could not work it all out for himself, is convinced that warrants could be supplied by someone in his community. In this usage "justified," like "rational," admits of degrees; one can be more or less justified in believing certain propositions.

Justification in this latter sense as predicated of belief is clearly a different and perhaps stronger notion than when we speak of a "justified" person. Characteristically a belief is justified when a case of some sort has been made in its favor. We might call this sort of justification "propositional justification." Often it is taken as tacit. Thus if I claim to have seen an elephant in the yard, it will suffice initially when challenged that I defend this propositionally by insisting that my eyesight was in good working order, that the light was acceptable, that there was nothing untoward in the environment like elephant cutout figures presented secretly as the real thing, and the like. I verbally lay out the relevant evidence in the light of this information. Normally we take the deliverances of intuition, memory, perception, deduction, induction, and testimony as forms of reliable belief-producing mechanisms. We also assume that these faculties operate against an overriding system in which coherence clearly plays a critical part. Thus if I claim that there is an elephant in my third-floor office, the conditions of success for justification are more stringent. Given what is generally known of the building in question and the laws of nature, it is physically impossible for there to be even a baby elephant in my office. In this case it will be more difficult to mount a propositional defense. Thus an element of coherence can readily come into play, and this can make the challenge more demanding. If I explain that my colleagues hired a crane, punched open the roof, and dropped an elephant in my office as a practical joke, I take care of the problem of coherence with physical laws. However, there will then be the added challenge of a different kind of coherence, namely, coherence with the character, actions, and intentions of my colleagues. Generally our practices of propositional justification are thoroughly contextual; we either tacitly supply the wider horizon or it is presented explicitly when requested.

The limiting case is supplied by legal practice. For this the requirements for justification are much more stringent. Here the production of specific and publicly recognizable kinds of evidence and the rebuttal of objections are indispensable. To be sure, legal practices operate with a tacit acceptance of perception, memory, testimony, and the like. Indeed, they could not work without them; it would be bizarre to have an epistemological debate in the court about their efficacy. The law, however, generally concerns itself with particular actions and with the descriptions of these actions as advanced by plaintiffs and defendants; evidence, objections, and rebuttals must then be directed for and against these particular, target claims. The standards are extremely high, so high that to apply them in everyday life would be otiose and silly.

It is interesting to note why this is the case. Generally such high standards are required because so much is at stake. Minimally the guilt or innocence of the accused is at issue, but a lot may hang on the verdict of the court, right up to the very life of the accused for capital offenses. It is precisely because we know that so much is in the balance that we have such stringent conditions for providing appropriate propositional justification in the courts. We are more concerned to avoid error than to secure the truth. Thus our efforts at justification in legal contexts are clearly governed by moral considerations; issues of human welfare are in the neighborhood and cannot be ignored.

This principle also applies in various contexts outside of the law. In the workplace we now generally insist on propositional justification for claims advanced in decisions about firing, hiring, and promotion. Managers often build a paper trail of evaluation and appeal to it when needed. In the education of students we provide settings in which they are required to explain why they advance the claims that they do. In parliamentary settings success in enacting legislation depends on making out a persuasive case. In philosophy it is a serious failure if there is no effort to provide an account of this or that philosophical position; appealing to this or that dogma is taken as a serious weakness in one's position. In political circumstances, where there is a risk from the use of the bomb and bullet, strenuous efforts are made to mainstream those tempted to use physical coercion to achieve their aims. One way to do this is to put pressure on terrorists and their political allies to explain their actions by drawing them into the discourse of explicit, propositional justification. In this manner known terrorists can be called to give an account of their actions in public terms, a fact not lost on terrorists themselves when they cloak their political aspirations in terms of public values, like peace and reconciliation, to advance their cause.[6] Even in ordinary circumstances we insist on explicit justification for this or that claim if the claim has significant consequences for our lives or for the community as a whole. Thus the practice of justifying belief is intimately tied to promoting peace and advancing the common welfare. Justifying our beliefs is not simply a luxury enjoyed by eggheads who take pleasure in thinking and discoursing; requiring justification in the sense of making a propositional case can be a matter of saving life and of curbing the urge to kill.

Yet it would be a mistake to say that providing such justification for a belief is always done in a context that has clear moral overtones or components. Thus persons may provide justification for various beliefs even when moral considerations are absent. They may do so out of an ideal of intellectual excellence, or for gaining intellectual competence in certain areas of their thinking, or to satisfy their curiosity, or because they think doing so is intrinsically worthwhile. Overall, providing propositional justification for one's beliefs is heavily influenced by contextual considerations and by the more general policies and interests of the agents involved.

Clearly one reason why we look for and request nonpropositional or propositional justification for belief is that we think this practice will more readily lead to gaining the truth and avoiding error. We clearly think the practice of justifying belief is better at gaining truth than other practices, like guessing, wishful thinking, or tossing coins. We believe that justification as a whole tracks truth, even though we know that beliefs that at one time were very well justified turn out to be false. Strident claims to provide explicit justification for our beliefs can sometimes be read as a legitimate desire to avoid gullibility, to inhibit the reaching for hasty conclusions, to minimize relying improperly on authorities, to proportion the level of assent to the evidence available, and the like.[7] It is a mistake to be intimidated beyond these entirely wise admonitions into making the ex-

---

6. Alternatively when caught and brought to trial, they are liable to dismiss the standing of the court and present themselves as victims of a show trial.

7. The celebrated and much quoted comment of Clifford comes to mind: "[I]t is always wrong, everywhere, and for anyone to believe anything on insufficient evidence" ("The Ethics of Belief," in *Philosophy of Religion*, ed. Louis Pojman, 2nd ed. [Belmont, Calif.: Wadsworth, 1994], 426).

plicit presentation of appropriate evidence a condition of rationality or even knowledge. Fear of error or of intellectual vice is in fact but one element in a well-rounded intellectual formation. We need to resist intellectual paranoia as much as we forestall credulity and superstition. As in much of life, if little is ventured, little is gained. In any case, as we have already seen, the delineation of intellectual virtue is far richer and subtler than this way of thinking begins to accommodate. For the moment we simply note that there is an obvious analogy between the practice of seeking propositional justification and the exercise of intellectual virtue. We generally believe that through them we are more likely to gain truth and avoid error.

Knowledge

The shift from justified belief to knowledge, at least on traditional accounts of knowledge, is relatively simple. One secures knowledge by adding justification to true belief; knowledge is justified, true belief.[8] Thus in the case of knowledge it is not enough to be in the possession of truth, say, by a lucky guess or by good fortune. For example, even though the clock in the hallway is broken, it will in fact tell the right time twice a day. So I wander past the clock at two thirty, when the clock shows that it is two thirty, and glancing upward, I form the belief that it is two thirty. It happens both that I do not know that the clock is broken and that I come to believe it is two thirty by glancing at the clock. In this case I come to believe the truth, but I do not know the truth; I do not have knowledge. On the traditional account of knowledge, the additional feature required for knowledge is that I also be justified in relying on the clock for knowing it to be two thirty. Given that the clock was broken, clearly I had no such justification; I had relied on an unreliable time-telling mechanism; therefore, I did not have knowledge. Knowledge requires properly justified true belief.

Once this general picture of knowledge is in place, the main problem centers on figuring out what constitutes justification. As we have already seen, we can think of justification in terms of either non-propositional or propositional justification. We can think of justification

8. Skeptics tended to raise the stakes by insisting also on certainty for knowledge.

along the lines of the person being justified in believing the truth because of tracking the truth causally by our faculties, or we can construe justification along the lines of the person having propositional evidence for the belief in question. In the former case we can know what is the case without knowing that we know what is the case or without having propositional evidence for the truth believed. Thus I can know that there is green grass in the yard so long as I have gained access to this truth through perception, memory, testimony, deduction, and the like. If I know something on the basis of perception, I do not explicitly have to go through the process of checking internally in my consciousness that perception is in fact reliable or that my particular perceptual faculties are functioning properly. I may, of course, do this and thus have knowledge about my knowledge, but I do not need to do this to possess first-order knowledge of the world. It is enough that I am hooked up in various ways externally to the world, that is, without having in addition internal access to the knowledge that I am hooked up to the world. So a person could be justified nonpropositionally and thus have knowledge without having explicitly to supply propositional evidence for the proposition under review. Clearly, if we insist on propositional justification as the relevant form of justification, we know a lot less than is permitted under the nonpropositional conception of justification. My own preference is to eschew the limiting of justification to this condition. Thus I am fully prepared to allow for justification of a nonpropositional kind.

This whole vision of the relation between justification and knowledge has been deeply complicated by the famous Gettier counterexamples that show that we can have cases of justified true belief that we would not in fact reckon as knowledge.[9] The crucial feature of these cases hinges on the person having appropriate justification, believing what is true, yet having access to the truth only accidentally or by luck. In fact, the cases often involve a sequence in which bad luck is followed by good luck. Suppose I am sitting in La Madeleine's, my favorite French restaurant, and I come to believe by looking across the room that Patrick is sitting in his usual place drinking coffee. The lighting is fine; my eyesight is working properly; I see a person with the bodily features I readily associate with Patrick drinking coffee; and I come to believe that Patrick is in the restaurant. Now it happens that the person I see is not Patrick but his twin

---

9. E. L. Gettier, "Is Justified True Belief Knowledge?" *Analysis* 23 (1963): 121-23.

brother Michael. I know about the existence of Michael, but I have good reason to believe he is in Ireland for the St. Patrick's Day celebrations in Dublin. Even though I am justified in believing that I have seen Patrick, I did not see Patrick but Michael; because knowledge requires that the belief entertained as knowledge be true, I do not have knowledge. It happens, however, that in fact Patrick is in another part of the restaurant drinking his favorite coffee. It is in fact true that Patrick is in the restaurant. So in this instance my belief that Patrick is in the restaurant is true and justified or warranted, but my belief, even though true and justified, does not constitute knowledge. Cases like this have motivated many philosophers either to add a further condition of success in order to secure knowledge[10] or to abandon the link between justification and knowledge and strike out in another direction entirely.[11]

I cannot resolve these disputes here, nor do I think all that much hangs on resolving them. Given that we do actually possess knowledge, I assume that we can in time find a way to solve the various Gettier problems. Even then, it may turn out that Gettier has hit on exceptions that prove the rule for a more general conception of knowledge. That we cannot reach agreement on the necessary and sufficient conditions for knowledge does not mean that in many instances we cannot rely on the conventional portrait. Our definitions are useful enough, even though they may be able to cope with complicated sequences of luck.

For the moment, it is worth repeating that we can well have first-order knowledge without having second-order knowledge about that knowledge; we can have direct knowledge without having iterative knowledge. This is central to particularism where the challenge in epistemology is not that we do not know a host of things about the world and ourselves but that we do not always know how we know what we know. Another way to make this point is to say that we may well have knowledge without having perfect knowledge. Yet again we might say that it is good to have knowledge, but we can improve our epistemic status by coming to know how we know what we know. Thus the quest in epistemology is not simply gaining the coveted epistemic status of possessing knowledge but of

10. This is the route taken by Keith Lehrer when he adds the condition of being undefeated to the standard analysis of knowledge. See his contribution to M. Clay and K. Lehrer, eds., *Knowledge and Skepticism* (Boulder, Colo.: Westview Press, 1989).

11. This is the route taken by Zagzebski, *Virtues of the Mind*.

gaining any increase in our epistemic status. Thus, to use the standard concepts of discussion, we can move from being rational to being justified, from being justified to having a justification, from having a justification to having knowledge, and from having knowledge to having knowledge that we have knowledge. The limiting case would then be perfect knowledge, that is, knowledge such that we know everything there is to know about the knowledge we possess. We might want to capture this by claiming that we rightly seek after not just rationality, justification, or knowledge but the maximum understanding possible. This quest is entirely laudable so long as we do not underestimate the epistemic goods we actually possess because we do not have the best of all possible epistemic possessions. We should be grateful for all the epistemic mercies, however small, that we receive.

I have already suggested that a canonical theist can lay claim to being rational, but not to being justified in terms of nonpropositional evidence. We can add now the possibility of being propositionally justified either in the sense of supplying propositional evidence for her position or in the sense of making a case for her position. The latter designation is somewhat broader than the first in that it allows for a combined appeal to both propositional and nonpropositional evidence. The latter clearly fits with the scenario already sketched where we noted the various kinds of evidence that can be adduced at different points in the journey into canonical theism. Thus a mature canonical theist is well able to deliver on the stronger challenge of justification. When challenged, the mature believer can provide a sound justification of her belief.

In fact, a canonical theist can press further and lay claim to having knowledge. Given that she may have a host of good reasons for believing that she possesses divine revelation, then, given the epistemically privileged position of divine revelation, she does indeed have knowledge. This is one point where the appeal to divine revelation radically changes the epistemic situation. If perception, memory, reason, testimony, and the like can rightly supply us with knowledge of the world, if these can act as sources of justification and, other things being resolved, can enable us to move from true belief to knowledge, this is even more so for divine revelation. If anything is worthy of trust, then divine revelation is worthy of trust; it thus can operate as the justification for claims to knowledge in theology.

We can capture this by noting afresh the dynamic of the discussion.

If we have crossed the threshold of divine revelation, then we must be prepared to revise or abandon any claim that is contrary to the beliefs thus secured. We can explore this claim by means of analogy, that is, in terms of testimony. Suppose I have human testimony of the highest order; the testimony is unimpeachable, for it rests on someone whose faculties are in good working order and who is totally trustworthy; I can think of no stronger testimony. On the basis of this testimony I believe that the dean is in the library. Over against this I have reason to believe that the dean is not in the library because I have evidence from conversations with him that he has a long-standing aversion to visiting libraries. In fact, the sight of books sickens him. In this case, I suggest that the testimony wins out against my reasoning. Change the scenario a little. I have the same testimony, and I think I have just experienced a fleeting glance of the dean sitting in his office; I now have perceptual evidence that he is not in the library. Again I think the testimony wins out against the evidence of my senses; given the status of my fleeting glance, I reflect that I must have made a mistake in my perception.

Note that we are not here speaking of just any combination of evidence and counterevidence; we are concerned with a particular scenario in which the highest human testimony is ranged among forms of weaker evidence. All that is needed for the argument is a case of human testimony trumping other forms of evidence. Add in now the extra factor that the claim in theology is to be in possession of divine revelation; the conclusion is even more secure. In this instance we do not have simply human testimony but divine testimony. In this situation, once we are genuinely over the threshold, then there is knowledge; indeed, it is hard to think of any higher form of knowledge than the knowledge given to us by God in divine revelation.

The case I have made here is intentionally formal in nature. Much of the resistance to divine revelation in the modern period has stemmed less from understanding the formalities of the case advanced and more from the material positions adopted. Thus much of it has stemmed from the quick and easy identification of divine revelation with the speech acts of God and with the hasty identification of divine revelation with scripture. Once we rework the material claims to focus simply on the actions and speech acts of God, the resistance should melt. To be sure, as I have argued, the move to the full contours of canonical theism depends on additional epistemic resources like religious experience and inference, but given that both experience and inference can also yield knowledge, the additional appeal to such sources in no way undermines the basic point being pursued here. Divine revelation yields genuine knowledge.

Given the continued existence of aggressive forms of fundamentalist theism, we can understand culturally and psychologically why theologians have great difficulty working their way through to this conclusion. In part because of a bad conscience, too many theologians have given up on the possibility of more sophisticated visions of divine revelation. There is a genuine worry of falling back into positions that do not do justice to the richness and manifold character of scripture. Moreover, given the importance of diachronic considerations in thinking about the epistemology of theology as well as the subtlety and complexity of the evidence and grounds involved, it is understandable that some theologians become intellectually disoriented and discouraged. The whole idea of securing knowledge in theology is so foreign that the advocacy for such a position will take time and patience, especially if theologians refuse to be as serious about epistemology as they are about, say, exegesis, or history, or politics, or cultural studies.

Note that other uses of the claim "to know" are also available to the mature canonical theist. Thus we can think of a claim to have personal knowledge of God in the sense of genuine acquaintance of God through personal experience of God in response to the gospel. Sometimes, drawing on the thought of Paul, this claim has been expressed in terms of the inner witness of the Holy Spirit.[12] The relevant point here is that the believer can experience a divine witness within giving assurance that one is genuinely forgiven and can address God from within as Father. Equally, we can think of a performative use of "know" where the claim to know is an invitation to explore the truth of the Christian faith together with risking one's cognitive reputation that those who seek will find the truth about God in Jesus Christ. In this instance the believer is giving her word that the faith is true and that others can find this out to be the case for themselves.

---

12. The critical text is Romans 8:16-17. Paul K. Moser has identified this kind of knowledge as filial knowledge of God. See his "Jesus on Knowledge of God," *Christian Scholar's Review* 28 (1998-99): 586-604.

Knowledge, Grace, and Virtue

Nowhere does the mature believer take credit for any of the knowledge gained in divine revelation or in contemporary religious experience. This is entirely proper given the role of divine revelation and the ongoing divine assistance in gaining knowledge of and about God. Divine revelation takes place by way of divine initiative, and characteristically in, with, and through divine action, not human action. While faith in divine revelation is a voluntary act, the whole weight of the causal conditions for faith clearly and rightly comes down on the side of divine grace, divine initiative, and divine action. Given this weighting of the causal factors, it is misplaced and even otiose for the believer to take credit for faith. Repenting, struggling with virtue, engaging in relevant spiritual practices, and the like are not conditions for gaining merit; they are appropriate cognitive conditions for encountering the holiness and mercy of God in divine revelation.[13]

In the light of such human cognitions in gaining knowledge of God, it is not surprising that we should think of faith not just as a form of knowledge but also as a virtue. Unfaith, or unbelief in the face of divine revelation, in turn is seen as a vice. Once we factor in divine revelation, we can see why this is exactly right. It is sin and not just a failure in cognition not to respond positively to divine revelation. Failure to respond positively is a way of staying in darkness and ignoring the light of God; it is a deliberate act of refusing truth when it is given to us. On the other side, responding to the truth of divine revelation is a good thing to do; it is both an act of cognition and a morally good act. Hence the move to think of faith as a virtue is on target.

We see in this how divine revelation enriches the way we need to think about the intellectual virtues. Having crossed the threshold of divine revelation, we now find ourselves drawn to a new network of virtues or into a transformation of those virtues we already accept. The fear of the Lord becomes the beginning of wisdom; it is the pure in heart who see God. Thus fear of God, purity of heart, loving God with all one's mind, resisting the lure of vain philosophizing, bringing every thought captive to

---

13. William P. Alston felicitously makes this point in a different context. See his "The Fulfillment of Promises as Evidence for Religious Belief," in *Faith in Theory and Practice*, ed. Elizabeth S. Radcliffe and Carol J. White (Chicago and La Salle, Ill.: Open Court, 1993), 10-11.

Jesus Christ, obedience in believing, and the like become central to the life of the mind.

Canonical theists are also likely to draw attention to the critical place of social relations and community in the cultivation of intellectual virtue. Thus the virtues are caught more than they are taught; they are learned by imitation over time in communities of intellectual virtue; their cultivation is heavily dependent on sympathy, patience, friendship, and collegiality. Within this more general framework, the disposition to take the life of the church seriously will be a marked feature of the virtues as seen within canonical theism. Particular attention will be given to the great intellectual exemplars of the tradition, most especially to the canon of theologians recognized by the church as articulating and capturing the deposit of divine revelation across space and time. This does not mean the intellectual failures or vices of the church will go unnoticed; on the contrary, they will be all too readily acknowledged in all candor. However, it does mean there will at times be a readiness to bind up the wounds of the tradition rather than to deepen them; one will approach the life of the church as a whole with a hermeneutic of sympathy and grace rather than a hermeneutic of suspicion and hostility.

Another way divine revelation alters the epistemic landscape of intellectual virtue is by reordering the internal intellectual balance of the believer. In a strange way knowledge itself may be relativized in a radical manner. The truly spiritual believer is not the epistemically sophisticated believer but the one who loves God with all one's heart, soul, and mind, and who loves the neighbor as oneself. Having climbed the ladder of divine revelation, we set knowledge aside, as it were. To be sure, epistemological sophistication may be important for some believers, given their professional duties, or their temperament, or the kind of ministry they are called on to exercise in the church as evangelist or teacher. However, the goal of believing is not to gain knowledge, including knowledge about knowledge; knowledge is a penultimate goal. Indeed, all too often the quest for knowledge and its attainment is the occasion for arrogance and a host of other intellectual vices. The final goal of all believing and knowledge is beyond all belief and knowledge; the final goal of faith is simply the deepening of love for God and the neighbor. Happily, work in epistemology may at times clear the way for this by removing roadblocks and by providing badly needed intellectual rest and assurance. So we need not play knowledge and love of God off against each other. Across the threshold of divine revelation we indeed gain knowledge, yet immediately it is displaced. In gaining access to divine revelation we discover that knowledge itself is put in its proper perspective, for not even knowledge can displace God from his proper place as Lord of everything.

Index